THE

50

TOUGHEST, MEANEST, SCARIEST

HARD-MEN

IN FOOTBALL HISTORY

BY EDDIE RYAN

HERO BOOKS

PUBLISHED BY HERO BOOKS
LUCAN
CO. DUBLIN
IRELAND

Hero Books is an imprint of Umbrella Publishing

First Published 2023

Copyright © Eddie Ryan 2023

A CIP record for this book is available from the British Library

ISBN 9781910827697

Cover design and formatting: jessica@viitaladesign.com
Photographs: Sportsfile

DEDICATION

To my inspirational partners-in-crime
Mary O'Shaughnessy Ryan & Freddie the 'Great'!

INTRODUCTION

'THE TRUE SOLDIER FIGHTS NOT BECAUSE HE HATES
WHAT IS IN FRONT OF HIM, BUT BECAUSE HE LOVES
WHAT IS BEHIND HIM'

– G.K. CHESTERTON

THEY WERE the 'Most Wanted'.

Fifty of the 'toughest', 'meanest', 'scariest' warriors ever assembled on a gaelic football field. A rare breed of men that had their county's colours coursing through their veins. Men whose deeds and misdeeds have left their fingerprints all over the history of the Sam Maguire Cup.

An elite band of warriors who never took a backward step, or ever bent their knee on the field of battle. They walked the line and took it to the very edge and sometimes beyond…

They were the sniping assassins who picked defender's pockets. They were merciless defenders, who placed a bounty on your head, then hunted you down to collect their blood money.

The men profiled in this book are no angels. They also, most certainly, are not demons. They were men who went to war with their hearts on their sleeves, their noble legacy forged in blood, sweat, and no little tears.

Wherever their county needed battles to be fought and conflicts to be won, these men of selfless courage helped turn the tide. Men who faced huge physical and mental battles, and even their own demons from within to answer their county's call.

Whatever sacrifices were asked, they delivered in spades. For the pride of their families and the honour of the parish. For the love of the GAA, and their unbridled passion for their county's crest.

They took the hits and returned them with interest, knowing no fear and willing to risk all consequences. They were the front-line soldiers, the first responders. The men who dared to venture… where angels fear to tread.

It was a responsibility they never took lightly, a cross they were willing to carry right to the very end. Even when all hope was lost, they were a shining light that raged against the swirling inevitability of defeat. They never gave up, as true warriors never do. When the end arrived, they all went out upon their shields.

The exchange between Colonel Nathan R Jessup (Jack Nicholson), and Lt Daniel Kaffee (Tom Cruise), in the movie *A Few Good Men* provides a startling insight into the mind of a highly trained US marine. It is, in essence, the story of every man-of-war, and of the GAA's 'Most Wanted'.

Jessup pulls no punches as he takes us deep into the psyche of a fighting machine, and even deeper into the darkness of war.

'Son, we live in a world that has walls, and those walls have to be guarded by men with guns. Who's gonna do it? You? You, Lieutenant Weinberg? I have a greater responsibility than you can possibly fathom. You don't want the truth because deep down in places you don't talk about at parties, you want me on that wall – you need me on that wall.

'We use words like "honour", "code", "loyalty". We use these words as the backbone of a life spent defending something. You use them as a punch line.

'I have neither the time nor the inclination to explain myself to a man who rises and sleeps under the blanket of the very freedom that I provide and then questions the manner in which I provide it.'

The players featured within these pages were the ones their county needed guarding the wall against enemy attackers. Men who used the words 'honour', 'code' and 'loyalty' not as a punchline, but as an ethos by which they lived and died during their magnificent careers.

It gives me great pleasure to introduce these remarkable men, whose incredible exploits have helped shape the course of gaelic football history.

The '50 Toughest, Meanest, Scariest, Hard-Men' in gaelic football history.

Eddie Ryan
September 2023

ACKNOWLEDGEMENTS

My thanks to my publisher, Liam Hayes, and all the hard-working team at Hero Books. Liam has set such a standard in the world of GAA, and journalism and publishing, it is an incredible honour to be able to collaborate on a subject so close to his heart.

To my wife, Mary, an amazing soul mate, thanks for all your hard work and endless support. Always smiling, always full of bright and breezy energy, your companionship is a gift that keeps on giving.

To my late mother, Mrs Dorcas Ryan, your love and courage, and incredible sacrifice is a debt that can never be repaid.

Thanks also to all the Cardiac Critical Care Unit and the Cystic Fibrosis teams at Limerick and Nenagh Hospitals, for their outstanding professionalism and loving care. Special thanks to my heart surgeon Dr Kiernan and Jacinta Glasgow, my nurse of 'endless patience' and excellence.

My thanks to *Ireland's Own* and my monthly editor, Shea Tomkins. Shea is a true sports fanatic and an incredible editor for the publication. To Sean Nolan and all the rest of the *Ireland's*

Own crew. It is a rare privilege to write for what is truly an Irish institution.

My thanks also to Mary's mum and dad, Val and Susan, who taught being parents was tough going – until their daughter landed them with the son-in-law from hell!

Thanks also to Anna Louise O'Shaughnessy – 'a true book lover.' Thanks to Mannie and Ruth, for all the craic and great days out. Special thanks also to my good friends, Oliver and Shelley, Lauren and Cathal, and to John Savage my manager!

Last, but not least, many thanks to all the good people of Roscrea... The town I loved so well.

Eddie Ryan
September 2023

CONTENTS

INTRODUCTION

PHOTOS AND TOP 50 LIST

KEITH BARR

(Height 6' 1", Weight 14.5 St)

Decade... 1980s/1990s

(Position... Centre-Back)

CHIEF CHARACTERISTIC... DELIVERING CAPITAL PUNISHMENT
FROM THE BOYS IN BLUE

TOP ACCOMPLICES... PADDY MORAN, CIARÁN WALSH, KEITH GALVIN,
PAUL CURRAN, MICK DEEGAN, PAUL BEALIN

KEITH BARR

'WHEN I STARTED, YOU COULD GO OUT AND HAVE A
PINT, YOU COULD COME OUT OF THE PUB, YOU COULD
HAVE A P*** BESIDE THE LAMP-POST.'
– KEITH BARR

'**O**NE kick from immortality…

Keith Barr was never a man to shirk responsibility. When the moment arrived, he stepped forward when many would have sought refuge in the safety of the shadows.

In the Green Corner… Meath, a curious green and yellow monster – that once beheaded instantly seemed to sprout another one. In the Blue Corner… Dublin, desperately trying to channel their inner Van Helsing and finally, slay the beast.

Labour's Aodhán Ó Ríordáin, a lifelong Sky Blue, summed up the rabid disdain these urban and rural cousins had coursing through their veins.

'At that time, we cheered for every county that played against Meath. We took no pleasure in seeing our closest neighbours bring glory home. They were a side filled with hate-figures and we sang our distaste at every opportunity. At the time I thought Mick Lyons should have been tried in The Hague for crimes against humanity.'

**HARD
MAN
RATINGS**

TOUGHEST:
9.1/10

MEANEST:
9.8/10

SCARIEST:
9.0/10

HARDEST:
19.2/20

TOTAL
HARD MAN
47.1/50

The endless late drama began to wear on everybody, after a while. The supporters' nerves were shot, players were running on empty, and management had gone to the well once too often. Everyone desperately sought inspiration only to find that the cupboard had finally been laid bare.

The penalty awarded to Dublin in 1991 came at what felt like a decisive moment in the extraordinary Leinster Championship preliminary round… game four.

As Keith Barr manfully took the ball and strode forward, he was stuck between a rock and a hard place. Penalties are a kind of sporting version of Russian Roulette. Sometimes you dodge the bullet, and sometimes you don't.

Keith Barr knew a miss would ensure a case of paradise lost on Jones' Road. Those were the days of one strike and you're out – no sliding doors or open windows. The only way to stay in the championship was through the front door. Every contest was a lottery – a high-stakes bet – on an unforgiving roulette wheel.

The next 10 seconds could make or break his legacy. Whatever the outcome, this was a kick that would resonate through the corridors of time…

He had a streak of Boston's rebellious spirit in his blood. The seat of America's resistance during the War of Independence had always been partial to residents with a bit of backbone, which was something Keith Barr could never be accused of lacking.

Barr had played minor with his native Dublin, before following the well-worn Irish emigrant trail to one of the oldest cities in America, and also one of the most Irish… Boston.

Sometimes you chase your destiny and sometimes destiny chases you. Barr had always harboured hopes of lining out with his native county, so when the Dublin senior team touched down in the famous city dubbed 'Beantown' in the late 80s, the wheels of an unlikely reunion had been set in motion.

Barr had been playing with the local club, Colmcille's in Boston, and Keith had a date with destiny as the 'Sky Blues' played a challenge against the locals. The metropolitan's supremo at the time was Gerry McCaul, and he was smitten with Barr's all-action approach. He invited him onto the panel and Keith, who was by now yearning for home comforts, set sail for Erin's green shores.

Dublin was inching ever closer to another tilt at Sam Maguire, the city side was on the cusp of something special, and Barr's arrival added a real layer of substance. The Erin's Isle centre-back was a gritty campaigner, who always brought a bit of 'Devil' to his defensive duties. Keith Barr's presence was oxygen for fellow teammates and Dublin supporters. He had a manic energy, that fizzed and crackled on match days. The nature of the beast often came back to haunt him, as in the All-Ireland semi-final against Cork in 1989, when his dismissal had a significant bearing on the outcome. Dublin and Keith dusted themselves down, winning Leinster titles and National Leagues, before eventually lifting 'Sam' in 1995. His penalty miss in 1991 never really defined him.

He had built up far too much credit in the bank at that stage and had already achieved cult status on the Hill.

{ SUMMER IN DUBLIN }

Clashes with the Royal County were still a regular on the Leinster banquet and the irascible duo were at it again in a 1997 classic Leinster quarter-final. That old dusty merry-go-round kept spinning through the decades, the football world reassuredly turning on its axis. Like ice cream cones and swimsuits, no Irish summer was deemed complete without a good old fashioned 'barney' between Dublin and Meath. The absence of endless scrutiny on social media allowed players to have a pint and unwind, without being dragged before the 'court of public opinion'.

It was a different, less intrusive world where you could answer the call of nature, without a trillion clicks on YouTube as Keith recalled.

'When I started, you could go out and have a pint, you could come out of the pub, you could have a p*** beside the lamp-post.

'You might get a f***ing kebab on the way home, or you'd chase a bit of skirt. You were allowed to grow up, to make mistakes, and to have fun.'

There was one constant that remained eternally the same. Keith and Dublin were always 'Public Enemy Number One' and nobody loved Dublin *very much* – but they never really cared.

The championship always seemed to ratchet up a notch when Dublin rolled into 'Croker.' They were the rock stars of the GAA, big and loud and always larger than life. The urban giants always seemed to exude an air of superiority, a self-inflated sense of self-worth. This was a balloon that everybody wanted to stick a pin in!

Keith's high velocity – lung-busting runs – were a feature of his decade with the Dubs. When the city rocked to the 'Boys in Blue', Barr was spinning the discs to that thumping summer soundtrack. All guns blazing, always up for the battle, dragging the opposition to hell in a handcart.

URBAN LEGEND

THE TOUGH-TACKLING centre-back played club football with Erin's Isle in the capital. He won two Dublin championships as part of the club's first-ever successful sides in 1993 and 1997. He also was a member of Erin's Isle's historic Leinster Championship-winning team in 1997.

He made his senior county first start for the metropolitans in a championship match against Wicklow in 1989.

He won two National League titles, in 1991, and again in 1992 against Donegal, coming on as a substitute in the drawn first encounter between the sides.

He helped Dublin to success in the 1995 All-Ireland final, with a narrow victory over Tyrone. The win ended a 12-year hiatus for the city without Sam visiting the capital city.

Barr was awarded two All Star awards, the first coming in 1991, and a second duly arriving in Dublin's All-Ireland winning year. He also won five Leinster medals.

He represented Ireland in the International Rules Series, securing a winning medal in Ireland's victory over Australia in 1990.

FRANCIE BELLEW

(Height 6' 1", Weight 14.5 St)

Decade... 2000s

(Position... Full-Back)

CHIEF CHARACTERISTIC... JCB OPERATOR WHO
DRILLED HOLES IN THE OPPOSITION

TOP ACCOMPLICES... PAUL HEARTY, KIERAN MCGEENEY,
AIDAN O'ROURKE, JUSTIN MCNULTY, PAUL MCGRANE

FRANCIE BELLEW

'NORMALLY, THE MANAGER SPEAKS, AND THEN THE CAPTAIN SPEAKS. I WAS THE CAPTAIN AT THE TIME, BUT I JUST THOUGHT, WHAT WOULD BE THE POINT OF ME TRYING TO FOLLOW THAT? THE MAN HASN'T SPOKEN IN 25 YEARS.'

– OISIN MCCONVILLE

FRANCIE Bellew was a cult hero on the famous Armagh side of the early 2000s. For well over a decade, the flame-haired Bellew was a tower of strength at the back for the Orchard County. His swash-buckling all-action style, allied with an almost superhuman physical strength made him a firm favourite with fans all over the country.

Francie was often labelled 'JCB' by adoring fans, as when Armagh needed digging out of a gaping hole, he could always be counted on to dig deepest and shoulder all the heavy lifting.

Not everyone was convinced of Francie's attributes, however, with some pundits distinctly underwhelmed by the big man's robust style of play.

At half-time in the 2002, All-Ireland final, things were looking bleak for Francie and Armagh. *The Sunday Game* analyst and Kerry legend, Pat Spillane offered a fairly withering assessment of one Crossmaglen defender in particular.

HARD MAN RATINGS

TOUGHEST: 9.5/10

MEANEST: 8.5/10

SCARIEST: 9.0/10

HARDEST: 19.7/20

TOTAL HARD MAN 46.7/50

'The problem (with Armagh) is in the full-back line which we have highlighted all year,' said the Templenoe native. 'Francie Bellew is a very ordinary club footballer, lacking in pace. I swear to God, my mother would be faster than most of those three fellows. And, jeez, she has a little bit of arthritis on the knee.'

Perceptions can be misleading, however, and the genial giant from Crossmaglen was a red-haired box of wonders, with razor-sharp gaelic football intelligence. There was so much more to his game than pure strength and fierce determination, as Crossmaglen's Donal Murtagh related. 'He is more of a stopper, an old-fashioned type of centre-half,' said his Crossmaglen teammate. 'He's a great man for reading the play. He knows when to come across and when to leave his man. He stops things happening before they do.'

Francie was known as the 'quiet man of the team, his shy and humble demeanour totally at odds with his combative on-field persona. He had never represented Armagh at any level and was known to be a notoriously reclusive individual, who had previously turned down offers to join the county set-up.

Former Armagh co-manager, Brian McAlinden revealed that Francie had turned down requests to join the Armagh panel. 'Based on his club championship performances we felt that Francie would have been suitable for the squad, but unfortunately, I think on several occasions, he turned down a request.'

Former teammate, Oisin McConville tells a tale about Francie's first ever training session with Armagh, and how his storied career almost ended… before it started.

Crossmaglen were managed at the time by Joe Kernan, who was also the manager of the Armagh senior squad. Kernan had seen

Bellew at close quarters and was fully aware of what an excellent addition he would be to the county panel. The problem was how to coax him into the fold – without scaring him off completely!

McConville gleefully picks up the story.

'Joe, having taken over the Armagh team in 2002, rang Francie and said: "Francie, I want you to be part of the Armagh team."

'Right, dead on Joe.'

'We're training Tuesday night,' Joe continued.

'Right. Dead on Joe. Whereabouts is that?'

'Armagh!'

'Right. See you there!'

Francie never turned up. Thursday night came… Francie never showed up. Kernan, however, was not a man to be put off easily. He was convinced his club man could be the missing link for what was already a very promising-looking Armagh backline.

McConville continues: 'So the following Tuesday, Joe called to his house and he wasn't there, he wasn't home from work. And Joe waited for him for 45 minutes. So much so that Joe was actually late for training that night.

He finally arrived with Francie Bellew and that was Francie's first training session.'

{THE RELUCTANT HERO}

Francie Bellew was a man who avoided the limelight like the plague! The reserved Bellew was best summed up by PRO Tom McKay. 'He is more talkative with those he knows, but he's naturally a shy person. You'd have to know him a long time to get 20 words out of him.'

It was a rare event if Frankie ever deemed the need to address his comrades in arms. There was one occasion, however, when another red-head's antics were the straw that finally broke the camel's back!

Colm Cooper of Dr Crokes had been in flying form during the All-Ireland Club Championship. The ginger magician would finish the championship with a very impressive total of 6-23. Cooper had 'skinned' Frankie a few times in the first half and the normally reticent Bellow was fuming at the break.

A man who had known him longer than most, Oisin McConville continues the story.

'I remember 2007… we played Crokes. At half-time I'd never heard Francie talking (in the dressing-room). I played with Francie from roughly six or seven years of age, and he never opened his mouth in the dressing room.

'Francie was annoyed because I think the Gooch skinned him a couple of times in the first-half. Francie just let go at half-time. That was the first time he ever talked. He'd never spoken before in the room.

'He said he was going to maybe leave something on the Gooch in the second-half. He also wanted the rest of us to step up and be a bit more physical. Normally, the manager speaks, and then the captain speaks. I was the captain at the time, but I just thought… *What would be the point of me trying to follow that? The man hasn't spoken in 25 years.*'

Francie's impromptu delivery had the desired effect as Crossmaglen eventually won the title, following a 0-13 to 1-5 defeat of the Killarney outfit in the All-Ireland final replay at O'Moore Park.

Francie Bellew was probably one of the most under-rated players in the Orchard County's march to ultimate glory. The quiet, unassuming 'Cross' man let his football do the talking, leaving his opponents lost for words!

FRANCIE'S FANTASTIC VOYAGE

FRANCIE BELLEW made his senior championship debut against Tyrone in 2002. It would turn out to be a year to remember for the Crossmaglen man as Armagh secured provincial honours winning the Ulster final by 1-14 to 1-10 in a tense affair with Donegal. His dream season continued as Armagh stunned favourites Kerry in the All-Ireland final to win their first-ever Sam Maguire Cup.

Armagh reached the 'Big Show' again at Croke Park the following year. Neighbours Tyrone provided the opposition in a first-ever meeting in a final between two counties from the same province. The 116th All-Ireland final would end in a defeat for Bellew and Armagh, on a day when they failed to fire on all cylinders. Francie picked up a fully merited All-Star award later in the year.

The following season saw Armagh and Bellew collect another Ulster crown. In 2005, Bellew helped Armagh win a National League title, beating surprise packets Wexford in the final.

The Armagh juggernaut rolled on as they completed a three-in-a-row of provincial championships in 2006. Francie won Ulster again in 2008, his fifth in total. Francie Bellew hung up his boots when retiring from county football in April 2009.

With Crossmaglen, Francie won 13 Armagh titles, eight Ulster Championships and five All-Ireland titles in an illustrious career.

COLM BOYLE
(Height 5' 11", Weight 14 St)

Decade... 2000s/2010s/2020s
(Position... Wing-Back)

CHIEF CHARACTERISTIC... HIS DEFENSIVE THERMOSTAT WAS
ALWAYS SET TO BOYLE - ING POINT

TOP ACCOMPLICES... LEE KEEGAN, CHRIS BARRETT, DONAL
VAUGHAN, PADDY DURCAN, TOM PARSONS, ALAN DILLON

COLM BOYLE

**'I WAS HITTING 34, CRUCIATE GONE, I WAS FAIRLY SURE
THAT WAS MY LAST YEAR. IT WAS EMOTIONAL'
– COLM BOYLE**

SEPTEMBER 23, 1951. The legend tells us that it was an innocuous event borne purely out of wild and impetuous youth… and good old-fashioned bad-timing. Perhaps in hindsight, they should have given Foxford a wider berth.

The graveyard was silent, except for a few final supplications to the heavens. The priest blessed the coffin, as a teary-eyed band of mourners bowed their heads against an icy September wind. The cleric's eyes narrowed in rage as the boisterous group of young men clutching the Sam Maguire Cup rolled noisily past in a truck. What manner of men would be laughing and joking in the middle of a funeral service?

The outraged priest almost choked on the fateful words in anger. For the football-mad residents of Mayo, that may well have been a mercy, as when he recovered all hell was unleashed on the sons of Mayo.

'For as long as you all live, Mayo won't win another All-Ireland.'

HARD MAN RATINGS

TOUGHEST:
9.0/10

MEANEST:
9.3/10

SCARIEST:
8.9/10

HARDEST:
19.0/20

TOTAL HARD MAN
46.2/50

The unwitting All-Ireland winning group was in high spirits when they accidentally stumbled upon a funeral service. Slightly perplexed, they soon left the irate clergyman in the rear-view mirror and continued on their merry way.

Unknowingly, the jubilant Mayo men had released a genie out of the bottle. Whatever poltergeist or piseogary they had unleashed was sadly of the disconcerting variety. As the football-mad county basked in seventh heaven, the angry priest's words had unlocked the gates of doom. As darkness fell along the borders of Mayo, and the bonfires lit up the western skies, something vile was stirring in the shadows.

The celebrating players paid little heed to the cleric's curse – but the fateful words would rise up on the freshening evening wind, and echo through the ages…

Colm Boyle shook his head in disbelief. Own goals in soccer were a rare enough event, but an own goal in an All-Ireland football final? Mayo had flown out of the blocks in the 2016 All-Ireland decider, only to be hit with two sucker punches in quick succession.

First up was the unfortunate Kevin McLoughlin, and it was deja-vu of the excruciating kind next, as Colm Boyle could hardly believe his rotten look as the ball cannoned off him past a bemused David Clarke.

On many occasions, the Castlebar native must have dreamed of finding the net in an All-Ireland final, but this was as cruel a twist on the 'be careful what you wish for' idiom, as it possibly gets.

Colm Boyle was a graduate of the Mayo successful All-Ireland under-21 class of 2006, a side that had yielded a rich harvest that included Boyle, Ger Cafferkey, Keith Higgins, Tom Cunniffe, and Chris Barrett.

This was the first of four All-Ireland final instalments that would end in mind-numbing defeat.

For Boyle, the agony was even prolonged by a week as Mayo somehow recovered from the concession of two own-goals to force a replay.

Colm's Mayo career, like so many valiant men before him was cursed with an impenetrable glass ceiling. Level eight is the highest grade of unbreakable glass and Mayo's ceiling had been soundly fitted out with a bulletproof roof.

That never deterred the full-blooded, single-minded defender in the slightest. Colm Boyle just shrugged his shoulders and went to the well one more time. His gung-ho style made him the darling of the fanatical Mayo following. Whenever Mayo were tethering on the ropes, he invariably led the charge, smashing through the blockades and breathing oxygen inducing energy into tired limbs and minds.

Nothing seemed to stem his perpetual battling motion. Having been hospitalised on the eve of his first All-Ireland final appearance in 2012 it seemed certain that Mayo would be shorn of Boyle's titanic presence in the decider.

Boyle shook off the virus and put in a magnificent shift against Donegal. This would turn out to be a recurring theme of the Castlebar flier's incredible career, as his manager James Horan reverently attested too.

'A very courageous guy. A week before the All-Ireland final, he was in hospital for a while, so it just shows you the level of commitment he has and what he is prepared to do for the team.'

{COMING OF AGE}

His career followed a wildly oscillating trajectory; when after being introduced in 2008, he flunked his audition in the Connacht final against a rampant Galway. A four-year hiatus ensued as it looked like Colm Boyle's career would not make it out of the blocks.

A string of epic displays from centre-back in his club's march to the All-Ireland Intermediate final, duly propelled him back onto new manager, James Horan's radar. The new regime was a shock to Colm's system.

'It's totally different, A different game. Everyone can see the professionalism that's in it. It's totally different. It's much more commitment, much more intense, it's much more specific.

Training is so game-specific. Everything we do is very much based on how we want to play.'

Colm was reborn as a county footballer, and the Mayo rollercoaster kept on spinning. Yet, wherever they turned, the curse surely followed.

Myth or dark magic?

The last surviving member of the 1951 side passed away in 2021, at the age of 95. Here's what the legendary Paddy Prendergast had to offer on the infamous event.

'I don't know whether there was or not. I saw people standing around the church but we didn't get off the truck because we couldn't get off the bloody truck.'

With all links severed to that fateful September evening, perhaps now, finally, Mayo's time has arrived? Mayo football has given us many gifts over the decades, and none more gratefully received than the dashing, courageous Colm Boyle.

A fighter whose career played out in two very different acts was at the epicentre of Mayo's years of resistance. When the green and red finally reach the promised shores, players like Colm Boyle will have hammered out the hard yards.

He may have been cursed by history, but gaelic football followers were truly blessed to have been graced by his majestic presence.

THE KING
OF
CASTLEBAR

COLM BOYLE was born on July 29, 1986. He is a native of Castlebar, County Mayo, and played his club football for Davitts. In 2012, Davitts won both the Mayo and Connacht Intermediate titles, and qualified for the All-Ireland final, where they were defeated by Kerry side Milltown-Castlemaine.

He was a stand-out underage player for the county and captained the minor side before winning an All-Ireland under-21 medal in 2006 as Mayo defeated Cork in a close encounter 1-13- to 1-11. He made his senior championship debut for the county two years later at right-corner-back against Sligo.

In a decorated 14-year spell in the green and red, he was part of the squad for seven All-Ireland finals, playing on the losing side in four - 2012, 2013, 2016 and 2017.

He has won six Connacht senior titles with Mayo and appeared on 120 occasions for the western county. He is the joint record holder of provincial medals and All Stars along with fellow legends Keith Higgins, and Lee Keegan.

He represented Ireland against Australia in the 2013 International Rules Series. He missed the 2020, and 2021 All-Ireland final losses to Dublin and Tyrone due to a torn anterior cruciate ligament.

NIALL CAHALANE

(Height 5' 11", Weight 15 St)

Decade... 1980s/1990s

(Position... Corner-Back)

CHIEF CHARACTERISTIC... CHIEF EXECUTIVE CORK
JERSEY TESTING DEPARTMENT

TOP ACCOMPLICES... TONY NATION, STEPHEN O'BRIEN,
DENIS WALSH, CONOR COUNIHAN, BARRY COFFEY, SHEA FAHY

NIALL CAHALANE

'THE WAY YOU MIGHT PUT IT IS THAT, BACK THEN, A
LOT OF CORNER-BACKS WERE F***ING PLUGS LIKE
MYSELF, A BIT OF BRUTE STRENGTH.'
— NIALL CAHALANE

'A MICKEY Mouse Final.'

The words had cut Cork to the marrow. The newly crowned Sam Maguire holders of 1989 were fuming – nothing quite riles a gladiator than questioning his manhood. The fact that the slight was delivered by Kerry's legendary leader, Mick O'Dwyer, almost sparked an all-out war.

Whether the Waterville maestro actually delivered such withering rhetoric was a matter for another day. Cork Manager, Billy Morgan had the bones of his 1990 All-Ireland final team-talk... sorted.

The 1990 version of the Rebels was a team that was firmly on a war footing. It was time to settle some old scores for a bunch of angry young men, and none played angrier than Castlehaven's, Niall Cahalane.

Cahalane and the word 'soft' were uneasy bedfellows. Since captaining the Cork under-21 side to All-Ireland glory, the 'Rock of Castlehaven'

HARD MAN RATINGS
TOUGHEST: 9.8/10
MEANEST: 8.9/10
SCARIEST: 9.1/10
HARDEST: 19.3/20
☠
TOTAL HARD MAN 47.1/50

had added a layer of granite to the belly of the Cork county team.

The Rebel supporters slept a little more easily in their beds the night before the 1990 All-Ireland final against Meath, though many would rightfully consider sleeping with both eyes open a necessity when locking horns with the Royals. Cahalane's presence however, was of the fully comprehensive insurance variety. Whatever cropped up during the course of the 70 odd minutes… Niall Cahalane had it covered!

Niall was a man that fed off criticism like a frenzied piranha fish. Slight and insults were the petrol of the unleaded variety – they turbo-charged his octane levels!

Kerry legend Pat Spillane is a man with a penchant for getting under even the toughest of skins and Niall recalled his first close encounter against the flying Templenoe icon with little fondness.

'I liked going up against good players. I remember the first time I marked Pat Spillane, I was about 20 and he got about 2-3… and afterwards, I was shaking his hand – a bit in awe – and he said, "You've an awful lot to learn, ladeen!" To this day, if I was asked for one thing which helped me to drive on to a higher level, it was probably that comment.'

Despite the perception that he thrived on fire and fury, he was also a shrewd operator – one who did his homework thoroughly on future opponents.

'With Colm O'Rourke, I knew he'd beat me to a few balls, he was big for a corner-forward and a good fielder but he was predominantly left-legged, so it was a case of turning him back onto the right. It never bothered me whether I was full-back, corner-back, wing-back… I just wanted to be on the team.

'Invariably, I'd have been a man-marker and, if I came off the pitch without having touched the ball and my opponent hadn't scored, you'd consider that a good return. That's probably how I became a bit of a journeyman in the backline; I played in all the positions. It didn't bother me sacrificing my game to mark a danger man.'

{ HOLDING BACK THE YEARS }

Great battles nearly always depend on even greater sacrifices, and going to the well against Meath was likely going to require the whole nine yards. The Royals took particular delight in raining on the Rebel parades. Cork had succumbed to Meath in the 1987 and 1988 (after a replay) All-Ireland finals, and Meath even had the temerity to twist the knife some more in an ill-tempered 1990 league quarter-final.

Cork manager Billy Morgan was reported to have fallen to his knees in the dressing-room, raised his hands to whatever sporting deities were on duty, and prayed that Meath would make it through to the All-Ireland final. Morgan was convinced Cork would uphold their end of the deal, and the stage was set for a heavyweight contest for the ages.

When the sides had last met in the 1988 final (replay) Meath had won out in the physical stakes, thanks in main part to Cork supremo, Billy Morgan.

He had ordered his charges to avoid off-the-ball confrontation and focus on playing the ball. It proved to be a fatal mistake against an opponent that was ready to punish even the slightest hint of weakness.

'It was the biggest mistake of my footballing life,' Morgan later admitted. 'Meath roughed us up afterwards and the boys didn't respond in kind because of my instructions. It was like giving them guns without ammunition.'

When the two by now bitter rivals eventually collided in 1990, Cork sustained a near catastrophic blow when they were reduced to 14 men. Taking the exact opposite route of their previous meeting, Colm O'Neill lashed out at Mick Lyons of Meath, a policy which, in general, most players avoided. O'Neill was handed his P45 for the indiscretion, and the game slowly descended into an arm wrestle, with the Rebels grinding out a two-point victory.

With Cork's manhood restored, Niall Cahalane had no intention of easing up.

Not many players manage to play at senior level aged 40, but Niall was always going to be involved for the long haul, as evidenced by his almost 50-year association with the Castlehaven Club.

Revered in the Rebel County, he never saw himself in the same exalted light as others.

'The way you might put it is that, back then, a lot of corner-backs were f***ing plugs like myself, a bit of brute strength.'

The kind of strength that generations of Cork football teams leaned heavily upon.

LIFE IN THE
COUNTY LANE

NIALL CAHALANE was born on September 25, 1963. His league and championship career at senior level with Cork spanned 14 seasons, from 1983 to 1997.

He hails from Castlehaven, and played his first competitive gaelic football at juvenile and underage levels with the club. He had a successful underage career which culminated in winning a number of divisional and county championship medals in all grades from under-12 to under-21.

He played senior football with Castlehaven, and in that time he secured three Munster medals and three county senior championship medals. He also played hurling with Cork giants, Blackrock.

Cahalane made his county debut aged 17 - when he was selected for the Cork minor football team, and was part of their 1981 All-Ireland winning side. He graduated to the Cork under-21 team and captained the team to the All-Ireland title in 1984.

He joined the Rebel senior ranks in 1979, gaining his first start during the 1983-84 league.

Cahalane won two All-Ireland medals back-to-back in 1989 and 1990. He was also part of the side that won seven Munster Championships, and one National Football League title.

He won two All Star awards, was selected as a member of the Ireland team for the International Rules Series in both 1986 and 1987.

PETER CANAVAN

(Height 5' 7", Weight 13.5 St)

Decade... 1990s/2000s

(Position... Corner-Forward)

CHIEF CHARACTERISTIC... 'PETER THE GREAT' BY NAME AND BY NATURE

TOP ACCOMPLICES... ENDA MCGINLEY, MARTIN PENROSE, BRIAN
DOOHER, STEPHEN O'NEILL, SEAN CAVANAGH

PETER CANAVAN

'THE MEDIA COMPARED TYRONE TO THE BRITISH ARMY
- ONCE WE CROSSED THE BORDER WE HAD NO POWER. I
THINK WE'VE A BIT OF POWER NOW.'

– PETER CANAVAN

WHEN a son was born to a Cossack family, his relatives present him with the gifts of an arrow, a bow, a cartridge, a bullet... and a gun. All of these items are then hung on the wall, over the boy's bed.

At the age of three, the boy is instructed on how to handle a horse. From the age of seven to eight, he is ready to fish and hunt with adults.

The first references to the Cossacks appear at the end of the 15th century, and their fame spread throughout Europe over the next 100 years. Their raids and robberies were legendary and daring – and their potential as a serious fighting force was unlimited.

The Cossacks were a volatile bunch, often hamstrung by internal disputes and local rivalries, but if properly united, they had a limitless capacity to wage war and emerge victorious.

'Peter the Great' was the first military leader of note to harness the power of the ancient band

HARD MAN RATINGS

TOUGHEST:
9.5/10

MEANEST:
8.5/10

SCARIEST:
9.4/10

HARDEST:
18.9/20

TOTAL HARD MAN
46.3/50

of warriors, as he mobilised them into a ferocious fighting force, winning the Battle of Azov in 1696.

The ability of astute leaders to recognise the potential of fearsome warriors and harness it into a potent and coherent fighting machine is as old as time.

Most occupants of Red Hand Country would claim there was only ever one who bore the illustrious title, 'Peter the Great'. Certainly, while the often much-derided Russian figurehead's place in the pantheon of the exalted military 'brains trusts' is debatable – there is no such conjecture about the 'real,' Peter the Great's place in the scheme of things!

Peter Canavan was Tyrone's Commander-in-Chief, and one of the greatest-ever warriors in GAA history. The leader of the Tyrone pack was cast in the likeness of his illustrious manager, Mickey Harte, exuding a quiet but firm authority, a man whom his Tyrone comrades would follow to the ends of the earth.

The Red Hand were like the Cossacks, a serious fighting machine that always seemed to be mired in local territorial disputes and in-house fighting. The county had probably the most unique demographic and area spread anywhere within the province. Suspicions of an east/west divide often lingered when it came to team selection, though it was likely borne out of domestic paranoia than rooted in any discernible reality.

Peter Canavan could tell a tale or two about local tensions, as he had to manoeuvre his way around a Gaelic Athletic Association by-law, because of a dispute in his parish.

The career of one of the most influential players in gaelic football history almost perished upon the rocks, scuppered by the incredibly intricate and equally infuriating GAA rule book!

Two club sides both claimed to represent his native parish, the established Ballygawley St Ciaran's club and the newly formed entity, which was then labelled Errigal Ciaran Naomh Malachai.

Players from the Errigal side of the fence were not recognised as being GAA members, because of an error in the registration process. Canavan was caught in the crossfire, as his unique status ensured exile from playing any meaningful football.

Peter's doggedness on the pitch was mirrored by a steely determination off it.

Undaunted, he registered as a member of the Killyclogher hurling club, even though he never held a camán or struck a sliotar in anger during his fledging GAA career. It turned out to be a piece of inspired improvisation, paving the way for his eligibility for selection for the Tyrone minors.

His ascent to the senior county throne would be of the more fractured variety – as Tyrone often resembled a one-man band – with Peter playing lead guitar! Peter was by now upholding his end of the bargain, as he replicated his scoring exploits from the under-21 grade, which saw him bag a staggering 13-53 in his four years there.

Having top-scored in the senior ranks in his first season in 1994, Peter became a target for the flesh-eating defenders, who brought the slogan, 'Ulster says No' to a whole new level!

While they reached the 1995 All-Ireland final with Canavan notching 11 points, the supporting cast kept fluffing their lines as the Red Hand's attacking unit miscued badly.

Peter continued to sparkle and by 1996, as a provincial top-scorer for the third time on the spin, he claimed a third successive All Star.

{ NO TO AUSSIE BULLYING }

The Red Hand's travails continued apace during the late 90s, at which time Peter donned the Irish jersey in the International Rules tests against Australia. He made his mark in more ways than one, when the wee Ballygawley man was sent off for tangling with another fiery campaigner in the shape of the Aussie, Jason Akermanis.

Canavan was a star turn for Ireland scoring 37 points in five career tests, with even the bloodthirsty Australian public appreciating his raw competitive edge against vastly superior physical presences.

Having won a first National League in 2002, it appeared Tyrone's All-Ireland credentials were on a more solid footing than previous incarnations, and they were installed as hesitant favourites in the eyes of the bookmakers for ultimate glory.

Defeat in a qualifying match to Sligo left even the normally indomitable Canavan reluctantly considering his future. On a personal level, he won his fourth All Star that year, making him Tyrone's most represented player on that Roll of Honour, overhauling Eugene McKenna.

When an emerging Tyrone finally landed the Sam Maguire Cup in 2003, 'Peter the Great' added yet another compelling layer to his incredible story.

Tyrone's top scorer on the day had left the field with a serious ankle injury, only to return with 10 minutes left to steer the Red Hand home. His return from the dead spooked fellow Ulster rivals Armagh, and cementing Peter's legacy for posterity.

Accepting the trophy, Tyrone's Peter reflected on the Red

Hand's turbulent journey.

'The media compared Tyrone to the British army – once we crossed the Border we had no power. I think we've a bit of power now.'

Power and this 'Peter the Great' always went hand in... Red Hand!

A LEADER'S LIFE

PETER CANAVAN was born on April 9, 1971, and is a native of Glencull, near Ballygawley. He played his club football with Errigal Ciarán, representing the famous club for nearly 17 seasons.

The club is a relatively new entity - having been formed at the dawn of the 1990s. They have enjoyed notable success in that period - winning eight Tyrone senior titles, and two Ulster Club Championships.

Peter Canavan was the driving force in their rapid ascent to the Tyrone club throne, and was on board for six county championships and two provincial titles.

His county life started at minor level as Tyrone won an Ulster Championship, and he was part of the all-conquering under-21 side that secured All-Ireland titles in 1991 and 1992.

Canavan began to make a serious impact in the Ulster Senior Championship in 1994, finishing as the top scorer in the province and earning his first All Star at the age of 23.

Peter would go on to become one of the most feared forwards of all time, winning two All-Ireland Senior Championship medals, and six All Stars awards, (more than any other Ulster player).

RICHIE CONNOR

(Height 6' 2", Weight 15 St)

Decade... 1970s/1980s

(Position... Centre-Back/Centre-Forward)

CHIEF CHARACTERISTIC... DISPROVING THE AGE-OLD
THEORY THAT NO MAN IS AN ISLAND

TOP ACCOMPLICES... LIAM CURRAMS, MARTIN FURLONG, SEAN
LOWRY, BRENDAN LOWRY, PÁDRAIG DUNNE, JOHNNY MOONEY

RICHIE CONNOR

'RICHIE CONNOR, HE WAS AS BRAVE AS
THEY COME, ONE TOUGH MAN.'
– BRIAN MULLINS

'**K**ING for a day…

King of Kings had an air of majesty as he left the stage for the final time. He had returned lame after the feature race, where many expected him to be crowned the king of them all.

When the horse had justified all the hype with a stunning turn of foot to win the Sagitta 2,000 Guineas at Newmarket in great style, the future seemed incredibly bright for the fleet-of-foot, Aidan O'Brien speedster.

Having clocked one minute and 14 seconds without being over-extended at seven furlongs in the Railway Stakes the year previously, it was clear the horse had an exceptional cruising speed and a blistering finishing kick.

Watching the magnificent steed being led painfully away after the Vodafone Irish Derby was a reminder of the fickle and unforgiving nature of elite sport. The crowds in the marquees were in high spirits, revelling in all the lavish trappings and impossible style of one of the biggest days in

**HARD
MAN
RATINGS**

TOUGHEST:
9.5/10

MEANEST:
9.2/10

SCARIEST:
8.9/10

HARDEST:
19.1/20

**TOTAL
HARD MAN
46.7/50**

the Irish equine calendar. The horse seemed to exude a certain sadness, like a superhero stripped of his powers.

Yet, the King of Kings had retained an air of majesty as he left the arena for the final time.

This was supposed to be a day of coronation; now the Ballydoyle superstar would never grace a racetrack again. If, when he grazed in some far-flung corner of a fertile field, did a distant memory ever flicker of the light of better days? Did he ever remember the time when he was crowned king for a day...

{ THROUGH THE CONVERGING CROWD }

Ritchie Connor burst through the converging crowd – running hard and running free. The game was over, and the Faithful had carried this most glorious of Irish sporting days.

There wasn't room to swing a cat, but Connor found space among the onrushing hordes.

That had been the story of the day as underdogs Offaly, navigated through narrow gaps to punish every Kerry indiscretion, while keeping the space among the Croke Park acres at a premium for the Kingdom. They had visited many plagues upon footballs High Kings, including assault and battery and, most scurrilous of them all, an act of grand larceny.

Kerry's Pat Spillane would lock himself in the Jones' Road toilet afterward and shed bitter tears, in truth if the whole county of Kerry could have squeezed into the tight cubicle, they would have cried a river along with him. It had been that sort of an emotional rollercoaster day in Croke Park. On one hand unbridled joy, and a thousand sorrows tattooed on the other.

It was a dark heavy day filled with swelling rain clouds, a day for men of real resolve, like celebrated Offaly fighter Richie Connor. The Walsh Island titan had put in some shifts in the county colours, as a centre-back and a roving midfielder. Now here he was on All-Ireland day, burning it up at centre-forward.

{ BORN OUT OF STRIFE }

Richie Connor, along with Matt his talismanic sibling, was born out of a crisis… of the footballing kind! The Eire Og club was a combination of Clonbologue, Bracknagh, and Walsh Island, but all the under-achieving combination side had to show for their endeavours was a county final appearance against Gracefield in 1970.

Dissatisfied with the parochial politics, Walsh Island decided to go it alone in the mid-1970s, and the seeds of an unlikely All-Ireland success were duly sown. The breakaway club spawned a remarkable dynasty that influenced the destination of the All-Ireland title in 1982. The Island qualified for an Offaly final in their first year of splendid isolation, narrowly missing on the title after a replay against Ferbane. Two years later, in 1978, they were back to win the Dowling Cup. From there they hoovered up an astonishing six in-a-row as Richie's towering presence lent a real backbone to the new kids on the Faithful block.

Offaly had made a major statement at the start of the 1970s with two All-Ireland successes in 1971 and '72, but they struggled to maintain the dizzying altitude they had reached, and they had soon plummeted back down to basement level within the provincial hierarchy.

The Metropolitans in sky-blue made capital gains and annexed six provincial titles on the trot, 1974 to 1979. By this stage, Offaly had regenerated and was captained by a barn-storming performer Connor.

When the two sides collided in the 1979 decider, the Faithful looked set for silverware as they kept their noses in front, with the sands in the hour-glass rapidly running out of grains.

Jimmy Keaveney had walked the plank after receiving a red, when Brian Mullins loaded the rifle cartridges for Bernard Brogan to shoot the Faithful hopes to smithereens.

Undaunted, Eugene McGee's warriors returned in 1980, and conquered the province before being squeezed out in the All-Ireland Semi by Kerry, despite a magical haul of 2-9 from Matt Connor.

Forewarned was not forearmed for the Kingdom, as after seeing off the Faithful in 1981 final, they were floored by Seamus Darby's sucker punch in a dramatic 1982 All-Ireland final.

As Richie Connor climbed the stairway to heaven, and lifted Sam into a grey Dublin sky the fickle hand of fate would decree that Offaly would never lift the famous old trophy again.

Yet, nothing would ever erase the shine of that spectacular victory, as Richie and the Faithful broke the chains that bound them, to gallop wild and free.

Kings for a day…

AN ISLANDER'S LIFE

RICHIE CONNOR was born in 1954 in Walsh Island, County Offaly. He was a powerful all-round presence, who lined out in a variety of guises including midfield, and at centre-forward and centre-back for his club, Walsh Island, and the Offaly senior football team.

He enjoyed a successful underage club career, with his first success arriving with the Erin's Hope team that won the Dublin under-21 title in 1974. He also helped them retain the title in 1975, and then won an Offaly under-21 medal with Walsh Island in the same year.

He was a colossal figure as the famed green and white hooped 'Islanders' dominated senior level, winning an astonishing haul of six county titles in-a-row from 1978 to 1983. He also captained Walsh Island to the 1981 and 1983 titles. Connor and Walsh Island contested two Leinster senior finals in succession in 1979-80, winning the title on both occasions, but never reached the All-Ireland final.

He spent almost 15 years with Walsh Island – hanging up his boots at the end of the 1989 Offaly Championship campaign.

He is best known as the man who captained Offaly to an historic All-Ireland win over red-hot favourites Kerry in the 1982 final, and it was also the last occasion the 'Faithful' ever lifted the Sam Maguire trophy.

He won one All-Star, along with three Leinster titles, to add to his 1982 Celtic Cross.

JONNY COOPER
(Height 5' 11", Weight 14 St)

Decade... 2010s/2020s
(Position... Corner-Back)

CHIEF CHARACTERISTIC... PESTERING INTER-COUNTY
FORWARDS INSIDE AND OUTSIDE CROKE PARK

TOP ACCOMPLICES... PHILLY MCMAHON, JOHN SMALL, MICHEAL
FITZSIMONS, JACK MCCAFFREY, STEPHEN CLUXTON

JONNY COOPER

"SO, SUCCESS ISN'T ALWAYS MEASURED ON THE SCOREBOARD.
INTER-COUNTY FOOTBALL IS FULL OF HIDDEN WINS, HAPPENING IN
THE BLINK OF AN EYE, UNRECOGNISABLE TO ONLOOKERS.

– JONNY COOPER

NEW YORK CITY. Sunday September 14, 1947.
The match poster boldly proclaimed... 'WORLD'S
GREATEST FOOTBALL GAME. It went on to detail the
event which was taking place in the heart of New York City...
'THE ALL- IRELAND GAELIC FOOTBALL FINAL'.

Coogan's Hollow stretched out lazily northward from 155th
Street in Manhattan. Anyone seeking higher
ground in the 'City That Never Sleeps' could
certainly take solace here. The suffocating
heatwave held the city in a vice-like grip, and the
stadium's pitch was a hard-boned bowl of dust. It
would not be a day for fancy football; luckily All-
Ireland's exist exclusively for the winning.

The decision to play the 1947 All-Ireland final
in New York was a goodwill gesture to mark the
centenary of the 'Great Famine' and to honour
members of the large Irish diaspora – most of
whom had been dislodged to the Big Apple.

A glance at old sepia images reveals a snapshot

**HARD
MAN
RATINGS**

TOUGHEST:
9.1/10

MEANEST:
10/10

SCARIEST:
8.9/10

HARDEST:
19.0/20

TOTAL
HARD MAN
47.0/50

of the host city for the football final. Scores of bustling commuters roam along 8th Avenue in Manhattan, a route well served by both bus and subway, a vibrant stretch that ran from the West Village up into Harlem.

A grainy image reveals a handful of migrants lingering outside Whelan's store by the Independent subway which served Uptown, The Bronx, and Queens. A magical old curiosity shop, where you could purchase anything from a bottle of Coke to a hairdryer!

The stadium was better known as a baseball venue and even the mere utterance of its name – evokes a sense of enduring wonder.

The Polo Grounds opened on April 19, 1890 and finally closed its stadium doors on December 14, 1963. The original Polo Grounds area in New York City meandered south and north by 110th and 112th streets, and on the east and west by Fifth and Sixth (Lenox) Avenues, just north of Central Park.

It was the first home of the famed New York Mets baseball team and after it was renovated in 1911, peering out majestically from its perch, on a steep escarpment that descends 175 feet to the Harlem River below.

The ageing poster was bang on the money as it urged you to purchase a ticket...

POLO GROUNDS NEW YORK CITY
ADMISSION 2 DOLLARS
RESERVE YOUR TICKET NOW
ENJOY THE THRILLS OF A LIFETIME AT
THE MATCH OF THE CENTURY

Mitchel Cogley enthused in the *Irish Independent* the next day. *It was a game worthy of a great occasion. The pitch was concrete hard, and the ball as lively as a kitten.*

Cavan defeated Kerry in the only final that has ever taken place outside Ireland. Simon Deignan was a member of the victorious Breffni side and would go on to win three All-Ireland medals.

It was quite a haul for the colossus from Mullagh, County Cavan, and he would participate in a staggering 12 All-Ireland finals, as a player or referee. He was one of the last surviving members of the famed Cavan side, when he passed away in 2006. Around that time, his grandnephew was about to set out on an extraordinary All-Ireland journey all of his own. The family connection with All-Ireland final day was only getting started.

{MAKING CAPITAL GAINS}

After Dublin's 2011 All-Ireland success, almost everybody in the capital was basking in the sweet afterglow of breakthrough success. Dublin was back in vogue, yet there was the odd unhappy camper!

Jonny Cooper had knocked on the door of the 2011 panel, but Pat Gilroy never let him in. He was desperate to jump onboard the Dublin Express; the runaway train was leaving the station, and hell or high water, the Na Fianna man was determined to be part of the journey.

The morning following Dublin winning the 2011 All-Ireland final, Jonny was mad for the road, and an impromptu training session followed!

'Because I knew the 30-odd guys that were my direct competitors weren't going to be training and I was trying to get the edge there, in my own small way.'

Edge was something Jonny provided in abundance and when

his former under-21 manager, Jim Gavin took over the capital sides reins in 2012, Johnny's cut and thrust was destined to be a large part of his future philosophy.

Those plans went out the window when Jonny's life was plunged into despair, as he was victim of a knife attack. It would take nearly two years for the mental scars of the traumatic event to heal.

That he returned to play such a significant part in Dublin's history-making six in-a-row success is a testament to one of inter-county football's truly courageous individuals.

Jonny Cooper will readily admit to not being much of a talker, but his psychology offers the kind of insight that takes you under the skin of the game. Sometimes a defeat is the essential ingredient that can lead to the building blocks of a football dynasty.

After the harrowing defeat to Donegal in 2014, Dublin became a different animal as Cooper revealed.

After that game, we became even more connected; we were challenging ourselves regularly but after that game, we tried to ask ourselves the right questions relentlessly; we felt the energy of our supporters up and down the country – after Donegal, we came to understand how to tap into that support to get us over the finish line many times in the following years.

So, success isn't always measured on the scoreboard. Inter-county football is full of hidden wins, happening in the blink of an eye, unrecognisable to onlookers. For players, however, they're completely obvious.

It's what they train for. It's a specific frequency that they operate on. When connected, it's powerful.

Connecting the dots was something Jonny Cooper did better

than most. He was the sword of fury, a swashbuckling pillar of defiance, a throwback to the gladiatorial battlefields of the 40s and 50s. Connecting the dots… all the way back to 1947.

AN URBAN LEGEND

JONNY COOPER was always destined to be a footballer. A grandnephew of triple All-Ireland winning Cavan great, Simon Deignan, and his grandfather was one of the founders of the Na Fianna club. Jonny was a decent underage hurler, before becoming an integral part of the Dublin under-21 side managed by future legendary Dublin coach, Jim Gavin.

Cooper won an All-Ireland 'A' hurling medal while playing with Dublin Colleges during their 2006 campaign, and secured a Leinster Minor Hurling Championship medal the following season.

Jim Gavin named Cooper as captain of the 2010 Dublin under-21 football team, but Cooper was hampered by a troublesome shoulder injury that required surgery. He kept playing through the pain barrier, but was not selected as part of Pat Gilroy's senior squad.

Cooper played a handful of games in the 2012 National Football League, but only a quarter of the Leinster Senior Football Championship quarter-final win over Louth.

He was part of the Dublin team that defeated Tyrone by 0-18 to 0-17 to win the 2013 National Football League, with Jim Gavin now at the helm. He won his first Celtic Cross when Dublin beat Mayo by 2-12 to 1-14 in the 2013 All-Ireland final.

In a glorious career, he won 10 Leinster senior titles, seven All-Irelands and six National Football Leagues, as well as two All Star awards.

CONOR COUNIHAN

(Height 5' 10", Weight 14 St)

Decade... 1980s/1990s

(Position... Centre-Back)

CHIEF CHARACTERISTIC... LEADER OF THE
REBEL RISINGS IN 1989 AND 1990

TOP ACCOMPLICES... NIALL CAHALANE, STEPHEN O'BRIEN, JIMMY
KERRIGAN, TONY DAVIS, JOHN KERINS, LARRY TOMPKINS

CONOR COUNIHAN

'DID I MISS IT FOR A WHILE? I DON'T MISS THE DEFEATS. THEY WERE HARD TO TAKE. I'D NEARLY HAVE TO WATCH THE VIDEO OF A DEFEAT THE SAME NIGHT TO SEE WHAT WENT WRONG AND TO START THE PROCESS OF WORKING OUT THE REASONS. IT BECOMES THAT ADDICTIVE.'

– CONOR COUNIHAN

THE journey out from the gaily painted buildings and shop fronts of Cobh takes a little more than 12 minutes. That's not a long wait to immerse yourself in 1,300 years of Irish history.

Nowadays, Spike Island can be a bewitching place – where you can enjoy two scenic walking trails, magnificent buildings, abandoned villages and convict cemeteries.

Spike Island has been host to a seventh-century monastery, a 24-acre fortress, the largest prison depot in the world during Victorian times, and a haven to centuries of rich and varied island life.

The island's website details the many different characters who inhabited the island, including monks, redcoats, captains and convicts, sinners and saints!

The star-shaped Fort Mitchel, which was home to 2,300 prisoners dominates the island, an ominous reminder of a darker past. It was the largest prison on the planet at the time, and there

HARD MAN RATINGS

TOUGHEST:
9.1/10

MEANEST:
8.5/10

SCARIEST:
8.9/10

HARDEST:
19.6/20

TOTAL HARD MAN
46.1/50

has never been a larger prison in Ireland or Britain before or since.

A day trip to the island is a must, and among the many and varied exhibits is a list of prisoners who were incarcerated on the island fortress. The names are drawn from all over Ireland – with a striking representation from County Cork.

The Rebel County has long been associated with the Irish fight for freedom – it's part of their DNA, a badge of courage that defines true 'Corkness'.

The Rebel County's 'Blood and Bandages' was born out of an act of grand larceny on the eve of the 1919 All-Ireland final when the forces of the crown stole the sacred jerseys of the Cork hurling team. Cork borrowed a set of red ones – won the final, and the legend of 'An Fuil agus an Bindealan' was born.

Over the decades, many sons of Cork have led the fight on the golden fields of our national games of gaelic football and hurling. If you were to pick a Rebel footballer that epitomised the Cork spirit with every fibre of his being, you could look no further than Conor Counihan.

Both as a player and a manager he fought tooth and nail to further the Rebel cause. If you could bottle Corkness and sell it as an aphrodisiac to the Rebel hordes, Counihan's name would be on the label!

Counihan made his first appearance in a low-key encounter against Waterford as corner-back in Dungarvin in 1981, but he was back doing 'bench service' by the time the Rebels inevitably faced Kerry in the Munster final. The Kingdom devoured Cork on the day, prevailing by 1-11 to 0-3.

Conor however, continued to burn brightly at club level with

Aghada and Imolkilly, and while the Rebels failed to make any significant inroads in the province until 1983, he became a regular cog in the Leeside defensive machine.

By the time Cork faced Kerry in the 1985 Munster final, he was captain of the side and gave a near flawless exhibition of the defensive arts when holding Denis 'Ogie' Moran scoreless.

Cork would finally put Kerry on the back-burner in Munster when winning four consecutive titles from 1987-90. The golden age of Cork football had arrived. With Conor's steely hand on the tiller, they would reach five All-Ireland finals (including the 1988 replay against Meath), winning two. Conor's tigerish tackling and tenacious tight marking was a key component in the Rebel army's march back to the top table. In his five All-Ireland appearances, he conceded a meagre tally of two points to his direct opponents – one of which was a hotly disputed free!

{ A REBEL RETURNS }

When he departed from the main GAA stage in 1993 they could have declared a week's mourning in Cork! Then in 2008, the county rejoiced, when after a few stints as a selector, he was appointed manager of the senior squad.

It was inevitable that any side fashioned in the likeness of the indefatigable Counihan would be custom-built for 'Operation, Sam Maguire'. Twenty long and painful seasons after Conor had lifted 'Sam', his fingerprints were once more – all over one of the biggest prizes in Irish sport. The 2010 victory over Down felt like it was written in the stars.

When his tenure came to an end in 2013, he had added

another three Munster crowns to the Cork trophy collection. For the warrior spirit that was Conor Counihan, the story was never about him – just always about Cork. As his side caved in against Dublin in 2013, he had decided that a fresh orator was required to stoke the fires in the Rebel dressing-room.

'We still have a good squad of players but after six years you have to ask yourself the questions, are you getting enough out of people and that sort of thing… and maybe I wasn't – that's for other people to judge. The important thing is that I step down and a fresh voice takes over and that Cork football reaches the pinnacle again.'

Just when every county in Ireland felt it was safe to go back to the cookie jar, Counihan was back on the horse again, when appointed the Cork County Board Project Co-ordinator for football in 2019. It seemed an inspired choice for the Rebel's five-year plan to regenerate and revive the county's ailing fortunes.

Had the old warrior missed his time away from the inter-county bearpit? There was one aspect he certainly did not pine for, as he soon revealed.

'Do I miss it? I don't miss it now because I'm engaged in this. Did I miss it for a while? I don't miss the defeats.

'They were hard to take. I'd nearly have to watch the video of a defeat the same night to see what went wrong and to start the process of working out the reasons. It becomes that addictive.'

It's an addiction the good people of Cork hope won't end any time soon. With Conor's steely hand back at the tiller, it won't be too long before the Rebels find their way back to real 'Corkness'.

THE
⟫ ⟶ CAPTAIN'S ⟵ ⟪
TALE

CONOR COUNIHAN was born September 28, 1959 in Aghada, County Cork. He was part of the Cork under-21 team, which reached the All-Ireland final, losing to Down in 1979. Counihan and Cork returned to the decider the following season claiming victory over Dublin.

He played his club football with Aghada and Divisional side Imolkilly. Imolkilly reached the final of the county Senior Championship for the first time ever in 1984, against Cork, kingpins St Finbarr's, claiming the title with a 2-14 to 2-7 scoreline.

Counihan was again a central part of their second title success in 1986, as they again edged the 'Barrs' by a single point. He helped Aghada to a fourth divisional junior medal of the decade in 1989. They later reached the final of the county championship against Knocknagree, winning by 0-8 to 0-4 to secure a Junior Football Championship medal.

After just two years at intermediate level, Aghada reached the county final against Ballincollig. A slender 0-9 to 0-8 victory gave Counihan an Intermediate Championship medal.

At senior level, Conor won two All-Ireland medals in 1989 and 1990. He also won four Munster Championships in-a-row 1987-90, and two All Star Awards.

He managed Cork to the All-Ireland football title in 2010, as well as three National Leagues and three Munster Championships.

COLM COYLE

(Height 5' 11", Weight 14 St)

Decade... 1980s/1990s

(Position... Corner-Back/Half-Back)

CHIEF CHARACTERISTIC... MEATH RIOT CONTROL
(RAPID RESPONSE UNIT)

TOP ACCOMPLICES... MICK LYONS, LIAM HARNAN,
KEVIN FOLEY, DARREN FAY

COLM COYLE

'HE'S AFTER DROPPING ABOUT SIX OF THEM!'
– UMPIRE FRANCIE MCMAHON

COLM Coyle was always a man you felt would go out with a bang. Coyle's glorious career was petering out in 1996, with a lot of the Royal's 'old guard' having ridden off into the sunset.

While the slippers and the fireside chair beckoned invitingly to him, he still felt the call of the 'wild' for one more spin on the roundabout.

Colm had provided so many talking points during his fantastic voyage, but he still had a couple more giant-sized rabbits to pull out of the hat!

It had started in innocuous fashion when, early in the 1996 All-Ireland final, Meath's full-back Darren Fay gathered the ball and looked to surge forward. A flying elbow floored him, and that was the signal for all hell to break loose. Croke Park had not witnessed a scrap of this magnitude since the memorable night it hosted the legendary Muhammed Ali's joust with Al 'Blue' Lewis back in 1972.

HARD MAN RATINGS

TOUGHEST:
9.3/10

MEANEST:
9.7/10

SCARIEST:
9.7/10

HARDEST:
19.1/20

TOTAL HARD MAN
47.8/50

Coyle recalled the flash point in the 1996 final vividly. 'He should have just given the free, but Pat McEnaney had told both teams he wanted a free-flowing game and would use the advantage rule,' said Coyle.

McEnaney decided he was going to send off two players, one from each team. In reality, he could have given marching orders to 20 more. An eyewitness in the form of umpire Francie McMahon made a bee-line to McEnaney, and offered an incriminating indictment of one Meath player in particular.

'Pat, you're going to have to send off Colm Coyle. He's after dropping about six of them.'

The umpire's intervention would prove costly for Royal's stalwart Coyle. He was dispatched to the line along with Mayo's Liam McHale.

Thankfully, the story for Colm would have a happy ending, as the ever-defiant Royals reigned supreme to reclaim Sam in a nerve-shredding conclusion.

Colm Coyle was a multi-talented performer who combined a hard-nosed defender's instincts with the natural predatory edge of a midfielder or scoring forward. Never were these attributes more in evidence than in the first game of the 1996 All-Ireland final when he somehow rescued a draw for Meath – with one of the most bizarre points in GAA history.

It had not been his finest hour in the famed green and gold jersey, and Coyle was glancing anxiously across at the sideline.

'I had an off day in the drawn final. I said to Sean Boylan that for around 55 of the 75 minutes, I kept looking over to see if he was going to call me ashore! I actually got into it for the last 15 or 20 minutes. That's the beauty of Sean. He'd say, "You were having a stinker, but I knew you'd come into it".'

Colm thundered into the game in the last quarter, but with time ticking away Meath were still losing by the bare minimum.

Coyle and his teammates were, however, finishing like a train. Sean Boylan had revitalised the panel during the winter months with an all-important injection of youthful energy.

'I was 33 in 1996. A load of young lads had come in, and training was tough, but brilliant. I'd never trained as hard. Dublin had beaten us in 1995 by 10 points and we'd lost a raft of players. Five or six had retired. Martin O'Connell asked me what I was doing, and I said,

"Jesus, I was half thinking of retiring, but there's too many lads gone". I gave it another shot and got a new lease of life. Those young lads just drove us on.'

The infusion of fresh blood was what the doctor ordered for a jaded-looking Meath outfit.

Despite the pessimistic expectations within the county, Sean Boylan's regeneration had the desired effect as they progressed to the decider for another tilt at Sam Maguire.

Mayo provided the opposition and Colm Coyle would be a central figure in a controversial drama in two acts. After a shaky first-half, Colm thundered into the contest but Mayo appeared to have weathered the storm. They were hanging on grimly to a slender one-point lead as time elapsed.

The 'Westerners' looked set to secure a first All-Ireland since 1951.

The Leinster kingpins launched one last despairing assault, but there appeared to be little danger as Colm Coyle's hopeful punt drifted in around the Mayo goalmouth.

What happened next defied all logic or reason? The ball hopped in a no-man's-land and somehow it evaded all and sundry. To audible gasps from the packed Croke Park stands, the bounce cleared the crossbar to restore parity, ensuring Sean Boylan's troops would live to fight another day.

{ KICKING JOE BROLLY UP THE ARSE }

Mercurial Derry forward, Joe Brolly had a fetish for blowing kisses to the crowd, which to the Meath legend was akin to waving a red rag at a bull!

Brolly recounted a hilarious example of Colm's disdain for prima-donnas in his *Gaelic Life* column. He had just scored a goal in the dying embers of a National League play-off, and began tousling the Meath goalkeeper's hair. Then he proceeded to blow kisses to the crowd.

What transpired next was reminiscent of an iconic episode from much-loved television series *Father Ted*, as a red mist descended upon Colm Coyle.

In that classic scene, Father Ted Crilly must kick his strict, overbearing superior, Bishop Brennan ('up the arse') as a forfeit set in the previous episode by Father Dick Byrne for cheating at a football match.

Colm booted Brolly up the backside, sending him crashing to the floor. The Derry talisman was transferred to the hospital to receive stitches.

Brolly's manager, Brian Mullins, seemed to concur with Colm Coyle's withering assessment of Brolly's antics. As Brolly was stretchered sheepishly off the sacred sod, he leaned over the stricken forward and whispered, 'You deserved that, you little bollocks'.

Like many before him, Brolly received 'The Order of the Royal Boot' as Colm Coyle replicated his enduring ability... to send forwards packing!

LIFE IN THE ROYAL LANE

HE PLAYED his club football with Seneschalstown, and Coyle won a Leinster Minor Football Championship medal with Meath in 1980. He made his senior debut for Meath in the 1981/82 National League.

He was part of an emerging Meath team which won the Leinster Championship in 1986, Meath's first since 1970. Having cut short a stay in the US, Meath introduced him off the bench in the 1987 final, Meath's first All-Ireland triumph in 20 years!

Coyle was a 'starter' the following year when the Royals won a second All-Ireland in-a-row.

For Meath, he played in a number of positions, including in the full-back line, half-back line, half-forward line, and full forward line. While he excelled in most positions a defensive berth probably suited his combative style most.

In a glittering career, he won five Leinster titles, two National Leagues and three All-Ireland medals. After retirement, he went into coaching and managed the Monaghan senior football team. He was also at the helm of his native county. The Meath County Board appointed Coyle on 11 September, 2006, and they reached an All-Ireland quarter-final in 2007 during his tenure.

PAUL CURRAN
(Height 5' 10", Weight 14 St)

Decade... 1980s/1990s
(Position... Wing-Back)

CHIEF CHARACTERISTIC... ADDING A REVERSE GEAR TO A
FORWARD'S REPERTOIRE

TOP ACCOMPLICES... PAUL CLARKE, CHARLIE REDMOND,
PAUL BEALIN, KEITH GALVAN, MICK DEEGAN, KEITH BARR

PAUL CURRAN

'HE WENT ON AND ON AND THEN ASKED ME, "WHERE
WERE YOU, PAUL, IN THE PLAY?"... TO WHICH I REPLIED,
"SITTING BESIDE YOU, PADDY'

– PAUL CURRAN

THE term 'skin in the game' originated in the financial world. To have 'skin in the game' is to have incurred risk (monetary or otherwise), by being involved in achieving a goal.

In sporting context, the word, 'skin' refers to the level of investment, and 'game' is the metaphor for actions on the field of play. Few have had more skin in the game than Dublin defender, Paul Curran. He invested a lifetime in the sky-blue jersey and the 'game' of football.

Regrets he had a few!

'I consider the era that I played all my inter-county football in to be the most competitive decade in the history of the championship.

'The 1990s produced no fewer than eight different winners in a 10-year stretch. I look back with some regret but also with great satisfaction at what Dublin achieved in that decade.

'My debut season was 1989 and that year, like most other years I played, we had some success but ultimately ended without the big prize.'

HARD MAN RATINGS
TOUGHEST: 9.1/10
MEANEST: 9.3/10
SCARIEST: 8.5/10
HARDEST: 19.0/20

TOTAL HARD MAN
45.9/50

That success included a hard-earned win over arch-enemies Meath, the defending All-Ireland champions who were going for three in-a-row and four Leinsters in-a-row in 1989, having beaten Dublin in the three previous provincial finals.

It would be a case of fourth time lucky for Dublin as Paul's debut season yielded a coveted Leinster title. The following season was over for Paul Curran before it began. From the high of a sparkling break-out season to the crashing low of a 'lost season,' as events off the pitch would deprive the Dubs of his services for the entire year.

He became embroiled in an argument that resulted in a serious injury, as he subsequently recounted. 'A year that I was looking forward to turned out to be a total disaster as I didn't kick a ball in that year's championship. A nasty eye injury meant surgery for a detached retina and a summer on the sidelines.'

Paul Curran had certainly been through the mill in his first two seasons playing football at the highest level. Win or lose, upon his belated return, he was by now just happy to be back playing, as a new and exciting gaelic football decade was about to throw in.

It certainly started in fine style, with Dublin winning the league title, but a nightmare draw which pitted them against Meath at the preliminary stage, was a clear and present danger to locating a missing person by the name of Sam Maguire.

The meeting has long since passed into GAA folklore, a sweltering four-game saga which ebbed and flowed before finally falling the way of the Royals.

Paul Curran took a heavy blow to the head and recalled little of a feisty second encounter, but one moment stood out that he felt could have changed the course of the enthralling narrative.

'The replay a week later again finished level and a further two periods of extra time failed to separate the teams. I actually don't remember too much about this game, having taken a blow to the head in the opening half, other than Vinnie Murphy's glorious chance to win the game at the end of normal time.

'Straight through on goal and only Mickey McQuillan to beat, a simple fisted score would have done the job but Vinnie went for the three-pointer, which was saved and the saga continued into extra time.'

It was a crushing blow for Dublin, but even in the midst of all the gloom, Paul Curran saw the funny side of an incident that occurred midway through the marathon mini-series of matches.

'There was very little video analysis back then, but between the third and fourth games we sat down after training one night to watch the VHS video of the second replay. I was dropped for the start of that third game and was sitting down the back of the room.

'After watching the first 15 minutes, manager Paddy Cullen pressed the pause button and started complaining about the lack of support from our half-forwards. He went on and on and then asked me, "Where were you, Paul, in the play?"… to which I replied, "Sitting beside you, Paddy".

'Needless to say, laughter broke out and the seriousness of the point was lost for another day.'

{ DESPERATELY SEEKING SAM }

Dublin dusted themselves down and got back on the horse with a routine opening-round win over Offaly the following season. Paul Curran had been relocated from the attack to the half-back line. For all his talents as an attacker, Curran revelled in his new home. He was strong, fearless, and always played with a sharp edge.

Dublin would account for surprise packets Clare in the All-Ireland semi-final, but they were ambushed by a well-drilled Donegal in the 1992 final. A first All Star softened the blow for Curran, but his sheer bravery would take its toll – as he suffered a broken jaw in 1994. Curran amazingly recovered for the All-Ireland final, but another Northern raider in the shape of Down plundered the silverware.

Paul Curran finally got his hands on Sam in 1995, as Dublin finally solved the burning 'Ulster question,' when they defeated a dogged Tyrone, to finally paint the capital city sky-blue.

Another All Star followed for Paul and he was also voted Texaco Footballer of the Year. He was in outstanding form in 1996, but Dublin failed to advance to another decider.

In 1997, he was involved in a much-publicised incident with Offaly player Finbar Cullen losing three front teeth. He was banned for 12 weeks, although he was not sent off during the match. Dublin were by now declining rapidly, and Paul would never climb the hallowed steps of the Hogan Stand again.

The 90s, what a decade!

Cork (1990), Down (1991, 1994), Donegal (1992), Derry (1993), Dublin (1995), Meath (1996, 1999), Kerry (1997) and Galway (1998) all lifted the Sam Maguire in the 90s. In a rollercoaster decade like no other, the tenacious and tigerish Paul Curran ensured Dublin always had… skin in the game.

MISTER SKY BLUE

PAUL'S FATHER, Noel Curran is also a winner of an All-Ireland medal; he was a full-forward on the Meath team which won the All-Ireland in 1967. Paul was a versatile player. In his first senior football year of 1990, he played at midfield for Dublin with clubmate Dave Foran.

In 1991, he was at half-forward, and the following season lined out at right half-back. Wherever Dublin had a need, Paul Curran fulfilled it. He was selected as a left half-back in 1993, and at centre-forward in 1994.

He also did a stint in midfield in 1995 alongside Erin's Isle's Keith Barr, although he played in the All-Ireland final for Dublin at right half-back. He was awarded Texaco Footballer of the Year that season too.

Curran won the National Football League with Dublin in 1991 and 1993. A model of consistency, he was an All Star on three occasions in 1992, 1995, and 1996. He also amassed six Leinster Senior medals in 1989, 1992, 1993, 1994, 1995, and 2002.

At club level, he represented Thomas Davis helping them to win three Dublin titles on the spin. He also managed the winner of the 2012 Dublin senior championship, Ballymun Kickhams.

MICHAEL FAGAN

(Height 5' 8", Weight 13.5 St)

Decade... 1980s/1990s

(Position... Corner-Back)

CHIEF CHARACTERISTIC... WON THE WAR IN
THE LAND DOWN UNDER

TOP ACCOMPLICES... LARRY GILES, MARTIN FLANAGAN,
JOHN O'BRIEN, JACK COONEY

MICHAEL FAGAN

'NOT MANY PEOPLE KNOW MY NAME IS ACTUALLY MICHAEL…
EVERYONE CALLS ME "SPIKE."'

– MICHAEL FAGAN

WANTED

HIT-MAN

JOB SPECIFICATION – A PROPENSITY FOR

HURTING AUSSIES

THE definition of a hitman as defined by the respected Dictionary Webster's and reads as follows… *A professional assassin who works for a crime syndicate.* The Free Dictionary definition adds a little more 'essential' detail!

A person, usually male (thus the 'man' part) who kills for money. Hired assassins are never suave, and they rarely wear suits.

People, organisations and entities have embraced and required the particular set of skills that a hitman embodies to chilling and ruthless effect over the centuries.

While there are very few living examples of a hitman's handiwork, there are numerous instances

HARD
MAN
RATINGS

TOUGHEST:
9.3/10

MEANEST:
9.0/10

SCARIEST:
8.4/10

HARDEST:
19.3/20

☠

TOTAL
HARD MAN
46.0/50

of their productivity resting under an array of headstones dotted at various junctures around the globe!

No prizes for guessing Harry Strauss of the infamous 'Murder Incorporated's' occupation. The mainly Jewish, Italian group had a varied portfolio including murder, illegal gambling, theft, money laundering, arms trafficking, fraud, fencing, kidnapping and armed robbery.

Harry was a man who carried out his work in a calm but surgical fashion, and his name can be associated with anywhere between 100-500… terminations!

The key message here is when you need a job done efficiently – hire a professional.

Kevin Heffernan was a man that appreciated players who had a very specific set of skills. 'Heffo' was planning an expedition with a rather significant headcount and he had given several men, in particular, a very specific instruction.

'KILL THE AUSTRALIANS'

Michael 'Spike' Fagan wasn't one of Heffo's hitmen; he was a helper, someone to clean up a mess and make everyone look good in the process. He was a man who took a certain pride in his workmanship, which as you might expect, is a very important component of being in a family of hitmen.

If you had ever thumbed through Kevin Heffernan's record collection it would have been safe to assume *Advance Australia Fair* was not featured on any of the playlists.

The International Rules Series was, on the face of it, a decent idea. The cross-code game would give Irish and Aussie players a taste of something that every elite sportsman inwardly craved… international recognition.

The historic first test in 1984 was played before a paltry attendance of 8,000 at Pairc Ui Chaoimh, and it certainly didn't lack fireworks, as an almighty melee which took place in the third quarter. This would prove to be the catalyst for decades of rather strained international relations! Australia won the game by two goals, and by the time of the third test the crowd at GAA headquarters had swelled to well over 30,000. The visitors clinched the series in an entertaining final test and the sides would next lock horns in 1986 – in a land Down Under.

Irish manager, Kevin Heffernan was keenly aware that the Aussies had out-muscled the locals in many of the key compartments in the opening salvo of the series, and was determined to add some serious steel for what was sure to be a highly confrontational tour.

{ DIARY OF AN ADVENTURE }

Micheal Fagan had chiselled out a fearsome reputation as one of the hardest and craftiest defenders in Leinster football. Despite the modesty of Westmeath's riches as a footballing county, Heffo extended the invite to the Mullingar Shamrocks' warrior, and while Fagan was honoured to be involved he was under no illusions about his place in the scheme of things.

'I knew coming from Westmeath it was going to be a long and hard fight to try to get onto the team,' he would recall. 'I told him (Heffernan) I couldn't make a training session because we were in a county semi-final and he told me if I wanted to get to Australia that I'd have to make up my mind what I wanted… and I knew then exactly what I wanted. Heffernan was right, you don't get a second chance to play for your country.'

The first test in 1986 was more of an all-in-wrestling contest – with five players receiving their marching orders, as the Aussies won the day.

'Spike' Fagan's selection seemed to be very much from left field but, as ever, Heffo, was one step ahead of the posse, and after a slow start to his tour he was about to grab centre stage.

The second test, on the face of it, involved a very straightforward scenario for the visitors. It was s**t or get off the pot time for the Irish at VFL Park. By this stage, Heffo's patience was wearing thin with the endless intimidation of the hosts and their intensely annoying coach, John Todd.

The unleashing of the 'Spike' caused such consternation, even normally abrasive Aussies were taken aback with the ferocity the small-sized Westmeath warlord was thundering into the fray with. The Aussies were shaken and soon they would be stirred! Heffo's master plan was taking shape… time to send on the cavalry.

Mick Lyons was sent into the fray with some very simple words of advice.

'… the fella with the moustache Mick… (Robert Di Pierdomenico), give him a thump!'

Mick could always be relied upon to give you a warm welcome, and that kicked off a serious downturn in international relations.

Michael Fagan was elevated to cult status when he was voted Man of the Match, as the Irish levelled the series. Some might claim he should have been nominated for *The Military Medal For Gallantry* – Ireland's highest award for services rendered on the battlefield.

Australia and motormouth Todd were by now a busted flush, as the visitors sauntered to victory in the third test.

Heffernan had demonstrated his sleight of hand, and given a masterclass in cartomancy. The selection of players like Wicklow's Pat O'Byrne, Brian McGilligan, and the irrepressible Spike had nullified Australia's heavy-handedness.

The trio spear-headed by Fagan were not in the business of starting fights – their main focus was on finishing them.

When Ireland's need was greatest, Kevin Heffernan turned to the services of an industry professional to finish the job.

For Michael 'Spike' Fagan it was just another day at the office!

⟩——→ THE LIFE OF SPIKE ←——⟨

MICHAEL FAGAN was born on April 28, 1960. He represented Westmeath kingpins, Mullingar Shamrocks at club level, and starred in both juvenile and underage grades for the club. He won a host of trophies as Mullingar won under-14, under-18 and under-21, and senior Westmeath titles during his time in their ranks.

He also played some rugby at junior level, winning a Leinster J2 medal. He made his senior county debut with Westmeath in 1982 against Wicklow in St Conleth's Park, Newbridge. The Leinster Senior Championship match ended in a draw, with the Lake County progressing to face Laois, after a hard-fought replay, 3-7 to 2-5.

Fagan became a permanent fixture in the sides starting fifteen until his retirement in 1995. He gave a string of impressive performances which led to his selection with the International Rules Series squad managed by Dublin maestro Kevin Heffernan. Fagan starred in three tests series against the men from 'Down under' in 1986, 1987, and 1990. He was voted Player of the Match in the second test in 1986, at VFL Park (Waverly Park), in Melbourne.

While his time with Westmeath produced little tangible success, his outstanding inter-county performances earned him a place on the Leinster provincial team where he earned a well-merited Railway Cup winners medal.

DARREN FAY
(Height 6' 1", Weight 15 St)

Decade... 1990s/2000s
(Position... Full-Back)

CHIEF CHARACTERISTIC... HEAD WARDEN HILL 16 AND CANAL END

TOP ACCOMPLICES... COLM COYLE, MARK O'REILLY, JOHN
MCDERMOTT, BRENDAN REILLY, ENDA MCMANUS

DARREN FAY

'THE YEAR BEFORE WE HAD TRAINED SO HARD IT WOULD
NEVER ENTER YOUR HEAD TO GIVE A FELLA A BOX BECAUSE IT
WOULD HAVE COST YOU SO MUCH. BUT, BECAUSE YOU ARE NOT
PUTTING IN THE SAME EFFORT IN TRAINING, TO TURN AROUND
AND GIVE A LAD A BOX IS MUCH EASIER. YOU LOSE YOUR
DISCIPLINE. NOW HE FELL DOWN A LITTLE BIT EASIER...'

– DARREN FAY

IN many respects, the 1996 All-Ireland football final was a rite of passage, a changing of the guard. The Royal County's second 'golden generation' had ascended to the throne.

Succession is part of the natural order. Kings are crowned and wars are won and lost. Mighty empires rise majestically from the rubble, then sink without a trace into the yawning chasm of time.

Yet for all the change – a natural order still exists. The King of full-backs, Mick Lyons was dead... long live The King. This would not be the end of a celebrated bloodline, but rather, a new beginning.

O'Brien, Quinn, Lyons... and now Fay. The Meath full-back had always been bestowed with the title of absolute power. They were the standard bearers, the ones who set the rules of engagement. Number three was the epicentre for all the

HARD
MAN
RATINGS

TOUGHEST:
9.5/10

MEANEST:
9.1/10

SCARIEST:
9.0/10

HARDEST:
19.3/20

TOTAL
HARD MAN

46.9/50

madness, chaos and carnage that this particular Royal Family invariably brought to the party.

In any era, the modus operandi remained unflinchingly the same… when Meath charged into battle… heads would surely roll!

This was the Meath way. The county had spanned generations of godless, demented warriors, whose names were whispered in dimly lit pubs and dark back alleyways.

Many feared they had signed a pact with the devil. Practicing pagan rites and drinking Sean Boylan's strange potions.

This county had produced some of the toughest, meanest defenders in gaelic football history. At a glance, it was like reading a 'who's who' of Gaelic Games' craziest.

Coyle, Foley, Harnan…

When the legendary Mick Lyons retired in 1992, many feared the Meath defensive wall would crumble, and finally come crashing down. Lyons had been a colossus for thirteen seasons, an unbreakable force who had repelled attackers from every corner of Ireland.

Meath's prospects looked decidedly grim without the Summerhill native's steady hand on the tiller. Was it to be a case of 'after the lord mayor's show,' for the land that had held the all-time copyright on full-backs?

Luckily for Meath, they had a leader who had been blessed with mystical powers. If it wore a pair of football boots, manager, Sean Boylan likely had a dossier compiled on him! The legendary Dunboyne oracle worker harvested the county's footballing seas and nothing was allowed to slip through the net. If you heard a rattle in your trash can at night, it was likely the intrepid Boylan searching for obscure clues that might unearth another member of his very exclusive Royal family.

If you were old enough to walk in footballing terms, Sean Boylan had no qualms about plunging you straight into the white-hot heat of inter-county action.

{ THE FOURTH KING }

Darren Fay's debut season would break all box-office records. A Leinster title, an All-Ireland crown, and the not-too-insignificant matter of being voted 'Young Footballer of the Year'. It was an entrance for the ages, as the 20-year-old from Trim had made the art of Royal succession look ridiculously easy.

Meath fans could have been forgiven for having to do a double-take at the player wearing uimhir a trí. Surely even Boylan hadn't managed to clone Mick Lyons or summon the spirit of Paddy 'Hands' O'Brien?

Fay always seemed to have a step on his opponents – like a chess grandmaster who was always operating a number of moves ahead of his opponents. He fitted seamlessly into what was fast becoming Meath's next winning generation, a prowling, almost aloof presence, strangling the life out of enemy forces.

{ DEFENDING THE ROYAL REALM }

Playing with Meath always dictated walking towards the wild side and for Darren Fay, his meteoric start to life with the Royals was about to come crashing back down to earth.

All appeared to be going to script the following season, as Darren and Meath started brightly when dispatching Dublin in a classic Leinster quarter-final encounter, but then they were blown out of the water when underdogs Offaly staged an almighty upset in the Leinster final.

En route to that 'Faithful' encounter with Offaly in the decider, Meath had to negotiate a tricky assignment with Kildare in the semi-final. Never a county to take the easy road, the Royals became embroiled in yet another trilogy of games – with a fired-up 'Lilywhites,' hellbent on taking the provincial and All-Ireland champions down. Meath eventually secured the victory, but at a heavy cost. A cohort featuring four players from both sides were sent off, and Darren Fay was one of the unfortunate quartet.

'The year before we had trained so hard it would never enter your head to give a fella a box because it would have cost you so much. But because you are not putting in the same effort in training, to turn around and give a lad a box is much easier. You lose your discipline. Now he fell down a little bit easy…'

Sadly for Darren, the Leinster Council placed him in cold storage for the Leinster final. Darren looks back on that turbulent period with more than a hint of regret, as he revealed in Phillip Lanigan's sweeping portrayal of Meath's finest full-backs, entitled Four Kings.

The book traces the Royals' full-back lineage through the lens of four of the finest defenders in gaelic football history.

'I can only speak for myself but most of the team were probably doing the same. I was going training, living off, "Oh there's Darren Fay. He won an All Star and an All-Ireland in 96."'

Lack of intensity had stolen up on Meath, like a thief in the night. There had been little or no warning sign as that silent, deadly, momentum killer put a straight-jacket on the defending champions' hopes of retaining Sam Maguire.

Meath's second generation didn't stay parked at the crossroads for very long, as Fay and Meath reclaimed 'Sam' in 1999.

Darren Fay remained a cauldron of raging defiance at the hub of the county's rearguard, for well over a decade, clocking up nearly 50 championship appearances. The crown had rested easily upon his head…

LIFE AT THE
ROYAL COURT

DARREN FAY was another glorious addition to the Royal County's pedigree line of full-backs.

He hailed from a footballing background, with his father Jimmy having played in goal for six seasons with Meath. He played his club football with the local side Trim and such was his versatility, he was regularly deployed around midfield.

He won an All-Ireland medal in his first season with the Royals. He was also voted 'Young Footballer of the Year' and rounded off a remarkable first campaign with a first-ever All Star Award.

After a successful decade with Meath, Fay made himself unavailable for selection,

but he returned to the Meath panel for the 2007 season. On July 23, 2008, Fay called time on his stellar career, announcing his retirement after a defeat to Limerick.

He won a host of individual accolades, including three All Star Awards in 1996, 1999 and 2001. At senior county level with Meath, he collected three Leinster Senior Championships medals, the first arriving in 1996, and further medals in 1999, and 2001.

He won two All-Ireland Senior Championships in 1996 and 1999. At underage level he won two Leinster under-21 Championships in consecutive seasons, and a Leinster Minor Championship medal in 1993.

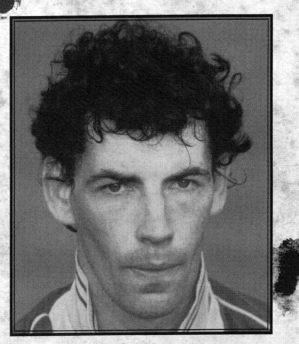

KEVIN FOLEY

(Height 5' 10", Weight 13.5 St)

Decade... 1980s/1990s

(Position... Wing-Back)

CHIEF CHARACTERISTIC... THIS CHEF DE PARTIE GUARANTEED
FORWARDS WERE ALWAYS ON THE CROKE PARK FINE-DINING MENU

TOP ACCOMPLICES... LIAM HARNAN, MICK LYONS,
BOB O'MALLEY, MARTIN O'CONNELL, GERRY MCENTEE,
TERRY FERGUSON, PJ GILLIC

KEVIN FOLEY

'I'M SURE TOMMY GOT A SURPRISE WHEN HE GOT THROUGH AND SAW ME AT THE EDGE OF THE SQUARE, BUT HE PASSED IT TO ME ANYWAY... BECAUSE THERE WASN'T ANYBODY ELSE HE COULD GIVE IT TO... AND THAT IS BASICALLY HOW IT HAPPENED.'

– KEVIN FOLEY

THE Korowai tribe eat many different things, including frogs, spiders, snakes, crocodiles and more. Included in a rich, varied diet, are yams, yam roots, and jungle fruits. The Papua New Guinea-based clan are a mainly indigenous group, with a slightly disturbing variation in their dietary theme.

They eat humans!

Despite the existence of many rumours of human consumption in the annals of the GAA, very few of these chilling claims have ever been substantiated. Dining out on the sacrificial attacking lambs of county football, in a literal sense, however, is a practice that has existed for well over a century.

One such tribe that has gathered unfettered notoriety hailed from the Royal County of Meath. Any exploration in the deep, dark recesses of the Meath backline should have carried a government health warning.

Head Chef Mick Lyons welcomed you to the

HARD MAN RATINGS

TOUGHEST:
9.0/10

MEANEST:
10/10

SCARIEST:
10/10

HARDEST:
18.5/20

TOTAL
HARD MAN
47.5/50

feast, as you were thoroughly grilled by Liam Harnan. Next, you were mounted on the spit, and thoroughly roasted, until ripe for consumption, by Bob O'Malley and Colm Coyle.

Then Kevin Foley… would eat you alive!

Being marked by the 'Trim Terror' was akin to a spiritual experience, as it was rumoured that many forwards discovered God during the 70-odd minutes spent in his company.

Being subjected to Foley's close attention for any extended period of time could have been likened to the title of a much-loved hymn, *Nearer, My God, To Thee!*

Such was the relish with which Foley attacked his opponents, it would have elicited little surprise to see him bundling body parts into his kit bag after the game – then depositing them in a cabinet freezer for consumption at a later date!

What was rare was wonderful for supporters of the Royals, and lifting Sam Maguire after a two-decade hiatus in 1987 was the most unexpected of gifts. Even less would have predicted Kevin Foley's meteoric rise, as the Trim native hadn't featured on any of the radars that covered the Royal's minor and under-21 squads.

Kevin Foley was a defender with many attributes, but scoring wasn't one of them.

If you had launched a poll to pick the identity of the match-winning goal-scorer from the marathon four-game series against Dublin in 1991 both goalkeepers, Micheal McQuillan and John O'Leary, would have occupied the slots ahead of the dynamic wing back.

Foley's forays into enemy territory rarely yielded any net gains; defending the Royal realm was his forte. The Royal County was particularly well-stocked in that department anyway, leaving Foley to focus on guarding the house. This was a task he carried out with a ruthlessly, chilling efficiency.

When Foley appeared in the guise of a fast finishing forward – in game four of the 1991, Dublin versus Meath saga – you could have drawn lots for which team members and supporters were more shocked!

After over 300 minutes of rip-roaring action, the identity of the match-winning assailant was about to be revealed. Move over Colonel Mustard in the dining room with a carving knife, here was an ending that even Agatha Christie in her heyday would have pined for!

The Meath Chronicle described the seismic score thus!

O'Connell to Lyons, Lyons to McCabe… McCabe to Harnan, Harnan to Dowd, Dowd to O'Rourke… O'Rourke to Beggy, Beggy to Foley… Foley to Gillic… Gillic to Dowd, Dowd to O'Rourke… O'Rourke to Dowd, Dowd to Foley… GOAL!!!'

It was a gaelic football version of 'total football' with nine different pairs of paws combining like a sea of synchronised swimmers, to torpedo Dublin's summer before it started.

Kevin explained his famous expedition from the Canal End to the Hill in typically modest fashion.

{ THE GOLDEN GOAL }

'As the play moved on, I was just inclined to drift forward. I just kept drifting forward and when I met Mattie (McCabe) in the middle of the field I was thinking that he should be the one to move forward and that I'd head back to defence, but Mattie was taking one of their defenders away from their defence and he told me to keep going.

'Not that I was famous for scoring goals, but I was still conscious of not ending up inside the square and I tried to make sure I was just arriving, running onto the ball rather than getting it standing still.'

Of course, the drama did not quite end there – as these two incurable show-offs treated the breathless punters to one last enthralling act... or two!

Meath's David Beggy was having a self-confessed 'shocker,' but he managed to drain off all the dirty petrol in time to add that essential coat of varnish, applying the coup de grâce.

The referee, Tommy Howard demurred on ending the contest, as Dublin won the obligatory replay-inducing fee. Jack Sheedy stepped forward and miscued, ensuring the umpire's hands stayed firmly in their pockets, and *ensuring* act five of the melodrama remained on the cutting-room floor!

Foley's unlikely intervention had diverted a contest that was wildly oscillating in the opposite direction. Of all the sucker punches the Dubs had endured at the hands of their most troublesome rivals, Kevin's goal would forever reside at Ground Zero!

Over the course of his astonishing eight-year shift with the Royals, Meath had many reasons to be cheerful about Kevin Foley's inspirational efforts.

For all the finesse, fire, and brimstone, Kevin Foley's part in the Meath footballing revolution would curiously never yield an All Star. Even though his trio of performances in 1990 against Messers, Duff, McHugh, and Tomkins were fashioned out of the top drawer. The fact that his ravenous displays against three of the most potent attacking weapons in the country was delivered in the unusual berth of centre-back was even more laudable.

A career spent eating forwards alive… metaphorically speaking, of course!

A RIGHT
>———→ ROYAL ←———«
EXISTENCE

KEVIN FOLEY was born on January 9, 1960 and is a native of Trim, County Meath. His league and championship career at senior level with the Royals covered eight very successful seasons, from 1986 to 1993.

He hailed from a football-mad family and took his first steps towards a career with Meath, playing competitive football during his school days at Trim CBS and St Patrick's Classical School in Navan.

He was also an avid soccer player, a sport he concentrated on during his studies at University College Dublin. He was also playing his club football with Trim. He won a county Junior Championship medal in 1978.

Foley never played at county level as a minor or an under-21, but was called into the senior panel for the 1986 championship. He won two All-Ireland medals in-a-row in 1987, and another in 1988.

He won a total of five Leinster Senior Championships (1986, 1987, 1988, 1990, 1991). Foley also won the National Football League on two occasions (1987-88, 1989-90), and was a member of the Leinster interprovincial team in 1988, winning his sole Railway Cup medal.

MARTIN FURLONG

(Height 5' 10", Weight 15 St)

Decade... 1960s/1970s/1980s

(Position... Goalkeeper)

CHIEF CHARACTERISTIC... ENSURING FORWARDS TOOK NO STEPS
FORWARD AND THREE STEPS BACKWARD

TOP ACCOMPLICES... NONE NEEDED (NONE APPLIED)

MARTIN FURLONG

'DON'T LOOK AT THE KICKER, BECAUSE HE CAN THROW SHAPES.
JUST KEEP YOUR EYES ON THE BALL.'

– MARTIN FURLONG

EAST Durham, New York.

Picturesquely located in the sleeping shadows of the famed Catskills Mountains is Tom Furlongs ale house.

Sporting images greet you as you step inside, where a warm Irish welcome always awaits in this New York State heartland. Everywhere you gaze are the badges of sporting war.

A genial Babe Ruth smiles down at you. There is also a picture of the Offaly minor football team that won the 1960 Leinster title. On the counter lies a burst football from the 1971 All-Ireland final.

The pub speaks of a thousand stories and the proprietor and his sibling could tell you a million more. Tom Furlong, and his brother Martin, know a thing or two about sporting highs and lows. Tom had travelled many decades ago, when only a freak injury had ended his career as a kicker in the NFL as an American Football player. Martin journeyed also, reuniting the footballing family in 1988.

HARD MAN RATINGS

TOUGHEST:
9.8/10

MEANEST:
9.9/10

SCARIEST:
9.7/10

HARDEST:
20/20

TOTAL HARD MAN

49.4/50

Blue Bloods, the hugely popular American police drama television series, has been airing on CBS since September 2010. It centres on the lives of the fictional Reagan family, a Catholic Irish-American family in New York City with a history of work in law enforcement.

The Reagan family gathers for Sunday dinner each week, to socialise and recount stories of days gone by, and the weekly Sunday supper is at the heart of each show.

If there ever was a gaelic football family of Blue Bloods, the Furlongs of Tullamore would be the perfect choice to play 'New York's finest' the much-loved Reagan crew.

There was a time when it would have been hard to remember an Offaly team-sheet without the Furlong name on it. For five successive generations, the family name had been a permanent fixture with the 'Faithful' county.

The Furlong siblings included Tom's older brother, Mickey and Martin the goalkeeper who had denied the Kingdom so famously in 1971 with his penalty save in Croke Park.

After the magnificent and history-altering save, Martin pumps the air with clenched fists.

It was a seminal moment that stirred the 'Faithful' from their slumber. It would spark a chain of events that would culminate in one of the most incredible endings in GAA history. Seamus Darby's late-late show would deny the Kingdom football's 'Holy Grail' of five in-a-row.

The nerveless custodian would be a witness to history from his perch at the Canal End, as not for the first time he hauled the county out of the fire.

Martin Furlong may have been a goalkeeper, but he might well have been an extra defender, such was the purposefulness with which he attacked the ball.

He had a granite-like toughness, that ensured any stray inside forwards were ruthlessly dealt with... man, ball, and anything else, it mattered little to the fearless son of Tullamore.

He was the last line of the Offaly rearguard and also its strongest.

The sight of Martin thundering off his line was a massive deterrent to any in-rushing enemy troops. Time and time again, he went where angels feared to tread, putting his body on the line, to answer the call.

Martin announced himself to the Irish sporting public, in the first minor All-Ireland final to be broadcast on television. The game concluded with the mother of all goalmouth scrambles. Cork and Offaly had gone to the wire, and young Offaly keeper Martin Furling had somehow scrambled to make a wonder save. Frantic Cork bodies piled in on top of the net-minder clawing for the ball, but Furlong held on.

Moments later, a shrill blast of the whistle ended the contest as the legend of Martin Furlong was born.

{ THE LAST LINE OF DEFENCE }

Martin's forays from goal quickly became the stuff of lore, with the aftermath resembling a demolition derby. He quickly developed the respect of his peers for his incredible shot-stopping ability, and the no-nonsense way he went about his business.

Whenever Martin left his line, alarm bells were ringing in the Offaly camp, never mind the opposition! Offaly defenders tended to need eyes in the back of their heads under a dropping ball as Martin called time on any potential crisis.

Donegal's Brian McEniff marvelled at the custodian's fearlessness after the 1972 All-Ireland semi-final.

'Furlong in goals, he was a great one. He was a huge shot-stopper and he was brave to a degree where it was dangerous.'

Furlong saw neither friend nor foe, and went about the housekeeping with serious intent.

Once he hit, you stayed hit as the Offaly full-back, John Smith could attest to after being left with broken ribs in a league game.

In 1989, Martin moved from Clonminch, Tullamore to the United States, following the request of his older brother, Tom to assist him in running his bar. The proud Furlong, footballing family, rubbing shoulders with New York's finest.

Perhaps that pair of GAA 'Bluebloods,' met up every Sunday for supper and if they did, what stories they would have had to tell.

THE FINAL FURLONG

MARTIN FURLONG was born September 14, 1946 in Tullamore. He was one of four Furlong brothers which included Mickey, John, and Tom. Martin would be one of three brothers, who would eventually have to emigrate to New York owing to the economic downturn.

He won three county football titles with his club Tullamore. He was the first-choice goalkeeper at senior level on the Offaly team from 1966 until 1985. And he holds a special place in Offaly GAA as he is part of a select cohort who won three All-Ireland SFC medals – in 1971, 1972, and 1982. He also won an All-Ireland Minor Football Championship in 1964. He was voted the Texaco Footballer of the Year in 1982 when his heroics between the sticks helped propel Offaly to an All-Ireland SFC win.

Martin was one of the greatest goalkeepers in GAA history and his enduring excellence was rewarded with four All Star awards. Offaly were at the peak of their powers during Martin's career and he also won an astonishing seven Leinster titles during the birth of a new footballing dynasty.

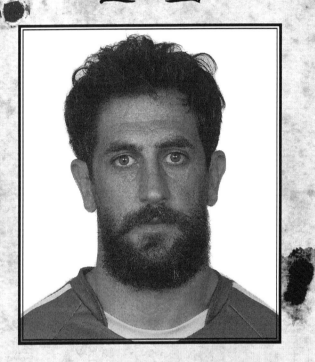

PAUL GALVIN
(Height 5' 11", Weight 14 St)

Decade... 2000s/2010s
(Position... Wing-Forward)

CHIEF CHARACTERISTIC... GIVING DEFENDERS
A GOOD DRESSING DOWN

TOP ACCOMPLICES... DARRAGH Ó SÉ, TOMÁS Ó SÉ, MARC Ó SÉ

PAUL
GALVIN

'STANDING MY GROUND WITH YOU IN
THE KERRY JERSEY WAS MY PRIVILEGE.'
– PAUL GALVIN

GRAND Designs…

He had always existed in a parallel universe, driven by a relentless pursuit of perfection. Years before he pulled on the sacred shirt and began his county journey, he studied the competition and formulated his grand designs.

The keen student of the game has done his homework thoroughly. Inter-county football had moved on, and left its founding fathers trailing in its wake. The Kingdom required a different type of warrior, and Paul Galvin would cut his cloth accordingly…

Kerry's football was wedged between two stools. Many within the county feared they were no longer built for the battlefield. A once proud race, cowed and bullied into submission.

Teams were playing with higher aggression and intensity, with Kerry gasping for oxygen at these strange, new, rarefied heights.

The rules of engagement had shifted alarmingly, with the likes of Tyrone bringing an unfamiliar

HARD MAN RATINGS

TOUGHEST:
9.2/10

MEANEST:
9.7/10

SCARIEST:
8.7/10

HARDEST:
18.5/20

TOTAL HARD MAN

46.1/50

type of war to the combat zone.

The Kingdom looked ill-prepared for the onslaught as they floundered against the three previous All-Ireland winners, Meath, Armagh and Tyrone between 2001-03.

Kerry were in urgent need of some dark magic, when a muscular, brooding destroyer stepped out of the shadows.

Lixnaw was an unlikely venue for a football saviour, as it was a land where the small ball was King. The local hurling club has won nine county titles, with the first arriving in 1933. Lixnaw native, Paul Galvin, was a decent hurler, who happened to possess a raging passion for football.

Galvin was cognisant of the fact that Gaelic football's next generation had moved on, and the Kingdom would need a different type of player to adjust to that shifting landscape.

Paul looked back on those seismic days when appearing on former teammate Tomás Ó Sé's podcast.

'I watched them closely, and it was highly physical, highly aggressive, rules were being bent and broken and particularly the Tyrone '03 semi-final... I was right on the sideline looking at a lot of the activity.

'It was so intense and aggressive, I just thought... *All bets are off here if you get in.* That was my approach always.

'I was just disgusted looking at Kerry getting roughed up and beaten and I said, *If I ever get in there, I'm going to match fire with fire.* I was only matching what I was seeing really. Then you try to take it up a level of course and wherever the game goes, you've got to try to take it a bit further. So, my position was part of the middle-third conflict.'

Galvin was introduced to the Kerry championship team versus

Clare in 2004 by legendary Jack O'Connor. The pair went back a few years and the admiration is clear, when Galvin speaks about his former manager.

'I think Jack saw me in a county schools final when I was playing for Causeway against what was then Cahersiveen Post-Primary. He was managing them and I got around five points from play from midfield. I was maybe 16 or 17 and I think I was in his head six or seven years later when he got the Kerry job. I was 23 then. So, he had me earmarked.'

The wily O'Connor certainly had, and Paul Galvin's addition reaped an instant dividend as Kerry trounced Mayo in the 2004 All-Ireland final.

It was some turnaround after being battered and bruised by the Red Hand of Tyrone, as Galvin recalled in another interview.

'2004 was exceptional. You'll remember that the 2004 team won an All-Ireland without Séamus Moynihan and Darragh Ó Sé. And you think of where they were in 2003 after Tyrone did what they did…

'If a fella was to say to you that in 12 months you'll have the All-Ireland won but you'll have no Darragh Ó Sé and you'll have no Séamus Moynihan on the day. You'd be saying to yourself, *you must have some exceptional manager or coach in mind if you think that's going to happen*. Right? And that's what happened.'

{ A FOOTBALLING EDUCATION }

Football was Paul Galvin's magnificent obsession; wherever he went the football came with him, and that even included the classroom!

'This was early in my career. I was obsessed. I did need a hobby because I was completely obsessed with football. I mean, I was in class and I'd often have the football out around the classroom.

'Tuesdays and Thursdays, I'd start my warm-up in the last class, I'd be doing my stretches and honestly now, it was some scene when I think back, students… I'd give an exercise to do and then I'd start to do my stretches for training.

'I wouldn't even waste time at training doing my stretches, I'd have it done so when I got there I'd be ready to go. I'd have a good bit of (ball) handling done in the daytime. Morning, noon and night, I was obsessed with what we were doing, what we were trying to do. I did burn myself out eventually… I took it way too seriously.'

Paul Galvin was just what the doctor ordered for Kerry's football, at a time when football in the county was firmly at a crossroads. He was a unique mix of nervous, raw energy, and ice-cold, glacier-like composure.

His glorious decade yielded a rich harvest of Munster and All-Ireland titles from a new type of Kerry footballer, who was built for the modern age. For all of Galvin's 'Dogs of War' mentality, he was as beautifully balanced a footballer as ever graced the glorious Kerry jersey. Smart and intelligent in possession, he was a lethal combination of the bomb and the ballot box.

There was never a dull moment when he was playing, and he kept up that theme in retirement, when entering the elevated, trend-driven high-stakes world of fashion.

In 2017, Kerry GAA brought him in to design their new O'Neill's playing kits. The 80s inspired home shirt and black away version were popular additions to a famous set of colours, that have inspired Kerry players down through the ages.

A life spent crossing the lines and pushing boundaries... Paul Galvin has always been cut from a different cloth!

FROM THE CRADLE TO THE CATWALK

PAUL GALVIN was born on November 2, 1979. He played for his local club Finuge, and at the divisional level for Feale Rangers. Galvan's county career spanned a glorious 11 seasons between 2003 and 2014.

Galvin hailed from Lixnaw, County Kerry, and also played hurling with the passionate local side. In 2002, Finuge qualified for the final of the county junior championship. Having lost their previous two finals, Galvin's men defeated Castlegregory as he won his first county medal in the grade.

In 2007, Feale Rangers reached the final of the county senior championship. Opponents, South Kerry were going for a remarkable fourth county title in succession. Galvin's side edged out the win by 1-5 to 0-6, in what was Rangers' first county triumph in 27 years.

At senior level, Galvin had a successful career with the gaelic football standard bearers, winning four All-Irelands, seven Munster titles, and three National League titles. He was also honoured as an All Star on three occasions and voted Footballer of the Year in 2009.

He also achieved a unique place in the pantheon of All Star Awards history, when selected the 1,000th All Star Award winner. He represented Ireland in the infamous 2004 International Rules Series against Australia.

GRAHAM GERAGHTY

(Height 6' 1", Weight 14.5 St)

Decade... 1990s/2000s/2010s

(Position... Wing-Back/Full-Forward)

CHIEF CHARACTERISTIC... CHIEF COMMANDER ROYAL'S
CHAOS AND MAYHEM DIVISION

TOP ACCOMPLICES... TOMMY DOWD, TREVOR GILES, JOHN
MCDERMOTT, JIMMY MCGUINNESS, OLLIE MURPHY, BRENDAN REILLY

GRAHAM GERAGHTY

'I NEARLY DIDN'T GET ON THE PITCH BECAUSE THERE WERE
THREE OF THEM WAITING ON THE SIDELINE FOR ME. I WENT TO
GET ON AND THEY SAID TO ME, "YOU KNOW YOU'RE GOING TO
GET IT TODAY". I WAS LIKE, "F**K IT, WHATEVER".'

– GRAHAM GERAGHTY

GRAHAM Geraghty knew what was coming once he crossed the white line. The Aussies were waiting as he took to the field. They lingered in little groups, nodding and gesturing in his direction.

It was pay-back time and it would not end well for one of Meath's finest. He always knew there would be repercussions. That was the thing about Graham Geraghty, he never shied away from the consequences. He shrugged his shoulders and made tracks for the field of play. It was time to pay the piper...

The bad blood generated from the First Test of the 2006 International Rules Series was about to boil over. Graham Geraghty had vague memories of being knocked out and ending up in an ambulance, during the course of an ill-tempered Second Test. He had lost consciousness when he became entangled with the Aussie Danyle Pearce and his hands and the rest was just a blur.

Some days you had to take your medicine,

**HARD
MAN
RATINGS**

TOUGHEST:
9.4/10

MEANEST:
9.8/10

SCARIEST:
9.0/10

HARDEST:
19.5/20

**TOTAL
HARD MAN
47.7/50**

but Graham always came back for more. From appearing in an Irish Kung Fu movie, to playing twice for Arsenal, and the very impressive honour of captaining an All-Ireland winning side, being Graham Geraghty is to have had a life less ordinary.

Throw in running for a seat in the Dáil, and battling life-threatening illness along the way and it has been a helter-skelter journey to this point.

His incredible Royal voyage began when he was starring for the under-21 side, earning rave reviews in the county rear-guard. Meath senior manager Sean Boylan, as ever, was looking at the bigger picture, and felt Geraghty had a future further up the field. It seemed an audacious plan, but it very nearly hit the rocks as Graham's 'tour de force' in the 1994 Leinster under 21 final impressed one of the greatest soccer managers of all time.

Playing at right half-back in that decider, 21-year-old Graham scored 1-2 in a match where Dublin eventually prevailed by a point.

Manchester United's Alex Ferguson was queried by Ger Canning on RTÉ if he was impressed by any of the talent on show.

'I thought the lad that scored the goal, the number five for Meath, Graham Geraghty, did very well.'

He was not the only famous soccer club wowed by Geraghty's athleticism and Arsenal offered him a trial out of the blue.

'I stayed in the hotel that night with the team and I got a phone call from my dad. I don't know how he actually found out I was there, and he says, "There's a fella from Arsenal coming to see you at 12 o'clock tomorrow, so you better be home".

'Alex Ferguson was at the game. I was playing wing back and I scored 1-2. They interviewed him after the game, and they asked him if anyone impressed him and he said, 'The blond fella playing number five, I like the way he gets up and down the field. He has an eye for goal'.

As ever the wily old fox, Fergie's shrewd observations would come to pass, albeit in a different sporting realm. Graham Geraghty certainly got up and down the field, and his eye for goal would propel him to the very top of the Gaelic football food chain.

His career spanned nearly two decades and was a captivating rollercoaster ride, filled with breath-taking highs and crushing lows.

Boylan's decision to make him captain in 1999 proved to be a masterstroke. The extra layer of responsibility inspired Seneschalstown's colossus to even greater heights as the Royals plundered Sam Maguire.

He was always up front in displaying his courage, there was never anything sneaky going on with Geraghty, as Dublin opponent Paddy Christie testified. 'Some forwards would be a bit sneaky, hitting from behind or tripping, but I didn't find that with Geraghty at all. He just hit you straight on. When he got the ball, he'd run straight at you which, when you've a fella that fast, with that much athleticism, you were wondering how you were going to stop him.'

{ ROYAL'S HIGH ROLLER }

Whenever or wherever Geraghty performed, it made for box office viewing. He had the rarest of qualities, that intoxicating X-factor appeal.

In 2002, he was flown by helicopter to Navan from a wedding reception. With Meath trailing and time almost up, Richie Kealy conjured up a goal to give them some faint hope. Having shed his top hat and tails, Geraghty donned his Superman guise and with Meath heading out of the championship, he somehow managed a miracle goal in injury time against Louth.

He was then flown back to his duties as best man at the wedding after dashing a heartbroken Wee County's hopes of a sensational upset.

He retired for a few seasons before briefly returning with another astonishing cameo in 2011 against Kildare. Sadly, his late winning goal was chalked incorrectly off, depriving him of the fairytale finish he so richly deserved. He remained the darling of the Meath sporting public and was voted Meath Player of the Year on two occasions, in 1999 and 2006.

The GAA community was rocked with the news that his life hung in the balance in October 2020, as he was diagnosed with a brain haemorrhage and aneurysm. Graham survived the shocking ordeal, displaying extraordinary courage in his darkest hours.

'The first week was horrific,' he admitted. 'On a scale of one to 10, the pain was probably about 15. I couldn't stick the pain really. I was on a lot of medication and painkillers. There'd be a lot of things going through your mind... *Are you going to see your family again, your friends.*'

In a Royal County flush with attacking brilliance, Graham Geraghty's swashbuckling and scintillating swagger might well have made him the most aristocratic of them all.

A ROYAL PILGRIMAGE

GRAHAM GERAGHTY played at club level with Seneschalstown, winning the Meath Senior Football Championship in 1994. He has also won the Meath under-21 Championship with his club in 1992.

He had a successful underage career with the Royals winning an All-Ireland Minor Championship in 1990 and an All-Ireland under-21 Championship in 1993.

He captained Meath to Sam Maguire success in 1999, to go alongside his maiden Celtic Cross from 1996.

On July 23, 2008, Geraghty initially retired following Meath's exit from the 2008 Championship at the hands of Limerick. But, in May of 2011, at the age of 38 he returned to the Meath panel after a three-year absence.

He entered the fray as a substitute in Meath's first game of the Championship against Kildare at Croke Park. Geraghty announced his second retirement soon after from the inter-county game, and became a selector.

A brilliant all-round athlete he had trials with London giants Arsenal as a teenager, and signed for Dublin club Bohemians in September 1994. He also played rugby for a season with Buccaneers Reserves in 2003.

He won three Leinster Championship medals, along with four Railway Cup titles with Leinster. Twice an All Star, he also won two National Football League medals.

T.J. GILMORE

(Height 6' 0", Weight 15 St)

Decade... 1970s/1980s

(Position... Centre-Back)

CHIEF CHARACTERISTIC... TURNING THE N17
INTO THE HIGHWAY TO HELL

TOP ACCOMPLICES... JUST THE ONE USUALLY NEEDED, BILLY JOYCE

T.J. GILMORE

'I WOULD BE CROUCHED OVER THE FIRST ROW, HAND ON THE WETTEST
THICKEST SOD IN THE BOG. YOU'D HEAR "TOMMY JOE GILMORE
IS A TOUGH BASTARD. HE ALMOST KILLED TJ KILGALLON LAST
SUNDAY". I'D LOOK UP. ALL YOU COULD SEE WERE HEADS BOBBING IN
AGREEMENT... TURF FLYING OUT BETWEEN THE OLD MEN'S LEGS.'
– JOHN DIVILLY

> *The boy stood on the burning deck,*
> *Whence all but he had fled;*
> *The flame that lit the battle's wreck,*
> *Shone round him o'er the dead.*

FELECIA Heyman's hauntingly poetic depiction of a young boy who stayed at his post to the very end is a timeless tale of heroic sacrifice.

Tommy Joe Gilmore had been on that burning bridge – more than a few times, as the good ship Galway slipped ominously below the waterline. The Cortoon Shamrocks legend filled the centre-half back berth, when the 'Tribe' lost three All-Ireland finals in four seasons to Offaly, Cork, and Dublin in 1971, 1973, and 1974 respectively.

The defeats rankled with him, the ship had finally sailed on his All-Ireland ambitions. When opportunity knocks 'tis best practice to always answer the door.

HARD MAN RATINGS

TOUGHEST:
9.2/10

MEANEST:
9.0/10

SCARIEST:
9.5/10

HARDEST:
19.7/20

TOTAL HARD MAN

47.4/50

As Pat Spillane colourfully once intimated after watching an Ulster final, and almost losing the will to live, sometimes it's best to call a spade… a *spade*.

'According to NASA, a blue moon occurs every two to three years. The last one arrived on August 31, 2023. So, it is a rare phenomenon. Well, I had my own 'blue moon' experience watching the Ulster final. At times the game was so boring, I couldn't think of a single note to jot down.

'I could describe the game as intriguing, tactical, enthralling, a fascinating game of chess football, but the readers of this column are a discerning bunch; they recognise bulls**t from a mile off.

'If it walks like a duck, swims like a duck, and quacks like a duck, then it probably is a duck.

The Ulster final was the same, it was a stinker.'

Tommy Joe Gilmore was also a man that talked and played… in monochrome. He wasn't in the mood for dressing it up. The failure to attain an elusive Celtic Cross had left a deep chasm within his soul. He could still see the fire and smell the smoke, as the burning vessel began to slip below the waterline. The Galway footballing great bemoaned the lack of a regular and reliable free-taker, to keep the scoreboard ticking over.

'It's a big disappointment to appear in three finals in four years and not win one. To get so close makes it harder to accept, but I firmly believe that the lack of a reliable free-taker cost us two finals. The 1971 result was upsetting because if we had put the ball over the bar from placed balls, like Tony McTeague did for Offaly on the day, then we'd have won out comfortably. A team must carry a free-taker who can get four out of five over the bar from within 50 yards.'

Tommy Joe had not failed for the want of trying. If he had been asked to play in goal, you could rest assured he'd don the gloves. He had almost filled every berth on the team from centre-back, to a famous cameo at centre-forward in a National League final.

In full-on tackling mode, Tommy Joe was unstoppable, and collisions were normally followed by a bout of mild paralysis… if you were lucky! He was one from the old school of football motoring. He took a belt and gave one, without breaking his stride.

Tommy, like any self-respecting Galway warrior, was weaned on tales of one of the GAA's most storied and bitter rivalries. He remained faithful to that narrative whenever the green and red came to town.

John Divilly a proud descendent of Galway's footballing aristocracy, captured the spirit of that very Western 'tribal' warfare in the *Irish Examiner*. Any reference to that most enduring of chronicles wouldn't have been complete without a mention of the 'bould' Tommy Joe Gilmore exploits.

{ KEEPING THE WEST AWAKE }

Galway and Mayo is everyday talk. Thousands of daily commuters migrate along the N17 to hospitals, universities, manufacturing and pharmaceutical plants, airports, courts and livestock marts. The big annual pilgrimages to Croagh Patrick, Knock, or the Galway Races.

We talk about beating each other on the field 365 days of the year, not just when the championship rolls around." I would be crouched over the first row, hand on the wettest thickest sod in the bog. You'd hear "Tommy Joe Gilmore is a tough bastard. He almost killed TJ Kilgallon last Sunday". I'd look up. All you could see were heads bobbing in agreement… turf flying out between the old men's legs.

Gilmore rubbed shoulders with gaelic football blue-bloods as an All Star in the early 70s, stepping out on the cat-walk with the likes of Seán O'Neill, Brian McEniff, Mick O'Connell and Jimmy Barry-Murphy, in what certainly was a very impressive 70s ensemble.

While Tommy Joe was a feisty campaigner, he had the ability to conjure up breath-taking moments of attacking magic.

He scored a memorable point in the All-Ireland final of 1973 versus Cork. It was vintage Tommy, as he careered up the field with half of the Rebel County in tow, before slotting the ball over the bar with aplomb.

The Rebels had been in the ascendency, and it looked like the Western raiders were going to be swept away early doors by a manic red tide. Galway was reeling and staring into the abyss, but Tommy Joe would soon have them performing jigs… instead of reels!

Michael O'Hehir was behind the microphone, as Tommy Joe lit up an already enthralling high-scoring affair.

'Tommy Joe Gilmore has it on his own half-back line, he goes past Dinny Long, 60 yards out from the Cork goals… 50 yards out… 40, 30… on the 21-yard line… and it's over the bar.'

The score reignited the maroon and white who pushed the Leesiders all the way to the finish line in a fiercely contested second-half, but the crafty Corkmen hung on grimly to take 'Sam' back home.

Tommy Joe reluctantly left the stage in 1984 after a lifetime of magnificent service. Wherever they turn a sod of turf in the county of Tribes, they'll raise a flask to Cortoon's finest.

A TRIBAL PRACTICE

TOMMY JOE'S career started in the late 60s, in the senior ranks of local Cortoon Shamrocks.

A small rural club, there was little by the way of tangible success during Tommy's time, but the club always punched above its weight and recorded two county semi-final appearances in 1975 and 1978.

He was a county minor in 1967 and spent two further seasons on the under-21 side, before he was selected for the county's senior team. While centre-back was his regular position, he was Galway's 'Mr. Versatility' and played in a variety of locations from full-back to full-forward. Whatever the day demanded, you could count on Tommy Joe to step into the breach as he famously donned the No 14 jersey to help his county to victory over Roscommon in the 1981 National League decider.

Gilmore arrived on the inter-county scene at a time when the Tribesmen had just completed a famous three-in-a-row of All-Irelands. It seemed a Celtic Cross was an inevitability for the Cortoon man, but that never materialised despite contesting three All-Ireland finals.

Tommy was left-empty-handed. He was one of the greatest players of his era winning All Star Awards in 1972 and 1973. He retired in 1984 having won six Connacht titles.

CONOR GORMLEY

(Height 6' 0", Weight 14.5 St)

Decade... 2000s/2010s

(Position... Centre-Back)

CHIEF CHARACTERISTIC... THE ROAD-BLOCK FROM THE RED HAND

TOP ACCOMPLICES... BRIAN DOOHER, PHILLIP JORDAN, RYAN
MCMENAMIN, BRIAN MCGUIGAN, SEAN CAVANAGH

CONOR
GORMLEY

'MICKEY [HARTE] WOULD HAVE TALKED TO US FROM U21
DAYS THAT IF YOU'RE NOT IN THE PLAY, GET BACK AND DO
SOMETHING AND BE HELPFUL. MAYBE THAT'S RUNNING
THROUGH MY HEAD, TO GET BACK AND HELP OUT.'

– CONOR GORMLEY

THE Wheel of Time...

The thin watery line of the Blackwater was all that divided them. In a few footfalls, you could cross the divide via the Charlemont Bridge, County Armagh, to The Moy, County Tyrone.

It was late afternoon on September 28, 2003. The Lontra canadensis surfaced just under the bridge, shaking himself.

He sniffed the air.

Intrigued by the silence, he slipped onto the bank. A distant echo began to swell on the Red Hand side of the suspension, the stirring of a primal roar. The notoriously shy mammal slipped back into the water startled by the alarming escalation of noise.

Unlike most of the inhabitants on either side of the bridge, the otter wasn't much of a gaelic football fan; or he could just have navigated his way across to the Armagh side. There the

HARD
MAN
RATINGS

TOUGHEST:
9.5/10

MEANEST:
9.0/10

SCARIEST:
8.6/10

HARDEST:
19.3/20

TOTAL
HARD MAN
46.4/50

aquatically endowed creature would have been guaranteed a very tranquil evening!

Around the time the otter surfaced, most of the residents that lived along the riverbank had migrated to Dublin... where 79,391 pairs of eyes could barely believe what they had just witnessed.

It was the dying embers of the 2003 All-Ireland football final. The Red Hand of Tyrone had the Sam Maguire Cup firmly grasped for the first time in history.

Ballistics is the study and science dealing with the motion and impact of projectiles, such as bullets, rockets, bombs, amongst other things, and the effects of firing on a gun or bullet or cartridge. What would the study of breaking balls in GAA be termed?

The prediction of the path of a football can be a perilous exercise. The laws of science hold no sway on All-Ireland final day. The break or bounce can be a bit of a lottery that equates to a very simple rule of thumb. Some days you get them, some days you don't.

After thousands of actions and inactions, Armagh's ace goal-poacher Stephen McDonnell was in possession of the football in the vicinity of the Tyrone goal. A goal was required to force a replay.

The 'wheel of time' had whirred and spun for the 70 odd-minutes, and rendered a rather curious judgment... nobody wins!

A loud beep on McDonnell's internal chronograph revealed the sands of time were about to expire. He duly checked his gun chamber, which was happily reporting a full house.

He took careful aim, squeezing his trigger finger and the likely path and trajectory of the bullet closely resembled the back of the Tyrone net!

In Robert Jordan's epic fantasy, *The Wheel of Time*, the wheel moves forward and backwards, its motion determined by the actions or inactions of humans.

Sadly for Stephen McDonnell he had not counted on the core of Jordan's story ringing true.

The actions of men can always turn the wheel back in the opposite direction.

There was a ghost in the machine that powered the wheel of time. A ghost named Conor Gormley...

{ THE GHOST IN THE MACHINE }

Of course, Conor Gormley's career wasn't all about his famous Jones' Road tango with Stephen McDonnell.

That said, given the magnitude of the occasion and the effect of his actions on the course of GAA history it was likely one of the greatest defensive interventions All-Ireland final day had ever witnessed.

The meeting of two teams separated by the width of a bridge was a tense, claustrophobic encounter, with Tyrone edging it by three as the stewards ringed the pitch.

With the Fat Lady about to sing for Armagh, Stephen McDonnell had the goal at his mercy.

'I wouldn't have done anything differently in the lead-up,' recalled McDonnell much later.

'Breaking the high ball down, peeling off, that's exactly what I would have done. That was exactly right. Tony Mac got a good ball back to me, very quick hands.'

Armagh knew the feeling of waiting an eternity for an audience with Sam Maguire, having won the trophy for the first time a year previously.

Conor Gormley and Tyrone were anxious to taste that most unique of moments when you finally get to come in from the cold.

'Mickey (Harte) would have talked to us from under-21 days that if you're not in the play, get back and do something and be helpful. Maybe that's running through my head, to get back and help out.'

To win any All-Ireland demands extraordinary sacrifice, and Conor Gormley would happily have blocked McDonnell's shot down... with his head!

Gormley was a product of Harte's school of motoring having impressed with the manager's stellar under-21 selection. Harte was a mystical presence on the Red Hand sideline. Quiet and unassuming – a deep-thinking coach – who saw everything in razor-sharp UHD. Harte loved a defender that could play a bit and Conor Gormley was a sensational 'baller'.

He was cast from the most durable of alloys. A proper street fighter very few ever got to the bottom of. Not even a double-leg break suffered in a club match in 2006 could derail the indestructible Carrickmore St Colmcille's talisman. No matter what chaos was inflicted upon the Tyrone rearguard, Gormley could make sense of it. He was the Red Hand's one-stop, problem-solving shop.

His dramatic game-saving cameo even earned him an iconic nickname, Conor 'The Block' Gormley. So how exactly did he deny the Orchard County in one foul swoop?

'I saw him lining up the shot and I got the hands down. Lucky enough, it hit my right hand. A couple of inches lower and I would have missed it... but it was my day and the rest is history now. It was great to be involved in such a big moment and remembered for Tyrone winning their first All-Ireland.

'Wow, I was part of that.'

For well over a decade, Conor Gormley's heroic efforts continued to bend and shape the fortunes of the Red Hand. His heroic actions changed the face of Tyrone's football history. With one magical intervention, Gormley and Tyrone finally moved... The Wheel of Time.

⇒——→ LENDING A ←——⇐
LIFELONG HAND

CONOR GORMLEY was born on October 10, 1980. He is from Omagh, the county town of Tyrone. He played his club football for Carrickmore St Colmcille's and won numerous senior titles, the first of which arrived in 1999 against Killyclogher.

Gormley played at both under-21 and senior level for the legendary Mickey Harte. The tough-tackling centre-back was one of the most consistent performers within the Red Hand machine and went on to collect three All Star Awards in 2003 and 2005, and a final gong completed the set in 2008.

Gormley played a starring role when Tyrone won a first-ever National Football League title in 2002, defeating fellow Ulstermen Cavan in a one-sided contest in Clones.

He was also part of the squad that retained the title the following season.

He was a rock of strength as Tyrone won a first-ever All-Ireland Football title in 2003, as they dispatched near neighbours, Armagh. He would go on to collect two further Celtic Crosses, in 2005 and again in 2008.

KEITH HIGGINS

(Height 5' 11", Weight 14.5 St)

Decade... 2000s/2010s/2020s

(Position... Corner-Back)

CHIEF CHARACTERISTIC... MANAGING DIRECTOR OF
MAYO'S COUNTER-RESISTANCE

TOP ACCOMPLICES... COLM BOYLE, PADDY DURCAN, LEE KEEGAN

KEITH HIGGINS

'I THINK IT IS REMARKABLE HE WAS ABLE TO PLAY IN THE FULL-BACK LINE FOR 15 YEARS BECAUSE THAT IS MENTALLY DRAINING FOR A PLAYER TO GO OUT THERE, TIME AFTER TIME, WITH THAT SOLE RESPONSIBILITY OF SHUTTING DOWN SOMEONE ELSE AS YOUR PHYSICAL ATTRIBUTES ALTER AND MAYBE WEAKEN.'

– BILLY JOE PADDEN

'FOR Red Sox fans, it wasn't always about winning… that was the province of the Yankee fans. It was about wanting to win. Hoping they would win. The weight of the wait. Which is why the fans came back, even after so many near misses. There was something at once noble and naive about the dynamic between the fans and their team. As decades passed, Red Sox Nation offered no asylum for those in need of instant gratification. Believing the Red Sox would win a World Series required an act of faith not unlike one's commitment to a Higher Being.'

The words of Dan Shaughnessy in *Reversing the Curse.*

Is playing for or supporting Mayo an evangelical thing? A show of extraordinary faith in pursuit of a greater cause and a higher purpose? In the *Curse of the Bambino*, author Dan Shaughnessy details

HARD MAN RATINGS

TOUGHEST:
9.6/10

MEANEST:
9.0/10

SCARIEST:
9.0/10

HARDEST:
19.8/20

TOTAL HARD MAN

47.4/50

the travails of the Boston Red Sox, and their never-ending search for a World Series Championship after the departure of their star player, Babe Ruth to the New York Yankees.

The curse was derived from the 86-year championship drought of the Boston Red Sox between 1918 and 2004, when within that period the once invincible dynasty of the 'Sox,' turned losing into an art form! So much so, that their supporters attempted everything from suggesting the exhumation of Babe Ruth's remains, to placing a Boston cap atop Mount Everest and burning a Yankees cap at its base camp.

Lastly, and even more bizarrely, the desperate fan base hired Laurie Cabot, the Official Witch of Massachusetts, who brought an end to a 10-game losing streak. While the losing streak ended, the *Curse of the Bambino* was not for turning!

The county of Mayo and its gladiatorial football team can take solace from Dan Shaughnessy's sequel to the above book, entitled *Reversing the Curse*.

When the Red Sox slipped 3-0 in a seven-game World Series against the Yankees in 2004, you would have received long odds-on Shaughnessy ever penning a sequel. The Red Sox duly sent the curse plummeting to the bottom of the Charles River, when winning four on the bounce – to finally clinch the precious pennant.

In Mayo, when one warrior falls on the battlefield, another picks up his lance to carry on the fight. Being a Mayo footballer is a curious thing. Always stranded in a no-man's land sustaining insurmountable casualties, eternally blinded by pyrrhic victories and endless false dawns.

They are seemingly cursed by history, yet blessed with an

extraordinarily regal footballing pedigree. Each narrow reversal is merely another building block, that fuels the myth and the romance of one of the most captivating journeys in Irish sporting history.

Keith Higgins played with uncommon bravery through the long and heart-breaking career he endured, and enjoyed, over the course of almost two decades… yes… *enjoyed!*

How else would Mayo have kept their chins up?

How else would they have continued to play and dream big?

'If you walked into our dressing-room an hour before training, you'd hear Barry or Andy Moran and Mickey Conroy and them boys telling stories and laughing their heads off,' he revealed midway through the epic battle that was his full career.

'The craic is already there. Then you've an hour on the field doing the hard work. Lads wouldn't play if they didn't enjoy it. There's a perception that it's like a military life. It is a lot of fun.

'That's why the nights out are important as well, so the stories gather up. There has to be a fun element to it or else why would you bother?'

{ SOUNDING THE AIR-RAID SIRENS }

They love their football and hurling in Ballyhaunis – a small town with a big soul – and none bigger than the lion-hearted Mayo football slugger, Keith Higgins. Despite only winning two senior county titles, Higgins' club, Ballyhaunis has supplied some notable additions to the Mayo senior side. The Red and Black has sent many soldiers into battle for the county, including Fergal Kelly, David Nestor and Tony Morley.

Keith Higgins became another addition to that illustrious lineage after he made his debut for Mayo during the 2005 season. The dashing and combative left corner-back was a man who knew his job specifications to the letter. Nobody attempted entry through the side door on Higgins' watch. He normally sounded the air-raid sirens and was first responder to any menacing hazards.

He could pick your pocket in the blink of an eye, and if any errant attacker left the door ajar... he was through in a flash, sprinting away to lead the Mayo counter-resistance. Of all the soldiers that have donned the sackcloth and armour, Higgins was the embodiment of the unquenchable Mayo fire.

Nobody fought their corner with more gusto than the Ballyhaunis express, winning four All Stars at corner-back. It was a high watermark in the annals of the awards scheme, the only defenders to have won more were John O'Keeffe, Páidí Ó Sé, and Tomás Ó Sé with five gongs each.

It was a blessing for the Mayo County Board that professionalism hadn't infiltrated the inter-county ranks during Keith's career. Nobody would have clocked more hours in the county jersey. He turned out in 75 championship games for Mayo and another 90 shifts in the league. Higgins also turned out in almost 50 National Hurling League games. Never mind the 'airmiles' expense charges, as he also racked up 43 hurling championship appearances – split between Christy Ring, Nicky Rackard, Senior B, and Junior games.

That would have added up to one hell of a pay-check after 256 senior county outings.

But the only currency Keith and his beloved Mayo ever wanted to be paid in was Sam Maguire's finest silver. The Ballyhaunis legend had certainly fully paid his dues in a rip-roaring and unforgettable tenure in the Mayo jersey... that was worth its weight in gold.

A QUINTESSENTIAL
▶──── GAA LIFE ────◀

KEITH HIGGINS played both gaelic football and hurling for his native county. When he retired from the football team in 2021, he stayed with the Mayo hurling panel.

The dual star with his local club Ballyhaunis was born on February 25, 1985, in Castlebar. He excelled at underage level for Mayo, representing both the under-21 hurling and football county teams as captain, and winning an All-Ireland under-21 medal in 2006.

In 2006 also, he was voted the Young Footballer of the Year, although injury ruled him out of the 2007 versions of both championships. He has the unique distinction of playing for Connacht in hurling's Railway Cup, and winning a medal, and then in 2014 he became the first Connacht player to win football and hurling Railway Cups, after Connacht won its first title in football since the 1968/69 competition.

Higgins won an unprecedented eight provincial titles in his football career. He also won a solitary National Football League medal.

On the hurling front, Higgins won a Christy Ring Cup All Star and was also nominated for the competition's 'Player of the Year' award in 2008.

OLLIE HONEYMAN

(Height 5' 10", Weight 14 St)

Decade... 1970s/1980s/1990s

(Position... Corner-Back)

CHIEF CHARACTERISTIC... ERECTING A LARGE STOP SIGN
FOR VISUALLY IMPAIRED FORWARDS

TOP ACCOMPLICES... NOEL CROSSAN, MICKEY QUINN, MICKEY
MARTIN, FRANK HOLOHAN

OLLIE
HONEYMAN

'I ALWAYS WANTED TO PLAY IN A CONNACHT FINAL AND
DEFINITELY HOPED TO DO IT BUT...'

– OLLIE HONEYMAN

LEITRIM football was flying... in more ways than one.
It was an era of household names, Big Tom, Seamus McMahon, Henry McMahon John Beattie, Ginger Morgan, Ronnie Duffy... and the rest of the band!

While 'Big Tom' and the 'Mainliners' and 'BB King' were strutting their stuff almost half-a-century ago, the Leitrim football squad took to the skies in pursuit of an elusive Connacht senior title.

Those football pioneers from the West were travelling in style from Dublin, as they boldly went (by airplane), where few GAA county sides had gone before, for their Connacht Championship opener against the 'exiles' of London.

It was an historic day for the visitors as they played their first-ever Connacht Championship match outside of the Emerald Isle... May 23, 1982.

On board, the plane for the novel trip was one of Leitrim's most celebrated kinsmen, and

**HARD
MAN
RATINGS**

TOUGHEST:
9.2/10

MEANEST:
8.5/10

SCARIEST:
8.9/10

HARDEST:
19.1/20

**TOTAL
HARD MAN
45.7/50**

one of the toughest nuts ever to 'suit up' in county football, the indomitable Ollie Honeyman.

Memories of Leitrim's ill-fated tango in Carrick-on-Shannon in 1977 came flooding back to him as the miniature of the city receded behind a fluffy bed of clouds. The scoreboard rarely lies, and... London 0-9 Leitrim – 0-6... was the cause of many sleepless nights for the Leitrim faithful, and a stain that simply had to be eradicated five years later.

For a county that had pretensions of reaching a Connacht final, the trip to Ruislip had the potential to produce a banana skin of epic proportions.

Despite their impoverished record in the province, Leitrim had always dented a reputation or two, despite the general perception they languished in the province's third tier, lagging behind the likes of Roscommon and Sligo.

A much-needed Connacht under-21 title in 1977 had been harvested by an impressive crop of talent, who had seamlessly integrated into the senior ranks. The shot-in-the-arm had hinted that the new kids on the block had even bigger fish to fry.

The London reversal took a lot of air out of the Leitrim tyres and was a massive reality check for any of the Leitrim flock who had been dreaming of provincial gains.

Honeyman was fully aware that failure was not an option, Leitrim simply had to escape from London with the win. Ollie was a man with a no-frills approach to his defensive duties... 'Thou Shalt Not Pass' was tattooed across his burly frame and broad shoulders. The Sean O'Heslin's talisman could put in a shift anywhere across the backline, and never fully got the merit his footballing skills deserved. Like all great exponents of the defensive arts, he was blessed with a sixth sense for impending danger. His party piece was 'lifting the siege' and the sight of Honeyman busting through the enemy lines clutching the ball was the clarion call to arms for the Leitrim supporters.

There were no tomorrows for any attackers that were foolhardy enough to test the strength of Ollie's jersey. He tackled with a bone-jarring ferocity and rarely came off second best in the physical stakes.

Thankfully for Leitrim and their 'Honey Badger,' they avoided any unwanted drama, with an added bonus of twisting the knife in the 'upstart' exiles, as revenge was certainly served cold in what was a complete mismatch.

Mission accomplished with a healthy 1-13 to 0-5, deposit in the accounts section.

{ KNOCKING ON HEAVEN'S DOOR }

It was a journey graced by some of the biggest names in world sport… albeit unwittingly!

Leitrim players and supporters were granted an audience with a number of unexpected guests, including snooker legend, Jimmy White, a man who was at the peak of his powers.

White obligingly posed for photos and signed some autographs en-route, when passing through the lobby.

The sporting royal audiences did not end there as Irish rugby legend and the then European Rugby Player of the Year, Tony Ward, who was attending the FA Cup final, added his signature to the growing number of names on the trip's A-List.

All that appeared to be missing was an appearance from Big

Tom, but BB King stepped into the breach as members of the squad attended a concert the night before the big match.

Up next for Leitrim was a horse of a different colour, the Connacht superpower empire that was Mayo football. Leitrim were the hosts but were missing a few key players, including influential forward Frank Smith. A golden opportunity to reach the promised land was spurned, as the home side was infected with the dreaded virus of profligacy and shot a staggering 18 wides, losing out on a score-line of 2-7 to 1-7.

Ollie and Leitrim kept panning for provincial silver but despite their Herculean efforts, never reached Connacht's 'lost city' perishing on the ill-fated journey to a footballing 'El Dorado'.

Ollie kept the show on the road. However dark the days, Ollie always seemed to shine. After one particularly chastening defeat against Galway in 1981, by 16 points, the Leitrim Observer paid tribute to his sterling efforts. 'Honeyman at centre half back" crowned himself in glory with a 'scintillating performance'.

Ollie Honeyman never graced the big stage. He never won an All Star or a coveted Connacht title. His hit-first-and-ask-questions-later approach made him the darling of the Leitrim public. He was a symbol of resistance to the world populated by the football elite.

In a sporting world of unequals, his enduring brilliance helped tilt that unhealthy balance back towards his barren homelands.

In a time when Leitrim rubbed shoulders with the West's aristocracy, Honeyman made the good football people of Leitrim walk a little taller. Most of all he made them feel a little better about being from Leitrim. His legacy was not measured in the bling of medals and trophies, but in the inestimable currency of raw courage and selfless dedication.

Hidden away in plain sight, players like Ollie rarely step into the glare of the footballing spotlight. Yet whenever Leitrim lovers toast their bygone days and immortal heroes, they will surely raise a glass to the 'Honeyman.'

A LEITRIM LIFE

HE PLAYED his club football with Sean O'Heslin's. The famous Leitrim outfit was founded as Ballinamore in January 1889, and is one of the few dual clubs in the county.

Local schoolteacher Seán O'Heslin was the man behind the club in its early years, and the club was renamed Ballinamore Seán O'Heslin's in his honour in 1953.

Ollie won numerous county titles with the club, who are one of the dominant forces in the county, having won 21 county championships.

His first four years with the Leitrim senior squad coincided with his days at UCC, where he played in the Sigerson Cup, making the side in his first year of study in the famous institution. His final year exams prevented him from lining out against Galway in 1983, the only blemish on a near-perfect attendance record for his beloved county.

He never played in a Connacht final, coming closest in 1982 - losing by a goal to Mayo in the semi-final - and enduring more agony in 1983, as lightning struck twice with Leitrim edged out by three points.

Ollie continued to excel despite the set-backs and was fittingly included in the Leitrim Team of the Millennium. In 2012 the *Irish Independent* selected the 'The GAA Giants' picking every County's best 15 championship performers for the years 1962 to 1994 and the name Honeyman was proudly present.

DJ KANE

(Height 5' 10", Weight 14 St)

Decade... 1980s/1990s

(Position... Wing-Back)

CHIEF CHARACTERISTIC... CITIZEN KANE ALWAYS
ENSURED DOWN'S STOCK KEPT RISING

TOP ACCOMPLICES... PADDY O'ROURKE, PAUL HIGGINS, BRENDAN
MCKERNAN, JOHN KELLY, AMBROSE ROGERS, CONOR DEEGAN

DJ KANE

'WHEN I GO OUT ON THAT FIELD, I PLAY MY GUTS OUT FOR MYSELF
AND FOR MY COLLEAGUES AROUND ME.'

– DJ KANE

CITIZEN Kane, the classic 1941 drama charts the rise and fall of Charles Foster Kane, an enormously wealthy newspaper publisher and industrial magnate. Regarded as one of the greatest movies of all time, it charts Kane's ascent and crashing decent during the 1929 stock market crash.

Down football's rise and crashing fall had left its very own 'Citizen Kane' staring into a footballing abyss. Ten years was a lifetime in sports. A jail sentence that might as well have had the key thrown away, for good measure. Ten seasons ploughing a fallow field had left him riddled with frustration and a belly full of regret.

If not now… it would be never.

For one of Down's most decorated heroes, the next hour or so would define his football life. Future be dammed! For now, it was all about the present. For the Mourne men, Down, the equation was very straightforward. It was a case of beat Donegal or bust.

HARD MAN RATINGS

TOUGHEST:
9.1/10

MEANEST:
9.9/10

SCARIEST:
9.1/10

HARDEST:
18.8/20

TOTAL HARD MAN

46.9/50

Ten years without an Ulster title was an itch that needed to be scratched.

The 1991 Ulster title win against Donegal showcased everything that Down football could and should have been. The Mourne County crew were superb footballers, who were often hamstrung by a split footballing personality. You never really could predict which Down side was going to turn up.

Inside the camp, manager Pete McGrath, had successfully managed to dial-down the white noise. Down were quietly confident and were bringing a serious intensity to the training pitch.

Training had been going well and as Ross Carr would later reveal, nobody was holding back – least of all DJ Kane.

'Some of the games in training were savage. Paddy O'Rourke would be marking Greg Blaney, DJ (Kane) would be marking myself, Paul Higgins would be marking Mickey Linden.

'There were incredible individual battles. And as time went on you were thinking if I can hold my own against some of these boys, then there's nothing coming down the line that's going to be an awful lot better.'

If Nostradamus ever needed a physic assistant he could have emailed Carr! His observations proved to be on the money as Down tore into a bewildered Donegal, with DJ Kane gobbling up the opposition attacks, and bristling with attitude when bursting forward.

Kane hared up the left wing, took a pass from Mickey Linden and fired an arrow straight over Gary Walsh's crossbar. When Kane wasn't knocking spots off the opposition attack, he always chipped in with a vital point or two. He had moved up-field to score crucial points in earlier rounds against Armagh and Derry.

Down were on a war footing, and the Newry Man-of-War, Kane was generating that sort of controlled fury which was his trademark.

Donegal wilted in the face of the raging Down inferno, and the race for Sam Maguire changed in one seismic shift. The long-awaited triumph, however, was merely an aperitif for what was to follow, as Down raced past Kerry in the All-Ireland semi-final to face Meath in the decider.

On a sunny afternoon at GAA headquarters Down, and the Royals, with into battle with the Meath men slight favourites, after lowering Down's colours in the 1990 National League final.

{ KANE WAS ABLE }

Ross Carr, though, stressed that while they respected the challenge ahead, they certainly did not fear it.

'We certainly wouldn't have viewed Meath as an unbeatable team. There was a serious respect for them, but there would have been no fear because we had played against them regularly in the previous four or five years. After the All-Ireland semi-final, there was no doubt in our minds that we were training to win an All-Ireland final, we weren't just turning up to enjoy the day.'

Despite Carr's confidence, DJ Kane and company started slowly. Meath looked in the groove early on when rattling off a few quick points; then as Down slowly settled, the game took a decisive turn. Down started to click and amazingly outscored Meath by a total of 12 points to one, in a frantic second and third quarter.

Meath roared back, boosted by captain, Liam Hayes' goal and then missed a couple of gilt-edged chances. Down and the resolute DJ. Kane fought a tenacious rear-guard action to grind out a hard-earned win, shading it by two points.

There was one more red-letter day as they won a coveted Ulster title in 1994, defeating a dogged Tyrone side. DJ Kane recalled a good day at the office with great fondness.

'The weather was absolutely brilliant, it was a boiling hot day... the people were out in their shorts and T-shirts, sunglasses. The whole day just was perfect as soon as the final whistle went the crowd were already on the sidelines. It was just pure euphoria and I suppose an element of relief as well that you had succeeded; you've got the job done, and now you can look forward to hitting Clones town and maybe having a few drinks. We were teammates; that probably doesn't happen anymore, as you have to go and recover and rehydrate. Our rehydration was probably a slightly bit different and there was a whole lot of enjoyment, receiving the cup and heading onto the team bus.'

The county football scene is an eternally shifting market of stocks and shares. The market is a volatile world filled with breathtaking highs and shattering, crashing lows.

At a time of fluctuating fortunes for Down football, their very own 'blue-chip' wing-back, Citizen DJ Kane, ensured that the Mourne County's stock continued to soar.

DJ'S

»———— GREATEST ————«

HITS

DJ KANE was born in Newry, County Down in 1964. He was a member of his local club, Newry Mitchels, before playing with Newry Shamrocks. He was from a strong footballing background, with his brother Val a replacement as Down won the Sam Maguire Cup in 1968.

DJ Kane would go one better than his sibling and lead the Mourne men to the All-Ireland title as captain, in 1994.

He spent a 'baker's dozen' years with the red and black, and in that period he accumulated three Ulster Championship medals. That famous win in the 1990 Ulster final ended a 10 year wait for the Anglo Celt trophy. He won two All-Ireland senior medals, and two National League titles (Division 2 and Division 3), and won an All Star Award.

DJ Kane did not feature for Down at minor level. He did, however, win an Ulster under 21 title when playing in the forward line, as Down defeated Antrim in the Centenary Year. They would later lose out to Cork in the All-Ireland semi-final.

In his first season attending Northern Ireland Polytech (now the University of Ulster Jordanstown), he won an All-Ireland Freshers medal and followed this up with Sigerson Cup winners' medals in 1986 and again in 1987.

HARRY KEEGAN

(Height 6' 0", Weight 14.5 St)

Decade... 1970s/1980s

(Position... Corner-Back)

CHIEF CHARACTERISTIC... PERSONALISED GET-WELL-SOON
CARDS SALESMAN - CONNACHT REGION

TOP ACCOMPLICES... PAT LINDSAY, SEAMUS HAYDEN,
GERRY FITZMAURICE, DERMOT EARLEY, EAMON MCMANUS,
TOM DONNELLAN, GERRY CONNELLAN

HARRY KEEGAN

'I'VE GOT THE BALL! I'VE GOT THE BALL!'. 'NEVER MIND
THE BALL, PUT OUT THE BLOODY FIRE!'
– JIMMY MURRAY

THE burnt football still hangs from the ceiling. The identity of the man clutching the famous ball – needs no introduction in this Western footballing hotbed.

He might as well have been in Croke Park fielding the ball – but Roscommon captain Jimmy Murray was standing in the middle of a burnt-out pub holding a very unique item.

This pub, like Roscommon football, had a history of survival, and Murray the proprietor was a publican with a very unique distinction. He is the only man in the history of Roscommon football to lift the Sam Maguire Cup, presiding over the Rossies' sole wins in 1943 and 1944.

The story of the football from the 1943 All-Ireland final features as part of the *A History of the GAA in 100 Objects* and a bit like the history of Roscommon football is of the against all odds variety.

In 1990, the football was hanging from the

HARD
MAN
RATINGS

TOUGHEST:
9.5/10

MEANEST:
9.0/10

SCARIEST:
8.9/10

HARDEST:
19.3/20

TOTAL
HARD MAN
46.7/50

ceiling of the pub – when a fire broke out destroying the much-loved premises. Such was the ball's standing in the community, that a fireman fighting the blaze is reported to have shouted, 'I've got the ball! I've got the ball!'

Jimmy's reply was in the priceless category, as he reminded the ecstatic firefighter about the job-at-hand.

'Never mind the ball, put out the bloody fire!'

No amount of fire brigades in Ireland would have been able to douse the flames of the bonfires that lit up Roscommon on October 10, 1943, when the Rossies won a first ever All-Ireland senior title.

It had been a long winding road to Croker for Roscommon, and after both sides could not be separated a couple of weeks previously, the late dismissal of Cavan's Joe Stafford provided the platform for Roscommon to seal the deal.

When they followed it up the following year, defeating aristocrats Kerry, the perils of Croke Park did not appear quite so daunting. Two years later, Roscommon were poised to strike again, when they led Kerry by six points with a few minutes remaining.

The final had been originally set for September 22, but was delayed for two weeks as part of the 'Save the Harvest' campaign. Volunteers and farmers had worked side-by-side in an extraordinary display of togetherness during the national emergency of 1946. The monumental effort helped ensure the survival of the harvest, which had been threatened by severe flooding.

Roscommon had a six-point lead with three minutes left, but Kerry survived courtesy of goals by Paddy Burke and Tom 'Gega' O'Connor. The Kingdom won the replay and the golden age of Roscommon football ground to an unceremonious halt.

The Rossies disappearance from centre-stage is one of gaelic football's greatest unsolved mysteries. Roscommon toiled in the wilderness for nearly 40 years seeking a 'saviour', and it would take until the end of the 1970s before one was at hand!

Harry Keegan cut an impressive figure. The lion-hearted defender would prove to be the cornerstone of the Rossies second wave of footballing greats. Strong and granite-jawed, the Castlerea Colossus was a man with an aversion to taking any captives on the field of war.

Tough and uncompromising were two words to describe him, and after serving a few years of apprenticeship on the provincial stage, Harry was ready to go forth and spread his gospel of 'Thou shalt not pass' to all corners of Ireland!

Harry would be joined on the pilgrimage by a number of warriors fashioned in his own combative reflection. Players like the legendary Dermot Earley, talismanic captain and flying wing-back Danny Murray, and Sean Kilbride to name a few players with real pedigree.

Roscommon football had finally got the show back on the road, the band was belatedly back together. The years between 1977-80 saw Roscommon bring its own version of 'Murder Ball' to the Western province. The twin peaks of Galway and Mayo were sent tumbling, as Harry's hair-raising defensive exploits left a lasting impression – on two rather perplexed attacking units of the vanquished provincial giants.

{ EMULATING THE CLASS OF 1944 }

His impactful performances quickly translated to the national stage as he garnered All Stars in 1978 and 1980. Coupled with Earley's towering performances in midfield, this was a version of Roscommon that contained real heart and soul, traits that signposted a clear path back to the glory days of September.

By now, Roscommon were greedily eyeing Sam. When a fourth Connacht crown arrived in 1980, opportunity knocked.

Roscommon had signalled their renaissance when narrowly succumbing to Galway in the 1976 Connacht final. The following season the tables were turned as the Rossies deposed the incumbents, and then the Tribesmen were defeated again in 1978. Heady provincial days followed as Mayo bit the dust in 1979, and again in 1980.

After taking care of provincial business, Armagh were politely ushered to the exit door in the penultimate stage of the All-Ireland series.

When Roscommon went five clear in the early stages of the decider against Kerry, it appeared that the stars were aligning. The game sadly turned out to be a damp squib – as the Kingdom grasped a lifeline provided by John Egan's goal, to narrowly claim the spoils.

It had not been a thing of beauty – a game proliferated with an astonishing 64 frees.

Harry Keegan's typically obdurate performances that season confirmed his status as one of the finest defenders of his generation. He was back on the All Star podium again in 1986, before he gracefully bowed out in 1988.

It had been a long winding road to 'Croker' following in the footsteps of his celebrated forefathers.

Perhaps Pól Brennan and Ciarán Brennan's atmospheric lyrics

can provide some solace for long-suffering Roscommon fans.

The song based on the title of a 1975 novel by Gerald Seymour, strikes the perfect note for one of the most celebrated chapters in Roscommon football history…

HARRY'S GAME.

»——→ A ROSSIES ROAD ←——«

HARRY KEEGAN was born on January 12, 1952. The corner-back made his debut for Roscommon in 1972, in a league game against Kilkenny, and became a permanent fixture in the starting 15 until his retirement in 1988.

He attended secondary school in Castlerea and played his club football with the local Castlerea St Kevin's side.

During that time as a member of the Roscommon senior team, he won five Connacht Senior Championship medals, and three All Star awards in 1978, 1980 and 1986.

He holds a unique place in the pantheon of Roscommon footballing greats as he is the only player in the history of a football-mad county that has won three All Star Awards.

In 1980 he was part of a star-studded backline including; John O'Keeffe (Kerry), Robbie Kelleher (Dublin), Tommy Drumm (Dublin), Ollie Brady(Cavan), and Paudie Lynch (Kerry).

He was also part of a dominant Rossies side that won four Connacht Championships in a row. He also won a National Football League medal in 1979, as part of the Roscommon squad that defeated Cork in the decider, although he did not participate in the final due to injury.

LEE KEEGAN

(Height 5' 11", Weight 14 St)

Decade... 2010s/2020s

(Position... Wing-Back)

CHIEF CHARACTERISTIC... DIARMUID CONNOLLY'S
PERSONAL TRAINER

TOP ACCOMPLICES... PADDY DURCAN, COLIN BOYLE, CHRIS
BARRETT, DONAL VAUGHAN, SEAMUS O'SHEA, KEITH HIGGINS

LEE KEEGAN

'TO WIN ALL-IRELANDS AND TO BE THE BEST, YOU HAVE
TO HAVE THAT BIT OF DARK SIDE IN YOUR GAME.'

– LEE KEEGAN

SPORTSFILE, Ireland's award-winning sports photo agency, has captured some of the most iconic events in Irish sporting history. Shortly after the strains of *Auld Lang Syne* drift away, the sleeping giant of our Irish summers will gently stir from its wintery slumber.

Pre-season competitions like the O'Byrne Cup, the Munster League, and the McKenna Cup, herald a low-key start to another exciting chapter in the GAA's never-ending story.

In sleet or snow, in hail or sunshine, Sportsfile 'snappers' will be there to take you between the white lines and into the heart of the action. From the banks of the Corrib to the Mountains of Mourne, a dedicated band of professional camera-people will capture every waking moment – in every nook-and-cranny across the Emerald Isle.

Every rivalry in every decade has a Sportsfile roll of film attached to it. Some images more than most encapsulate the essence of the battle. Some

**HARD
MAN
RATINGS**

TOUGHEST:
9.3/10

MEANEST:
9.8/10

SCARIEST:
9.0/10

HARDEST:
19.0/20

**TOTAL
HARD MAN
47.1/50**

portray a story within a story. A last duel, a final struggle, a fight to the death…

Lee Keegan was the smiling hitman of an exceptional Mayo side that came within a whisker of immortality. Nobody raged harder against the oppressive nature of the footballing gods than the highest-scoring defender in championship history.

Not content with rendering most of his victims scoreless, Lee Keegan would add insult to injury with his terrifying raiding runs into enemy territory. He scored an astronomical 6-40 in 54 championship starts, as his sorties in the opposition half, were invariably followed by an almost inevitable white or green flag.

Keegan was the cure for all of Mayo's ills. He was a street fighter who at his core had a hefty layer of pragmatism. Brilliant defending… check. Transitioning and scoring… check.

Practitioner of dark arts… check.

An incident in the 2017 All-Ireland football final highlighted the Westport Wonder's total dedication to the green and red jersey. With the game tied at 1-16 apiece, Dublin's unerring place-ball specialist Dean Rock lined up a possible game-winning free as time expired, in a classic decider.

As Rock was shaping to kick, Lee Keegan threw his GPS at the Dublin forward in an effort to put Rock *off*. Keegan's quick thinking didn't have the desired effect; Rock's effort flew over the bar and Mayo were yet again condemned to the house of pain.

Lee Keegan was reflective about the incident, but was also unrepentant. In Mayo's darkest hours, desperate times required desperate measures.

'It's probably an unfortunate thing that it happened. You know, I always say, "If you were in my shoes, what would people have done?" Would they have come up with something else?

'Obviously, it's very unsportsmanlike and I totally accept that. But, I suppose, you're looking into losing your fourth All-Ireland… and to be fair to Dean Rock, he never batted an eyelid. 'As I think he said in the paper, he went through his routine and it just sailed over the bar. That's the mark of how good he is!'

Keegan went on to talk about the ruthlessness of the top teams and argued that a 'dark side' is necessary to be successful in the modern game. 'To win All-Irelands and to be the best, you have to have that bit of dark side in your game.'

{ KEEGAN VS CONNOLLY }

Lee's battles with Dublin forward, Diarmuid Connolly were a mirror image of the wider dynamic that existed between two incredible football teams. It was not inconceivable that Mayo could have worn the mantle of the 'GOAT' (greatest of all time), if only…

Scorelines between the two sides in the major finals and semi-finals indicated how thin the line between immortality and inconsequentiality genuinely are.

Lee Keegan was Diarmuid Connolly's shadow in a high-stakes game of poker with neither prepared to blink. The rivalry between Keegan and Connolly turned nasty at times, with both men locking horns like two rutting stags, as both teased both the best and the worst out of each other's locker. Keegan collected a black card while marking Connolly in the 2016 final replay, and in the 2015 semi-final Connolly saw red for throwing a punch at the Mayo man.

Both men had a healthy respect for each other's abilities, with Keegan warm in his praise for the Dublin talisman. Singling him out as his toughest assignment, having found himself on the wrong side in four All-Ireland finals at the hands of Dublin between 2013 and 2020. Connolly returned the compliment with an effusive tribute when news broke of Keegan's retirement.

'It was a bit of a shock to me to see him hang up the boots so early to be honest. He's a guy, I really admire; when he played at No 5 he was really hard to stop, he took your focus because he liked going forward a bit and getting on the scoreboard.'

'He caught me on the hop in the All-Ireland final replay in 2016 when he got a goal off the run of play and that can knock you for six. We were lucky to win that game; they didn't get over the line against us, so it may be disappointing for him never to get a Celtic Cross medal.

'He may have been sent to man-mark me but sometimes I ended up doing the marking. I don't believe I was a better player than Lee Keegan, I just played a different game. He was a top player for the Mayo side and they'll miss him this season.'

Sportsfile's image of Lee Keegan holding onto Connolly remains one of the defining images of one of the greatest individual and inter-county rivalries in the modern game.

It's the 2016 All-Ireland semi-final... Lee Keegan grasps Diarmuid Connolly, almost tearing his shirt off. Keegan is down on one knee... but never lets go of the shirt.

Lee Keegan and Mayo remind us more than most of Robin Island's 'Most Wanted', prisoner number 466/64 and the great Nelson Mandela's famous words... 'The greatest glory in living lies is not in never falling, but in rising every time we fall.'

THE LIFE OF LEE

LEE KEEGAN was born on October 25, 1989, and is widely regarded as one of his county's greatest-ever footballers. He is the highest-scoring defender of all time and is the only player to win five All Stars without winning an All-Ireland medal. He holds a unique record of having scored a goal against Dublin goalkeeper Stephen Cluxton in three consecutive championship matches.

Keegan played school football for Rice College. He had a passion for rugby union and he was part of Connacht Rugby underage academies.

Keegan was part of the Westport side that won the 2009 and 2016 Mayo Intermediate Football Championships, and also won a Connacht Intermediate Club Football Championship. In February 2017, Keegan won the pinnacle of titles in the grade when the Westerners won the All-Ireland Intermediate Club Football Championship title, defeating Meath's St Colmcille's by 2-12 to 3-8.

In October 2022, he won a Mayo Senior Championship, which was Westport's first county senior title.

Keegan did not feature at minor level for Mayo. He was voted Footballer of the Year in 2016.

Tim Kennelly
(Height 6' 0", Weight 15 St)

Decade... 1970s/1980s
(Position... Wing-Back)

CHIEF CHARACTERISTIC... HEAD BOUNCER CROKE PARK

TOP ACCOMPLICES... JIMMY DEENIHAN, PÁIDÍ Ó SÉ,
TOMMY DOYLE, JOHN EGAN, SEAN WALSH

TIM
KENNELLY

'IN MANY WAYS, HE WAS THE HEART AND SOUL OF THAT TEAM. SO
STRONG, SO WHOLE-HEARTED, BUT ALSO A VERY GOOD FOOTBALLER.
HE WAS A GREAT LEADER, WITH A FIERCE PRESENCE ABOUT HIM.'
– MIKEY SHEEHY

KERRY would not have been Kerry without him. If Kerry were the 'Irresistible Force,' he was the 'Immovable Object'. He was woven from solid oak. A defiant and imposing presence, who formed the backbone of the famed kingdom rearguard. A colossus dubbed lovingly 'The Horse'.

The warrior spirit within players like Tim Kennelly is a rare, yet wonderful thing.

He was once described by a former teammate as 'the first guy you'd want with you in the trenches'.

Tim was also a truly accomplished footballer with an intelligent football brain. His distribution was excellent, and his potent mixture of power and skill was a strength Kerry relied heavily upon.

The man saw no fear in terms of physical engagement. There were no half-measures. Every challenge, every tackle, was made with unwavering courage and incredible ferocity. When Tim Kennelly played for club or county, he was willing

**HARD
MAN
RATINGS**

TOUGHEST:
9.9/10

MEANEST:
8.4/10

SCARIEST:
9.0/10

HARDEST:
19.9/20

TOTAL
HARD MAN
47.2/50

to risk life and limb to do justice to their hallowed jerseys.

One perfect example of his lion-hearted approach came when he was playing for his divisional side, Feale Rangers against a much-vaunted Austin Stacks in the county final in 1980.

Tim was involved in a collision in the opening period and was diagnosed with a broken collarbone at the half-time interval.

It was a crushing blow to a side that leaned heavily upon their celebrated talisman. Tim Kennelly had other ideas, and despite being in excruciating pain, he tucked his arm across his chest and came out to play the second half.

Like a wounded soldier who refused to withdraw from the battlefield, Kennelly fought on with little regard for his own plight. It was a torturous 30 minutes, but he would not yield, his comrades on the front line needed him.

The sight of Tim Kennelly marching back out onto the field emboldened his ailing team. The symbolism of the 'Horse's' return was not lost upon Austin Stacks players; Tim Kennelly and Feale Rangers had laid down the gauntlet. Tim played the second-half just like the first one. It was possible he could have been minus two arms and still ploughed on.

Feale were by now totally energised by Tim Kennelly's unprecedented act of defiance, and the writing was on the wall for 'Stacks'.

The injury sustained on the day forced Kennelly out of football for six months, but he soldiered on and inspired Feale Rangers to register an unlikely victory. In doing so his club had the privilege of nominating the Kerry captain for the following year, Kennelly's good friend and future TD, Jimmy Deenihan.

Conor Heneghan recalls an exchange between the two

legendary Kerry warriors directly after the game. Once the game was over Kennelly walked up to Deenihan and said to him, 'There you are Jimmy. You're Kerry captain next year. I didn't let you down'.

Jimmy Deenihan remembered the 'Listowel Lion' as one of the Kingdom's true greats.

'I have played both with and against Tim over the past 40 years and, without doubt, he was one of the greatest centre-backs the game ever produced. Most dear to me are my memories of playing alongside Tim for Feale Rangers, which we did for nearly 10 years, when we won the county championship twice.'

For the club, for the county, for family and friends; Tim Kennelly was a man that would never let you down.

{ THE KEEPER OF THE FLAME }

In the 'Wonder Years' of the 1970s and early 80s, their names burned brightly. They were the 'chic', slightly 'uppity' residents of Jones' Road. Celtic Crosses collected like spare shirt buttons. They were the ultimate 'Kings of September'.

Mikey Sheehy, Jack O'Shea, Pat Spillane, Ogie Moran, Eoin 'Bomber' Liston... all style, substance, and infinite swagger.

They were standing on the shoulders of a giant named Tim Kennelly. The proud son of Listowel was the very beating heart of all that was great about Kerry's football. He was their enforcer, their Lord Protector, and he set the terms of engagement.

Former GAA President, Sean Kelly described Kennelly as a legend in GAA circles.

'He was among the best defenders the county ever had; a man

who excelled in a team that included some of the greatest players of all time,' he said.

Away from the gladiatorial arena of county football, Tim was an incredibly self-effacing and charming presence.

Upon the sad and untimely occasion of his passing, Billy John Keane, son of the legendary John B. Keane paid a poignant and moving tribute to a fellow son of Kerry in the *Irish Independent*.

'It was, I suppose, appropriate his heart gave out in the finish because he was all heart. That was the essence of the man, but there was no way the heart of a lion could be sustained by the body of a man, even a man called The Horse.'

Tim's legacy is alive and well in his family as his two sons also played for Kerry.

Noel Kennelly won an All-Ireland medal in 2000, while Tadhg Kennelly claimed a winner's medal in 2009, having earlier become the first Irish person to win an AFL Premiership medal with Sydney Swans.

Tim had safely passed the torch onwards. Future generations of Kerry youngsters would hear tales of a Listowel giant, who powered his team to an unlikely victory with one arm.

Kerry football was built upon great heroes and epic stories that echoed across the sands of time. Tim Kennelly always knew he was just passing through, and keeping the acclaimed jersey in safe-keeping for someone else. He understood and embraced the ancient traditions of the Kingdom, built on courageous deeds, not words.

He had written yet another glorious chapter with his warrior spirit. When he lifted the 'Holy Grail' in 1979 as All-Ireland winning captain, it put the seal on his amazing journey – from

Listowel Emmet's junior side to divisional kingpins, Feale Rangers.

Tim Kennelly was so many things to Kerry football, but most of all... he was the 'Keeper of its Flame'.

»——→ THE MAN'S HAUL ←——«

TIM KENNELLY was born in Listowel on July 6, 1954. The farmer and publican was one of the unsung heroes of one of the greatest football teams in GAA history.

He made his county debut at the age of 17 for the Kerry minor team. After two Munster final reversals in the grade, Kennelly subsequently joined Kerry's under-21 team, winning two All-Ireland medals as a substitute in 1973, and playing a starring role in 1975.

He graduated to the senior ranks on the eve of yet another 'Golden Generation' for Kerry football, when donning the famous green and gold geansaí during the 1974-75 National Football league.

Over the course of the next decade, Kennelly won five All-Ireland medals, beginning with a sole triumph in 1975, before a magnificent record-equalling four championships in-a-row from 1978 to 1981. The Kingdom were masters of all they surveyed in that era and he also won nine Munster medals, three National Football League medals, and claimed back-to-back All Stars in 1979 and 1980.

In the twilight days of Railway Cup football, he was a mainstay on the Munster interprovincial team, lining out for the first time in 1977.

Kennelly was at the peak of his powers and during that period added four Railway Cup medals to an already embarrassingly full chest of riches.

EOIN LISTON

(Height 6' 2", Weight 15.5 St)

Decade... 1970s/1980s/1990s

(Position... Full-Forward)

CHIEF CHARACTERISTIC... ON-FIELD AND ON-BOARD TERRORISM

TOP ACCOMPLICES... JOHN EGAN, PAT SPILLANE,
MIKEY SHEEHY, OGIE MORAN, JACK O'SHEA

EOIN
LISTON

'I WAS UP AT THE FRONT AND ONE OF THE LADS, TO GET MY
ATTENTION, CALLED OUT "BOMBER". THE AIR HOSTESS MUST HAVE
GOT A BIT CONCERNED... SHE REFERRED HIM TO THE PILOT'
– EOIN 'BOMBER' LISTON

HE was the most successful fighter pilot in the history of aerial warfare. Erich Hartmann flew 1,404 combat missions and engaged in aerial combat on 825 separate occasions.

Hartmann waged, at times, what appeared to be a one-man-war on the Allies during WW2, shooting down a total of 352 aircraft – 345 Soviet and seven American, during the course of his career with the German Luftwaffe.

Hartmann appeared to possess nine lives as he was forced to crash-land his fighter 16 times, due either to mechanical failure or damage caused by the multitude of aerial skirmishes he was involved in. Such was Hartmann's aerial prowess, he was never shot down by direct enemy action.

Erich Hartmann was also well known for attacking at very close range. He often appeared ghost-like out of the clouds. Most of his victims never knew anyone was there until one of their wings ripped off or their engine blew up.

Eoin Liston was another 'Bomber' who

HARD MAN RATINGS

TOUGHEST:
9.3/10

MEANEST:
9.1/10

SCARIEST:
9.7/10

HARDEST:
19.4/20

TOTAL HARD MAN

47.5/50

certainly won his fair share of aerial duels and wreaked havoc from close range. While Hartmann's astounding feats would ultimately have little impact on the course of the war, Liston's introduction would alter the course of gaelic football history.

His arrival would herald a new departure for The Kingdom, as they unveiled a frightening new weapon within their already formidable arsenal. Kerry so often the master of the ground offensive were about to unleash a terrifying new form of attack as Liston became the focal part of a devastating assault from above.

After winning the All-Ireland in 1975 with a blossoming youthful line-up, hopes had been high within the Kingdom hierarchy that it would launch a new period of Kerry ascendency.

Those lofty ideals were quickly quelled by the re-emergence of Dublin under Kevin Heffernan as the Metropolitans hoovered up Sam Maguire in 1976 and 77.

The crafty old footballing fox, Mick O'Dwyer knew the Kerry gateaux was lacking a vital ingredient. The Kingdom needed a different dimension and he turned to the bustling seaside resort of Ballybunion for the final segment of the Kingdom cake.

Eoin Liston's considerable frame did not at first glance fit the profile of a typical Kerry footballer. He was a huge man, whose undeniable gifts as an elite attacker did not include blistering pace.

O'Dwyer, however, already had plenty of jet fuel in the Kerry tank. Liston possessed the X Factor that the Kerry supremo inwardly craved.

He was a rare mix of size and silk. A man who could batter the door down, or tip-toe into the opposition house. A JCB with the stealth of a cat burglar wasn't something most enemy defences had ever witnessed on their radar before.

Liston was not to the manor born in footballing terms and did not feature on the Kerry minor team. He did make an instant impact at under-21 level in 1977, when they defeated Cork and Down en-route to collect an All-Ireland title.

'Micko' was never afraid to cast the net far and wide, and called Liston on board to bolster the squad for a tilt at Sam.

The 'Waterville Wizard', ever a man to see the wood from the trees, knew the big man's inclusion would be viewed as an act of desperation and the addition of nothing more than heavy machinery.

O'Dwyer happily traded in a currency of smoke and mirrors. Liston's soft hands and lazy skills were totally at odds with the public perception that he amounted to nothing more than a one-trick pony. Micko had the perfect foils in Mikey Sheehy and John Egan to extract the maximum for the genial giant.

He knew Liston's arrival would not only put The Dubs on high alert but it would also create the perfect state of flux for The Kingdom to make hay.

Dublin and Kerry were a GAA war like no other. The urban and rural cousins were chalk and cheese. It had raged bitterly for decades, a clash of two very different worlds that reflected an ever-widening urban and rural cultural divide.

Dublin were steaming towards three-in-a-row and Kerry were hell-bent on derailing them.

Major conflicts are invariably fought upon ideological differences, but their outcomes always hinge on the battle plans of generals and the deployment of their soldiers. Liston's deployment was about to put the 'mother of all spanners' into the works and change the course of a GAA rivalry that had fascinated and endured like no other.

When O'Dwyer took the 'nuclear option' and selected Liston at full-forward in his first championship decider, the fall-out for the incumbent metropolitans would be spectacular.

While a close encounter was predicted, the Bomber laid waste to the Dublin backline and at the full-time whistle Kerry prevailed by 5–11 to 0–9. Bomber proved to be the game-changer as Kerry imperiously wrestled back the crown and went on to complete four on-the-spin.

{ LIVING UP TO HIS NAME }

He bombed the opposition in major finals, amassing a staggering 3-10 in seven All-Ireland finals. He also scored 16-67 in 65 league games and 20-50 in 39 championship appearances.

The Bomber was well used to creating havoc at elevated and rarified heights so it probably came as little surprise when he caused quite a stir on board a flight from Cardiff to Cork.

'I was up at the front and one of the lads, to get my attention, called out "Bomber". The air hostess must have got a bit concerned… she referred him to the pilot. We knew there was a bit of a problem. I waited until everyone was off the plane in Cork.

'Some of the crew interviewed the fella who called me and they Googled me to confirm that I was known as "Bomber". They explained the protocols but they accepted the explanation, they just realised what had actually happened.'

Creating havoc in the air was, of course, a Bomber's prerogative!

THE SKY WAS
THE LIMIT

LISTON PLAYED his club football with his local club Beale. They were a powerhouse of the northern division, winning it on six occasions with the big man leading the charge.

He lined out in the county championship with the Divisional side Shannon Rangers. In 1977 he was a member of the side that won the battle of the 'Rangers,' when they defeated Feale Rangers to take the county senior championship title. It would prove to be Eoin's only victory in the county championship.

He won two All-Ireland under-21 titles before lining out with the Kerry senior team in 1978. His arrival into the senior ranks kick-started a period of total Kerry domination, with Liston's towering assault and soft skills rewriting a full-forward requirements for inter-county CVs.

The Bomber could well have opened an exhibition to showcase all the awards and trophies he accumulated in his dazzling Kingdom road trip. All Star awards were secured in 1980, 1981, 1982, and 1984. He won a magnificent seven All-Ireland medals, two National League medals and two Railway Cups between 1978 and 1986.

He played in a total of 15 Munster finals, winning 10, as well as contesting eight All-Ireland deciders.

He was the perfect size and stature as Ireland came calling for his services in the International Rules Series of 1984, 1985, and 1990.

THE 50
TOUGHEST, MEANEST, SCARIEST
HARD-MEN
IN GAELIC FOOTBALL HISTORY

Conor Counihan gets the job done against Meath's Bernard Flynn in the 1990 All-Ireland final

Francie Bellew brings order to the Armagh defence against Sligo in the 2002 All-Ireland Championship

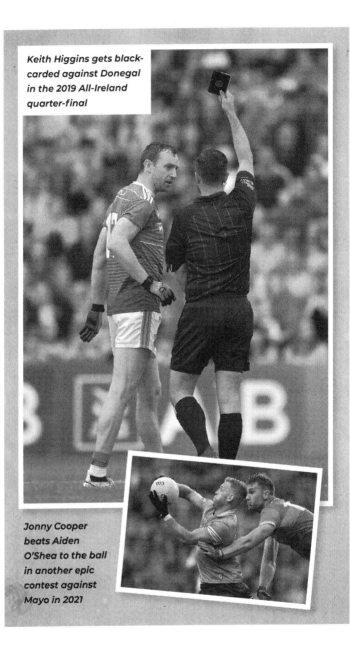

Keith Higgins gets black-carded against Donegal in the 2019 All-Ireland quarter-final

Jonny Cooper beats Aiden O'Shea to the ball in another epic contest against Mayo in 2021

Against arch enemy Cork, Paul Galvin is on the receiving end from Paudie Kissane and Noel O'Leary

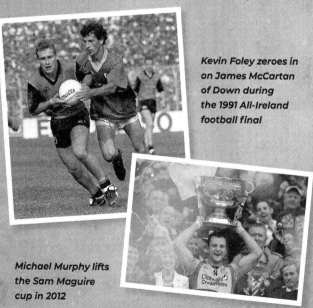

Kevin Foley zeroes in on James McCartan of Down during the 1991 All-Ireland football final

Michael Murphy lifts the Sam Maguire cup in 2012

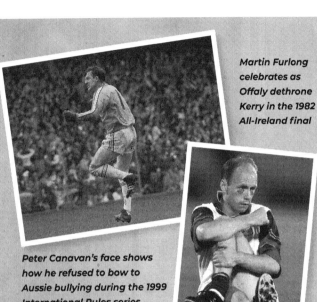

Martin Furlong celebrates as Offaly dethrone Kerry in the 1982 All-Ireland final

Peter Canavan's face shows how he refused to bow to Aussie bullying during the 1999 International Rules series

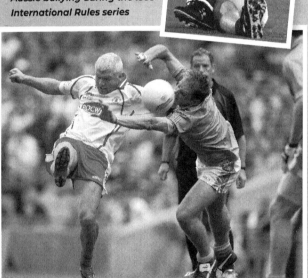

Darren Fay tangles with Owen Mulligan of Tyrone in the 2007 All-Ireland Championship

Colm O'Rourke takes on most of the Dublin defence in the 1987 Leinster final

Before the storm of the 1982 All-Ireland final, Richie Connor's shakes hands with Kerry's John Egan

Kieran McGeeney brings Stephen O'Neill to earth in the 2003 All-Ireland final against Tyrone

*Mick Lyons zones in on Mikey Sheehy of Kerry in the
All-Ireland semi-final in 1986*

*Jack O'Shea on the run against Cork in 1988 (left) and
Colm Boyle helps Con O'Callaghan to his feet in the
All-Ireland final against Dublin in 2017 (right)*

THE COUNTDOWN TO THE TOUGHEST MEANEST SCARIEST HARD-MAN IN GAELIC FOOTBALL HISTORY

SCORE OUT OF

50

50. Ollie Honeyman	45.7		29. Anthony Molloy	47.0
49. Paul Curran	45.9		28. Tony Scullion	47.0
48. Michael Fagan	46.0		27. Keith Barr	47.1
47. Conor Counihan	46.1		26. Lee Keegan	47.1
46. Paul Galvin	46.1		25. Niall Cahalane	47.1
45. Colm Boyle	46.2		24. Colm O'Rourke	47.2
44. Ryan McMenamin	46.2		23. Tim Kennelly	47.2
43. Peter Canavan	46.3		22. James McCarthy	47.3
42. Conor Gormley	46.4		21. T.J. Gilmore	47.4
41. Neil McGee	46.4		20. Stephen O'Brien	47.4
40. Johnny Nevin	46.5		19. Keith Higgins	47.4
39. Richie Connor	46.7		18. Michael Murphy	47.5
38. Francie Bellew	46.7		17. Eoin Liston	47.5
37. Harry Keegan	46.7		16. Kevin Foley	47.5
36. Martin O'Connell	46.8		15. Graham Geraghty	47.7
35. Larry Tompkins	46.8		14. Noel O'Leary	47.7
34. Darren Fay	46.9		13. Tomás Ó Sé	47.8
33. DJ Kane	46.9		12. Colm Coyle	47.8
32. Sean Lowry	46.9		11. Barnes Murphy	47.9
31. Glenn Ryan	46.9			
30. Jonny Cooper	47.0		**AND...**	

10. Jack O'Shea	48.2
9. Kieran McGeeney	48.3
8. Brian McGilligan	48.4
7. Paddy McCormack	48.5
6. Brian Mullins	48.5
5. Gerry McCarville	48.6
4. Gay O'Driscoll	48.6
3. Páidi Ó Sé	48.9
2. Mick Lyons	49.0
1. Martin Furlong	49.4

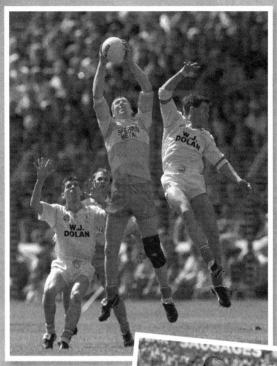

Brian McGilligan
proves unmovable
under the dropping
ball against Tyrone
in 1995

Nobody strode the
hallowed turf of Croke
Park quite like the
thoroughbred footballer
that was Brian Mullins

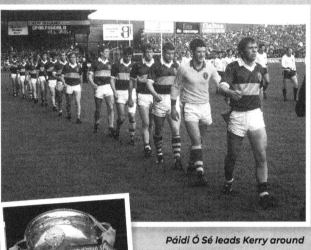

Páidi Ó Sé leads Kerry around the field before the 1985 All-Ireland final against Dublin

DJ Kane lifts the Sam Maguire Cup high after Down defeated Dublin in the 1994 All-Ireland final

Niall Cahalane wraps up Colm O'Rourke of Meath in the 1990 All-Ireland final

Diarmuid Connolly tries turning the tables on Lee Keegan in the 2016 All-Ireland final replay

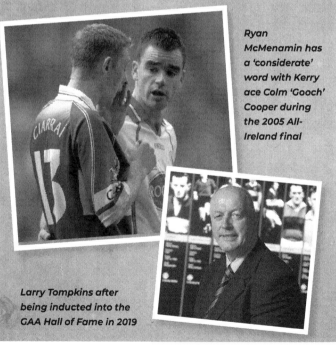

Ryan McMenamin has a 'considerate' word with Kerry ace Colm 'Gooch' Cooper during the 2005 All-Ireland final

Larry Tompkins after being inducted into the GAA Hall of Fame in 2019

James McCarthy soars through the air against Kildare in 2023 in the Leinster Championship

Glenn Ryan leads Kildare to the All-Ireland final in 1998

*Keith Barr in typically
defiant mood in Croke
Park in 1997*

*Stephen O'Brien goes
highest in the 1995 Munster
final against Kerry*

Graham Geraghty marks one down

Tomás Ó Sé races onto the field at the start of the 2011 All-Ireland final against Dublin

SEAN LOWRY

(Height 6' 1", Weight 15 St)

Decade... 1970s/1980s

(Position... Centre-Back/Full-Forward)

CHIEF CHARACTERISTIC... 'BOMBER' DISPOSAL UNIT.

TOP ACCOMPLICES... MARTIN FURLONG, PADDY MCCORMACK,
EUGENE MULLIGAN

SEAN LOWRY

'I MENTIONED CROKE PARK AS MY FAVOURITE GROUND, BUT THERE
REALLY IS SOMETHING MAGIC ABOUT IT. I REMEMBER THAT DAY
WHEN WE CAME OUT ONTO THE FIELD I LOOKED UP AT THE CLOCK... I
SAID TO MYSELF AT 5.35 PM IT WILL ALL BE OVER.'

– SEAN LOWRY

SEAN Lowry grasped the ball tightly to his chest. The time was 5.35 pm. He knew it was over, but still, he clutched the ball. How could you let go of history?

Penny for Sean Lowry's thoughts before the 1982 All-Ireland football final. It was the calm before the storm, he made a mental note of the time... death or glory beckoned.

All-Ireland's take on a strange life. Kerry was a raging favourite but somehow, Offaly held onto their coat-tails.

There was a strange feel to the day.

It was supposed to be a coronation, with Kerry sauntering to an unprecedented five in-a-row.

The skies overhead were dark and foreboding, and a lingering feeling of infamy hung on the swollen rain-heavy clouds. It felt more like a funeral than a wedding and Kerry's relationship with Sam was about to be cruelly terminated after four long seasons.

HARD MAN RATINGS

TOUGHEST:
9.2/10

MEANEST:
9.4/10

SCARIEST:
9.3/10

HARDEST:
19.0/20

TOTAL HARD MAN
46.9/50

Offaly centre-back Sean Lowry recalled how the final pulsating seconds panned out.

'The match went on anyway and Darby scored the goal. I knew Kerry would get a chance at some stage. Kerry's chance came and Furlong ended up out of the goals trying to clear it, but he lost it. I ran in to cover him and the ball came in.

'I think there was snow on it because it went that high and just seemed to stay in the air. I just remember hearing this shout "There's nobody behind you Lowry!"

'I caught it in my chest instead of over my head after that shout… in case I dropped it.'

Sean Lowry's crucial grab ensured that the Faithful would not be crying over spilt milk, as he safely secured the sodden and slippery ball.

It was at that moment he remembered his pre-game preamble and he glanced up at the famous old clock.

'I looked up at the clock for that split second and it was 5.35 pm. Well, I mean, if I had to run from there to Hill 16, or through Hill 16 for that matter, I would have because no way on earth was that ball leaving my hands.

'I think I faked a pass to one of my teammates twice but even they weren't getting it. Kerry had had their chance and I finished with the ball in my hands.

'Even when the supporters rushed the field, I couldn't let it go out of my hands.'

{ THE LAST KING OF MAYO }

It certainly was a sporting life less ordinary. One of a select band of Offaly men with three precious Celtic Crosses. A Connacht medal, and a near-miss with Mayo were packed into a tumultuous career spanning 15 incredible seasons.

He hailed from a family of Ferbane footballing brothers and the British Open golf champion, Shane Lowry is his nephew. He is, of course, fondly remembered in the Faithful County as a tenacious tackling centre-back and an equally robust and combative attacker.

The untold story of Sean Lowry is in many ways stranger than fiction. He was the last Mayo footballer to have won an All-Ireland medal. That incredible scenario transpired when he upped sticks and headed out to the footballing Wild West for work purposes.

It wasn't long before he caught the bug again and started playing some ball with the local side, Crossmolina.

'I had decided when I went down there, I was going to forget about (playing with) Ferbane because it was too far... it was 100 miles and I had a new family.

'It was a great way of getting into the community anyway and they were so welcoming and looked after us.

'I had given up (inter-county) football and was just playing with Crossmolina.'

Word spread around the county quickly. Before long, Mayo boss Liam O'Neill came calling.

Sean's versatility and inner steel were a major factor in the surprise visit from the Mayo supremo. He had forged a reputation for being rugged and uncompromising for his native county, and that allied to a brilliant football brain was a combination the Mayo boss felt was too good to pass upon. While ultimately

Mayo would again miss out on Sam during Lowry's term, a Connacht title was secured to add yet another coat of polish to a truly remarkable playing career.

THE FAITHFUL SON

SEAN LOWRY was born on February 24, 1952. His league and championship career at senior county level with both the Offaly and Mayo teams spanned an impressive 15 seasons, beginning in 1971 and ending in 1985.

At club level, he represented Ferbane, lining out with his brothers Mick and Brendan, who also were members of Offaly's 1982 Sam Maguire triumph.

Ferbane were one of Offaly's premier sides and won a very competitive Offaly championship three times, in 1971, 1974, and 1976, during Sean's playing tenure.

After a fruitless minor career, Lowry migrated to the Offaly under-21 team, winning Leinster medals in 1971 and 1973. He was also a member of the Offaly senior team, having been a late addition to the extended panel during the 1971 championship.

Lowry won three All-Ireland medals, beginning with back-to-back championships in 1971 and 1972. He was part of the side that engineered a spectacular smash 'n' grab raid to shoot down Kerry in the 1982 All-Ireland final.

He also won six Leinster medals, and one Connacht medal with Mayo. He picked up two All Stars, as both a defender and attacker, a ringing endorsement of his all-round versatility, and highly adaptable footballing skills.

MICK LYONS

(Height 6' 1", Weight 14.5 St)

Decade... 1970s/1980s/1990s

(Position... Full-Back)

CHIEF CHARACTERISTIC... REPRISING A YOUNG VITO CORLEONE

TOP ACCOMPLICES... (NEVER NEEDED ANY)

MICK LYONS

'PLAYING FULL-BACK IS A BIT LIKE BEING IN THE MAFIA... IT'S KILL
OR BE KILLED. ONE MISTAKE, ONE BULLET, AND YOU'RE GONE!'

– MICK LYONS

MEATH football has had a 'Royal' lineage in full-backs, with a pedigree selection of household names like Paddy 'Hands' O'Brien and Jack Quinn patrolling the house. Dubbed 'The King of full-backs' Mick Lyons was another towering addition to that rich heritage during the halcyon days of the Sean Boylan era.

Mick Lyons in particular was a nemesis to great rivals Dublin and he always seemed to produce his very best performances against the neighbouring metropolitans.

The Dublin and Meath rivalry was already at its zenith, but in 1991 it entered an even more exalted stratosphere. The four-game series stopped the nation, as Leinster's two 'Fantastic Beasts,' could not be separated after a series of pulsating draws.

Tensions, however, were running high down on the pitch as both sets of players tired of spending such an extended period of time in their bitter

HARD
MAN
RATINGS

TOUGHEST:
9.8/10

MEANEST:
9.8/10

SCARIEST:
9.9/10

HARDEST:
19.5/20

TOTAL
HARD MAN

49.0/50

rivals' company Dublin player Tommy Carr best summed up the mood in both camps, with the old adage of 'familiarity' breeding contempt never ringing with greater accuracy.

'You'd almost wish someone, anyone would end it now. It has gone beyond a joke.'

The draw for the 1991 Leinster Championship certainly had delivered an 'outlier,' when finalists for the previous five seasons, Dublin and Meath were dramatically paired together. To add insult to injury for Leinster football bluebloods, the fixture was deemed to be a preliminary round… for the right to enter the main draw!

The remarkable pairing certainly read like a punchline but for the two protagonists the prospect of an early exit was now a distinct possibility. Meath would eventually edge an epic affair after Lyons inevitably played a starring role.

Nobody enjoyed plunging the knife into the 'Dubs' more than Lyons. An incident nine minutes from the end of a compelling fourth act really drew the wrath of the city side's masses congregated on Hill 16.

Dublin were awarded a penalty and a golden ticket to finally escape the clutches of Sean Boylan's tenacious troops. In truth, justice was about to be served as Dublin had been the more cohesive outfit. If the contest had been judged on Marquis of Queensbury Rules, Dublin were clearly ahead on points over the course of the marathon, but had failed to land a telling knockout blow.

Keith Barr of Dublin missed his kick as Mick ran alongside him while he was taking the penalty, with the kick never retaken. Barr made reference to the incident much later, and seemed unperturbed by Mick's proximity while he took the kick.

'Everyone remembers my missed penalty in the fourth game, although I'd like to forget it! I struck the ball fairly well but it just clipped the outside of Mickey McQuillan's post. Much was made of Mick Lyons running alongside me as I went to take the kick, but to be honest, I didn't see him at the time, although TV pictures do suggest he nearly got to the ball before I did!'

The GAA took a rather dim view of the incident, however, changing the official pitch markings to include a semi-circle exclusion zone around from where a player takes a penalty kick.

Iconic sports journalist Con Houlihan summed up the Meath full-back's vice-like grip over an array of Dublin full-forwards over the course of the intensely fought quartet of games.

Dublin had another obvious flaw: they lacked a Lyons tamer: In this generation the goalkeepers got their Magna Carta: now they cannot be challenged inside the small box. There is no law which says that Mick Lyons cannot be challenged inside a certain area, but it seems that way.

Lyons was a man inspired and it continued a particular theme against the side from the capital, where Lyons had barely conceded a score in the eight previous meetings of those two fierce rivals.

Houlihan continued his observations in the *Evening Press* in his own inimitable style.

I wouldn't be surprised to hear that there are small boys in Dublin who believe that Mick is kept in a cage above in Summerhill and fed with raw meat. In fact, Mick is as mild a man as you could find in the world outside football. His main fault on the pitch is that, at times, he is reluctant to turn the other cheek. Nevertheless, a section of Dublin's followers have appointed him as Public Enemy Number One.

{ CAPTAIN FANTASTIC }

When Meath ended a 20-year famine in 1987, Mick Lyons was their 'Captain Fantastic' as he carried his troops on a never-to-be-forgotten All-Ireland winning odyssey.

All-Ireland titles can often rest on small margins, and Lyons made a critical intervention early in the first-half to prevent a certain Cork goal.

Cork had burst from the traps and caught a lacklustre Royals outfit cold. A Jimmy Kerrigan solo run knifed through the centre of the bewildered Meath rearguard. For once, the usually vigilant and unforgiving Royals' defence seemed to have been caught flat-footed.

For the Meath faithful who thronged Jones' Road, it was a chilling sight. Thousands offered silent prayers and some novenas were uttered. Kerrigan housed an executioner's eye and coldly pulled the trigger. The county of Meath held its breath and waited for the net to dance. A shadow appeared astride the Corkman as he put his foot sweetly through the ball. Mick Lyons had sniffed the danger, but Kerrigan had a crucial few steps on him.

Kerrigan closed the ground towards the goal and prepared to apply the kill shot. Mick Lyons dived full length and, somehow, blocked a startled Kerrigan's effort to prevent what could have been a fatal blow to the Royal's ambitions.

It was the catalyst for the Meathmen to awake from their

slumber and a Colm O'Rourke goal set them on the road to victory.

Mick Lyons' death-defying leap was one of the highlights of the gaelic football season.

When the GAA produced a coaching video the following year, Mick's famous block rightfully took pride of place, in a career filled with outstanding highlights.

THE WONDER
▶━━━▶ YEARS ◀━━━◀

MICK LYONS was born in Summerhill, Co. Meath, an area close to the Kildare border. His Father, Paddy lined out against Meath in the 1949 Leinster Championship for Kildare.

On the Meath team of the late 1980s and early 90s, Mick ensured it was a family affair when playing alongside his brother, Padraig and cousin, Liam Harnan.

Lyons made his championship debut for Meath in 1979 against unfamiliar opponents Kilkenny, playing at centre-back. He won two senior All-Ireland medals in 1987 and 1988, captaining the team in 1987 (Meath's first title in 20 years), as well as winning a bumper five Leinster Championship medals

and two National League medals.

In 1984, he was part of the Meath team which won the Centenary Cup, a competition which was contested to celebrate the GAA's 100-year anniversary. He was also on the losing side in the 1990 and 1991 All-Ireland finals. Mick Lyons never shirked a tackle, and his full-on style of play often put him in the firing line.

The Meath chieftain was sorely missed when sustaining a broken wrist in 1984, and a broken leg in 1989 – interestingly summers when Dublin took advantage of his absence to defeat Meath. He also won two All Stars in 1984 and 1986.

JAMES McCARTHY

(Height 6' 1", Weight 14.5 St)

Decade... 2010s/2020s

(Position... Midfield/Wing-Back)

CHIEF CHARACTERISTIC... PROVING THAT DURACELL
BATTERIES ARE DISTINCTLY OVERRATED

TOP ACCOMPLICES... BRIAN FENTON, CIARAN KILKENNY, PHILLY
MCMAHON, JOHN SMALL, STEPHEN CLUXTON, JONNY COOPER

JAMES McCARTHY

'IT'S HARD. YOU'RE COMING BACK A LOT OF THE TIME BROKE UP,
INJURED, CARRYING SOMETHING, YOU'VE BEEN ON THE GO FOR EIGHT
YEARS, PLAYING REPLAYS AGAINST MAYO OR KERRY AND YOU'RE
JUST TIRED AND IT'S REALLY HARD TO TRY AND GET GOING.'
– JAMES MCCARTHY

THE more things change, the more they stay the same…
The year is 3099.

The old stadium had fallen into disrepair. The Hogan stand had collapsed first, followed by the Davin, and the 'Hill'. One proud pillar falling onto the next. The domino effect followed swiftly, as the last man standing… the Cusack, finally caved in.

The small band of supporters shuffled away nervously, avoiding the curfew. The All-Ireland final had followed the same path as the last 50 – a mismatch of epic proportions.

The motley collection of factory droids, clones, and washed-up inter-county footballers, known as 'The Rest of Ireland' had been demolished by The Blue Wave.

The machines had been programmed for every eventuality, bar James McCarthy. The Ballymun legend had been engineered from a superior technology, a relentless, smooth-running gaelic football appliance!

**HARD
MAN
RATINGS**

TOUGHEST:
9.7/10

MEANEST:
9.1/10

SCARIEST:
9.1/10

HARDEST:
19.4/20
☠

**TOTAL
HARD MAN**

47.3/50

The strains of Brian Ferry's *Same Old Scene* spluttered out over the rusty tannoy – an inspired choice by the stadium DJ, or in mitigation, a blast of gallows humour?

The blood sport of gaelic football is dying on its feet. At its zenith in the mid-2000s, it was played on every habitable planet in the galaxy. Now there are just small pockets of the game, enacted on a remote planet called Earth.

'Team Dublin' boarded the mothership with the precious cargo in tow. The Sam Maguire was tucked safely away in the cargo hold. James McCarthy smiled at the irony of the lime-green graffiti, scrawled unevenly along the decaying stadium walls.

WHERE WE ALL BELONG.

The intergalactic vessel sped away. Another town, another train. The Blue Wave was running out of worlds to conquer…

All-Ireland Football semi-final

Croke Park, Dublin

July 2, 2023.

Deep in the heart of injury time, Dublin surged forward – after another Mayo attack was swallowed up by the relentless blue tide. The Leinster champions charge of 'The Light Brigade' often resembles a sea of rapidly moving sky-blue parts.

Unlike the ill-fated historical dash that took place at the Battle of Balaclava, the only ones riding in the valley of the shadow of death would hail from Mayo!

Leading the charge is the Ballymun Kichams' powerhouse, James McCarthy. The clock is ticking towards 75 minutes – a time when most 30-somethings would likely be running on empty. McCarthy, however, has left a trail of Mayo bodies floundering in his wake.

The hordes on the Hill bayed out their homage to a true Dublin blue. In a footballing nation where there is no country for old men the old warhorse is still bucking the trend.

With the Mayo supporters leaving in droves – desperately seeking solace, and the gastronomic comforts of a tasty fish & chip in Beshoffs, McCarthy is still at the coalface, putting out fires, and loading the ammo.

The ultimate big game hunter has always reserved his finest vintage for those hardy battlers from the western province. He was voted *The Sunday Game* Man of the Match in the 2017 decider, as an inspired late intervention derailed the fast-finishing Mayo Express.

Calm, and unfussed, he is the relentless face of one of the greatest winning machines in GAA history, leading the charge from pillar to post. McCarthy is Molly Malone wheeling her wheelbarrow, as reassuringly Dublin as a steaming hot bowl of Coddle.

He rarely seeks the headlines despite acquiring a propensity for being consistently brilliant. Happily operating like a front house projectionist, central to the smooth running of the show's success, but rarely demanding an encore on screen. McCarthy's enduring excellence is one of the few certainties as this crazy old world keeps spinning on its axis.

Death, Taxes, and Magic McCarthy.

The more things change, the more they stay the same…

{ LIKE FATHER, LIKE SON }

His dad recalls a story about a cross-country schools' race where James McCarthy was in the lead. Then disaster struck – when he took the wrong course. With a hundred guys ahead of him, the young McCarthy never wavered, to incredibly finish a couple of yards off fourth.

John McCarthy was a former Dublin great who marched the hard road to three All-Ireland titles with Heffo's Army, the kind of man that would never be blinded by parental bias. The penny had dropped about his son, after his sensational gallop around the Baldoyle track revealed, he had been cast in his old man's steely likeness.

'That's when I knew,' he simply stated.

Like father, like son. Both were destined to become darlings of the Hill. The footballing fortress was populated by one of the most knowledgeable fan bases in inter-county football. They know their football on the Hill, and rejoiced in the acquisition of a couple of instant cult heroes, for one of inter-county football's most discerning audiences. Watching the galloping McCarthy Jnr cover every blade of grass can be an exhausting experience. He is a study in perpetual movement – blessed with the uncanny knack of making every hard yard expended… a worthwhile one.

He is Dublin's beating heart and the desire to scale the peaks of Sam Maguire once again still burns brightly in a true warrior's soul. He stands on the Pantheon of the immortals – along with Mick Fitzsimons and Stephen Cluxton. The trio now exist in the realms of the fantastical – the only men in history to win an unprecedented nine All-Ireland senior football medals.

Before this season's decider, he spoke of his desire to reclaim 'Sam'.

'I'd love to win an All-Ireland medal, there's no doubt about it. That's why we are all still playing and going hard at it. Is it at the back of my mind and do I think about it every day? No, but is it something I want to do? Absolutely.

'It's more the last two seasons and how they went that's motivating for the group than anything else.'

A Dublin side harnessing a McCarthy engine – sounds like an ominous theme. The sky blue machine, yet again scaling the peaks of the Maguire Mountain, the Galaxy, and the Universe!

MCCARTHY'S HIGHWAYS
▶━━━▶ AND BYWAYS ◀━━━◀

JAMES McCARTHY was born on March 1, 1990. He was a student at Sacred Heart BNS, and St Kevin's College in Ballygall. He went to college at DCU, where he won both Sigerson Cup and the O'Byrne Cup medals as a defender.

He played his club football with Ballymun Kickhams, winning the Dublin Senior Football Championship on two occasions, in 2012 and 2020. He also landed a Leinster Senior Club Football Championship medal in 2012.

Ballymun then defeated Dr Crokes in the All-Ireland semi-final, before losing the 2013 All-Ireland Senior Club football final to St Brigid's of Roscommon.

After playing at minor level for Dublin, he won the 2010 Leinster and All-Ireland under-21 Football Championships with the metropolitans. He made his full senior championship debut for Dublin against Laois in the quarter-final of the 2011 Leinster Championship. He won his first Leinster Senior Football Championship against Wexford at Croke Park, in July of that year. Dublin advanced to All-Ireland final against Kerry, with McCarthy winning a first All-Ireland Senior Football Championship on a 1-12 to 1-11 scoreline.

McCarthy has won nine All-Ireland titles and is currently one of only three only players in the history of the football championship to win nine All-Irelands. He has also won 13 Leinster Championships, six National Leagues, and four All-Stars.

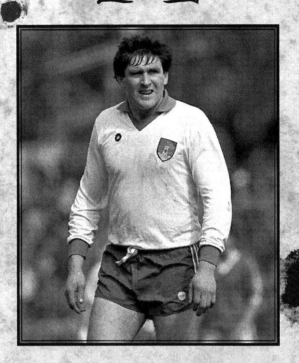

GERRY McCARVILLE

(Height 6' 0", Weight 15.5 St)

Decade... 1970s/1980s

(Position... Full-Back/Midfield)

CHIEF CHARACTERISTIC... MONAGHAN LIFE
INSURANCE SALES DEPARTMENT

TOP ACCOMPLICES... HUGO CLERKIN, FERGUS CAULFIELD, DECLAN
FLANAGAN, EUGENE SWEENEY, PADDY LINDEN

GERRY
McCARVILLE

'WHEN I WAS PLAYING AGAINST GENE SHERRY, GERRY
MCCARVILLE, AND FERGUS CAULFIELD, I WENT TO TWO MASSES,
CHECKED OUT THE LIFE INSURANCE POLICY, AND POINTED THE
CAR FOR HOME BEFORE THE GAME. SOMETIMES YOU HOPED FOR A
HAMSTRING, BUT THEY HAD NOT BEEN INVENTED BACK THEN.'

– COLM O'ROURKE

STILL crazy after all these years…

He waded his way carefully through the sea of severed limbs, glancing around the deserted stadium. The last of the survivors huddled together, trembling like startled sheep.

Nothing could have prepared them for the horrors of Ulster football. They searched vainly for a hint of mercy behind those dark demented eyes – but mercy was always in short supply in the Killing Fields of the Northern provincial championship.

The opposition supporters had long since scattered, seeking refuge in the hills. It was late evening, when the King of Monaghan rendered his judgment; amnesty had never been one of his fortes. Gerry McCarville's blood-stained fingers carefully removed an impaled head from the corner flag. The lightning flashed and the thunder quickened in the eye of the gathering storm.

'KILL THEM ALL,' he thundered…

HARD MAN RATINGS

TOUGHEST:
9.8/10

MEANEST:
9.8/10

SCARIEST:
9.5/10

HARDEST:
19.5/20

TOTAL HARD MAN

48.6/50

Championship contests against Monaghan have always tended to be the stuff of nightmares…

There is something primal about facing the Farney in the trenches – chilling, claustrophobic, hand-to-hand combat is always assured. Gerry McCarville's fearsome reputation was built upon creating struggle and strife. Monaghan was a county that examined your Championship credentials forensically and Gerry provided the litmus test for the perils that lay ahead.

He was furrowed out of the 'Stony Grey Soil of Monaghan'. The birthplace of Kavanagh is not renowned for sweeping peaks or expansive lakes, but is home to a race of hard-boned, hardy warriors.

The County is the location of one of the most feared forces on the harsh, unforgiving, rocky landscape of the Ulster football.

Monaghan have never won an All-Ireland title or ever featured in a final, but they have always distinguished themselves on the battlefield. The Farney box above their weight division, and routinely outpoint bigger and better opponents. The key pillar of any Monaghan side preparing for battle is efficiency – from back to front. Their indomitability will always seem to find a way; they persevere when others normally wilt.

Gerry McCarville was one of those pillars during the 70s and '80s when the Farney brewed up a storm on the national stage winning Ulster titles and National Leagues, and featuring in the exalted terrain of the penultimate stages of the All-Ireland series.

Meath maestro Colm O'Rourke, a man never prone to tip-toeing through the tulips, readily admitted to a certain unease about getting up close and personal in the Farney County, as he would reveal in his writings.

'Monaghan were proper hard men and their image in my eye is always one of backs. When I was playing against Gene Sherry, Gerry McCarville and Fergus Caulfield, I went to two Masses, checked out the life insurance policy and pointed the car for home before the game.

Sometimes you hoped for a hamstring but they had not been invented back then.

'A league match in Ballybay, Castleblayney or Clones was a trip to the lion's den and you needed to be hard in mind and body. Monaghan were honest and hard-working, and in the mid-'80s were boxing close to the top. Their football was a reflection of the place, there was a bit of raw hardness about it.'

Gerry McCarville, one of the patents of the Monaghan football brand, was painstakingly hewn out of. Selfless in his deployment, he would have been happy to hawk hot dogs or punch tickets for the Farney faithful.

His 'have boots, will travel' all-action mode saw him unleashed in every line of the battle-field. He was often underestimated in his odd-job capacity, and mistaken for an unskilled labourer, often with fatal results.

One of his finest hours arrived with partner-in-crime, Hugo Clerkin, when the dynamic duo gained a points decision in the midfield sector in the 1979 All-Ireland semi-final – when pitted against the much-vaunted Kingdom engine room of Jack O'Shea and Vincent O'Connor.

Ultimately, the Farney were submerged in a green and gold tide as Kerry waltzed into yet another decider, but McCarville refused to go under.

Gerry's enduring graft and excellence was rewarded with the

coveted Monaghan Player of the Year award in 1980. 'Big Gerry' was not so much a rock, as a boulder in the Farney rearguard, as he inspired them to a first National senior title, winning the 1985 National League.

Such was his grip on opposing attackers, he was being mentioned in the breath as the much-vaunted duo, Mick Lyons and John O'Keeffe at the top of the full-back food chain.

Like his fellow county men, Gerry's mantra has always been a 'What doesn't kill you makes you stronger variety', and by 1985, when they won the Ulster title again, Monaghan were again being ranked as serious contenders for Sam.

They again locked horns with Kerry in the last four of the All-Ireland series, and there would be no whitewash on this occasion, with the Kingdom winning an arm-wrestle 2-9 to 0-9 – after the teams had drawn the first day out.

Croke Park would turn out to be a graveyard for Monaghan's ambitions, time and time again.

The wide expanses of Jones' Road were a difficult environment to adequately ring fence, as the combative Monaghan side was often caught between two stools – their structured, compact style failing to lend a large enough dividend on the scoreboard.

When McCarville retired, opposition forces still checked under the bed at night just to be sure the 'bogeyman' had finally left the building!

The fire, however, never really diminished within the McCarville furnace. There were suspensions when his playing days were over, and in 2006, when he was part of Séamus McEneaney's Monaghan backroom, he was suspended (some say a little harshly) for six months.

Most agreed, Gerry's reputation had preceded him. But, as ever, there was nowhere to hide when Gerry was wearing his Monaghan war paint!

A FARNEY LOVE AFFAIR

GERRY McCARVILLE played his club football for Monaghan powerhouse, Scotstown. The club has won the Monaghan Senior football title (The Mick Duffy Cup) on 21 occasions, with McCarville featuring in 14 of those successes.

He was also part of the side that won three consecutive Ulster Club Championships in 1978, 1979, and 1980. Gerry and Scotstown missed out on an All-Ireland club title on St Patrick's Day 1979, falling at the final hurdle against Cork kingpins, Nemo Rangers in the decider.

After starring for the county under-21 side during the Ulster Championship, Gerry migrated to the senior ranks, making his debut his Monaghan debut against Westmeath in a Division Three National League match back in 1977.

He starred at midfield for Monaghan when they ended a 41-year Ulster Championship hiatus in 1979 – and by 1985, when they repeated the feat again, he featured at full-back.

Unlucky never to win an All-Star, he won a National Football League in 1985, and played for Ulster against Australia in the early years of the International Rules.

PADDY McCORMACK

(Height 5' 11", Weight 15 St)

Decade... 1950s/1960s/1970s

(Position... Full-Back)

CHIEF CHARACTERISTIC... ENSURED FORWARDS
GOT THEIR DAILY SUPPLY OF IRON

TOP ACCOMPLICES... MARTIN FURLONG, PETER DALY, WILLIE NOLAN,
JOHN EGAN, TOMMY CULLEN, MURT CONNOR

PADDY
McCORMACK

'PERHAPS THAT TEAK TOUGH PERSONA HELPED US TO THOSE ALL-
IRELAND WINS. WE WERE HARD AS F**CKING NAILS.'
– PADDY MCCORMACK

WHEN American business magnate, inventor and ingenious scientist, Anthony Edward Stark suffers a severe chest injury during his abduction, the sinister reason soon emerges behind the kidnapping. His captors instruct him to build a weapon of mass destruction as Stark's life reaches a defining moment.

In desperation, he is driven to somehow save his life by creating a mechanised suit of armour, and he flees captivity.

Stark conceals his identity at first before publicly proclaiming his alter-ego, *Iron Man*.

He vows to use his special attire, to protect the world. *Iron Man*, the ultimate comic-book hero, introduced himself to the universe, in *Tales of Suspense* #39 (cover dated March 1963). The character created by Stan Lee was the founder of the other-worldly, *Avengers* superhero team which featured *Thor*, *Ant-Man*, *Wasp* and the *Incredible Hulk*.

HARD MAN RATINGS

TOUGHEST:
9.8/10

MEANEST:
9.2/10

SCARIEST:
9.9/10

HARDEST:
19.6/20

TOTAL HARD MAN

48.5/50

They know a thing or two about superheroes in Offaly, with the county's football and hurling teams both securing multiple All-Ireland titles in the latter part of the millennium.

Uíbh Fhailí could well lay claim to having the 'Original' *Iron Man*, who hailed from the famous Offaly football nursery of Rhode.

Once Paddy McCormack donned his cape the Faithful County became an indestructible force. Like his *Marvel* namesake, McCormack was a human shield forged from a cold, impenetrable metal. He provided a steely protective ring around the Offaly goalmouth that proved a major deterrent against any uninvited guests.

McCormack was an unsettling presence once he donned the battle guise and suit of Iron, a formidable barrier that was unlikely to be breached.

Rhode is situated in the north region of Offaly and shares its parish border with Croghan.

It's the closest of the two to another football heartland, Edenderry.

Paddy McCormack was a native of Croghan, but lined out with Rhode. He excelled for the county minors in 1956 and 1957, where they lost out to All-Ireland champions-elect, a very formidable Meath side.

Paddy quickly became a bedrock of the Offaly rearguard at full-back. Judge, jury, and executioner too! He was joined by the core of the Faithful underage side and future partners in crime including Peter Daly, Willie Nolan, John Egan and Tommy Cullen.

Offaly's fans were dreaming of bigger things as they watched their 'kids' develop into men.

There was a special feel around the group, but as ever for Faithful followers it was time to address the 'elephant in the room'.

Offaly had always produced players with plenty of flair, but the matrix elements always lacked a finishing product. Paddy was well aware of the burden of high expectations, as he revealed on the Hogan Stand website.

'We could always produce good players, as good if not better than any other county, but we struggled to put it together as a team.'

In 1960, Paddy and Offaly would finally crack the code and win a first-ever Leinster title.

Dublin had won the All-Ireland in 1958, and the 'Leinster' in 1959. The city outfit had a swagger, and when they easily bowled over Longford in the first round in 1960, it appeared a mere formality that they would saunter to three in-a-row.

Any over-exuberance within the Offaly ranks had been tempered by a limp performance as they struggled to overcome Carlow in the first round. The Faithful then ripped up the script to emerge from the long grass and obliterate the Dubliners with a fully merited three-goal victory in the semi-final.

Paddy had been a colossal presence in their run to what would be a first-ever Leinster title. While they tested their supporters' pacemakers in the final with a slender one point to spare over Louth, Offaly had finally found a home for the famous provincial trophy.

Offaly would lose out to Down in the most controversial of circumstances in the semi-final, with a decision Paddy McCormack will never forgive, or forget.

'No way was it a penalty. McCartan tucked the ball under his arm and headed for goal. Four of Offaly's defenders stood firm, but to our amazement, the referee awarded a penalty.

'When we heard the whistle, we were positive it was a free out.'

Tony Hadden then added a Down point, and while Offaly responded with an equalising point, the damage had been done, and Down escaped with a replay.

The Iron Man from Rhode would have to wait 11 long years for a Celtic Cross, as Offaly were edged out by Down in 1962, and Kerry in 1969. Injury ruled Paddy out of the 1970 campaign, but he lived up to his name as he returned in 1971 at the ripe old age of 30 to finally get his hands on Sam.

{ LAYING DOWN THE LAW }

One young Armagh forward, who shall remain nameless, committed the most grievous of sins when skinning a bemused Paddy for a goal. This event was as rare as a curate's egg, and Paddy was to put it mildly… fuming!

The 'new sheriff in town was beaming from ear to ear; so much for the perils of being shackled by the so-called 'Iron Man from Rhode.'

Paddy had a quiet word with the ecstatic young man, as he accepted the heart-felt congratulations of his teammates on his return journey from the dastardly act.

Then in a brief exchange, Paddy offered the dismayed young forward a one-way ticket to Boot Hill, if he ventured over the 21-yard line again. Paddy was never a man that issued idle threats, so the stark advice was instantly acted upon!

For the young forward, it was a rude awakening, but when

Paddy McCormack laid down the law it was probably a wise course of action to avoid Dodge City.

The passing decades have not diluted the apprehension his presence inspired, which left even the most seasoned of county warriors quaking in their boots.

NO ORDINARY
»——→ HERO ←——«

PADDY WAS born in 1939 near Rhode, and gave two decades of unrivalled service to the local outfit.

He was promoted to the senior panel for the 1957-58 National League and made his championship debut in 1958. Offaly had never won a Leinster title, but Paddy would feature in no less than five championship-winning sides in the province.

Paddy, Greg Hughes and John Egan rapidly became one of the country's most formidable full-back lines, as Offaly broke the mould when winning a first Provincial crown in 1960.

Offaly had only ever contested three finals in the association's history and Paddy was revelling in his role as an enforcer at the heart of the backline.

The Faithful were by now a wily and formidable outfit and despite the setback of another heart-rending reversal to Down in the 1961 All-Ireland final had established themselves as one of the elite sides at county level.

Paddy and the Faithful kept knocking on the door but failed to unlock Sam Maguire, with another loss in the decider, this time against the mighty Kingdom in 1969. At half-time against Galway in the 1971 All-Ireland final Offaly trailed by five points, and stared down the barrel of another huge disappointment.

Murt Connor's goal turned the tide, as Paddy and the Faithful finally reigned on the sport's biggest stage. They returned the following season, retaining the cup, as the Iron Man collected a second All-Ireland medal.

NEIL McGEE

(Height 6' 1", Weight 15 St)

Decade... 2000s/2010s/2020s

(Position... Full-Back)

CHIEF CHARACTERISTIC... 'CHIP OFF THE OLD BLOCK' AND
'STUMBLING BLOCK' ROLLED INTO ONE

TOP ACCOMPLICES... KARL LACEY, NEIL GALLAGHER,
FRANK MCGLYNN, PAUL DURCAN

NEIL McGEE

'WE PLAYED A CHALLENGE GAME AGAINST DERRY AND AS I CAME
OUT ONE OF THEIR PLAYERS CAME ACROSS TO BLOCK ME. AS
I KEPT GOING, ALL I COULD HEAR BEHIND ME WAS A...THUMP,
THUMP... AND SOMEONE SAYING "DON'T TRY THAT AGAIN". THEY
DIDN'T! NEIL ALWAYS HAD YOUR BACK.'

– PADDY MCGRATH

THIS is football country. The razor's edge between land and sea. As the raven flies, a meandering coastline stretches lazily outward, basking in the swirling blue blanket of the Atlantic Ocean. You could picture him there... a towering, brooding, Donegal soldier.

Gweedore nestles in the shadow of Mount Errigal, Donegal's highest peak. The Irish speaking parish is known by its Gaelic name, Gaoth Dobhair. Gaoth refers to an inlet of the sea at the mouth of the Crolly River, known as An Ghaoth, and Dobhair is an old Irish word for water. Gaoth Dobhair nestles close to the lofty peaks of Errigal. The tallest mountain in Donegal is ring-fenced by the deep terrain and sapphire lakes of the Poisoned Glen.

It is one of the most densely populated rural places in Europe and the largest Irish-speaking parish in Ireland, with a population of over 4,000.

HARD
MAN
RATINGS

TOUGHEST:
9.0/10

MEANEST:
9.1/10

SCARIEST:
8.8/10

HARDEST:
19.5/20

TOTAL
HARD MAN
46.4/50

For many decades it was the county's most successful gaelic football club, but time and tide chipped away at that rich veneer, before they clawed their way back to the top in the early throes of the new millennium.

Their re-emergence was helped in no small way by the arrival of a very special kind of warrior by the name of Neil McGee.

His teammate the lion-hearted Kevin Cassidy recalled his remarkable efforts in his first county final, which ended a 41-year hiatus for the club to be reacquainted with the Dr Maguire Cup in 2002.

'Neil was 17, and was detailed to mark Brendan Devenney, one of the best forwards in the country at the time and kept him scoreless from play,'

When Gaoth Dobhair won the title again in 2006, McGee was already part of the Donegal senior side, manager Brian McIver giving him the corner-back berth against Down in the championship.

'I had gotten word of him,' McIver explained. 'Neil had played a club match for Gaoth Dobhair against Dungloe and done a brilliant marking job on Adrian Sweeney… this kid from Gweedore doing a job on Sweeney, an All-Star in 2003. I put him straight into a league match in Omagh.'

Cassidy also revealed the security blanket provided by the indomitable McGee was almost impenetrable.

'Before a big game, when you assess the opposition, you always felt that whoever Neil was looking after was one less person you had to worry about. He wasn't dirty, as some might say, but he knew how to lift it a notch if you want to put it that way.'

For Neil, there was simply no compromise in the heat of

battle. Tall and physically imposing, he took it to the very edge, occasionally sailing too close to the eye of the volcano.

In 2016, he lost his appeal against a red card, and a subsequent two-match ban was picked up in a fiery Ulster Championship quarter-final win over Fermanagh.

Two years later, the red mist descended again as he lost his appeal against a red card he picked up for an alleged knee into the back of an opponent in the Ulster semi-final win over Down. It proved to be a costly one as he missed Donegal's 2018 Ulster Championship final victory over Fermanagh.

{ THE LONG HAUL }

McGee racked up a record number of appearances in a 15-year-long Donegal odyssey. Only three county footballers had made their debut in the same season or earlier than the remarkable McGee. Ross Munnelly, Offaly's Niall McNamee, and Antrim's Michael McCann.

In his 192nd appearance, disaster struck as he sustained a serious back injury in 0-23 to 1-14 loss to Tyrone in the 2021 Ulster semi-final. It appeared to be the end of the road for the Gaoth Dobhair stalwart, but as former manager Declan Bonner revealed, Neil McGee was never going to buckle.

'Only Neil could come back from that. For someone that never shouted a lot, when he spoke, people listened. Even in later years, he was an incredible presence in the dressing-room.

'At training, sometimes we would have Neil paired off against Michael Murphy. The battle between the two of them was incredible to watch at times.'

Bonner was entirely grateful for McGee's stellar input, on and off the field, as Donegal struggled manfully to emulate Jim McGuinness's 2012 All-Ireland-winning regime.

'There was a lot of talk about transition. But Neil was having none of that. He believed that we, although with a young squad, had what was needed to compete with the best in the province and further afield.

Paddy McGrath, who soldiered with McGee, benefited from the shelter of the Gweedore colossus wing when he first entered the seething cauldron of inter-county football.

'I was almost in awe of Neil and his brother Eamon, Karl Lacey, guys like that, when I first trained with the seniors. We played a challenge game against Derry and as I came out one of their players came across to block me. As I kept going, all I could hear behind me was a… THUMP, THUMP… and someone saying, "Don't try that again". They didn't! Neil always had your back.'

He excelled for Ireland as he thrice represented his country against Australia in the International Rules Series. Kerry legend Eoin Liston summed up the incredible power McGee brought to the party, saying he was 'tailor-made' for the rough and tumble of International Rules football.

His county and club journey was given extra spice by the fact his brother, Eamon was with him nearly every step of the way, and he summed up his unique sibling's undoubted qualities.

'You ask the likes of Ryan McHugh, Paddy McBrearty, and any younger players… he would definitely have looked after them, and they knew that.

'That's part of the reason why they all looked up to him, because he was so protective of them. That was one of Neil's strengths, I believe. He was very, very loyal to his teammates.'

In a county of football giants, even the mighty Mount Errigal was dwarfed by the towering presence of Neil McGee's shadow.

HIS DONEGAL ROAD TRIP

NEIL McGEE was born on November 13, 1985. Gaoth Dobhair has a long and storied history and has won 15 county titles, with Neil playing a significant part in three of those successes.

McGee got his first start for Donegal seniors under the tutelage of legend Brian McEniff, who handed McGee the jersey for his Donegal senior debut against Fermanagh in the 2005 Dr McKenna Cup. He played in the 2006 Ulster Championship final at Croke Park.

McGee was part of the Donegal senior team that won the county's first National League title against Mayo in 2007. It was the first major piece of silverware the county senior team had lifted since 1992.

Neil had developed a reputation as one of the finest defenders in the country and he was rewarded with his first All Star award in 2011, and claimed two more before retirement.

He achieved a major personal milestone in 2013, when he made his 100th appearance for Donegal in the county's National League game against Kildare at Croke Park.

He represented Ireland against Australia in the International Rules Series in 2011, 2013, and 2014. He retired in 2022 having won five Ulster titles.

KIERAN McGEENEY
(Height 6' 0", Weight 15 St)

Decade... 1990s/2000s
(Position... Centre-Back)

CHIEF CHARACTERISTIC... THE ORIGINAL FOUNDER
MEMBER OF THE GAA 'DEATH STARE'

TOP ACCOMPLICES... FRANCIE BELLEW, ENDA MCNULTY, KIERAN
HUGHES, MCENTEES X 2, PAUL MCGRANE

KIERAN McGEENEY

"THIRTY-TWO YEARS OF UNBROKEN SERVICE AT INTER-COUNTY
LEVEL AS A PLAYER, COACH AND MANAGER IS INCREDIBLE."
– JUSTIN MCNULTY

OCTOBER 19, 2009. A hush fell over the crowd in the
Carlow Arts Centre. The guest speaker had an aura about
him... a real sense of presence. He spoke powerfully, choosing his
words carefully, the audience hanging on his every word.

That was the thing about Kieran 'Geezer' McGeeney as a
player, or a manager – he was quite simply box office.

'A few years ago, a friend gave me the loan of a
book called *The Battle of Thermopylae*, he said. 'It's
the book that the film 300 is based on, and it's
about the Spartans.

'What I took from it, more than anything else
was their motto... "Come home with your shield
or upon it".

'The Spartans were renowned as the greatest
fighting army in the world and they carried their
shield in their left hand, with their spear in their
right.

'They carried the shield in their left hand so
that they could protect the man beside them.'

**HARD
MAN
RATINGS**

TOUGHEST:
9.8/10

MEANEST:
9.2/10

SCARIEST:
9.6/10

HARDEST:
19.7/20

**TOTAL
HARD MAN
48.3/50**

It was an inspiring and rousing story, and one you could well say it summed up a certain Armagh and Mullaghbawn warrior. Kieran McGeeney was that man you wanted next to you in battle, the man who carried his shield in his left hand.

To tell Kieran McGeeney's story you have to begin in the middle, because he was always a manager, even when he was playing. For all the fighting spirit and blazing eyelids, McGeeney was also calm and very thoughtful. A natural-born leader.

Not many can manage a seamless transition from their playing days into coaching, but McGeeney took the leap with consummate ease, stepping straight from the frying pan into the managerial fire after he retired in 2006.

He took no nonsense as a player and certainly doesn't suffer fools as a manager, as an recent exchange with BBC journalist Mark Sidebottom graphically illustrated.

In a post-match press conference after the Galway Vs Armagh All-Ireland quarter-final, McGeeney responded to a question that he felt was of the 'loaded' variety with a barely concealed contempt.

Sidebottom asked if there was a duty on the player to not get involved in any 'afters'? McGeeney fired the question straight back at the bemused interviewer.

'What happens if somebody pushes you?' he asked.

'Do you push back? What would you do? What would you do? I'm asking, it is a very simple question.'

Sidebottom struggled to muster a reply, and McGeeney knowing his opponent was on the ropes, landed the knockout blow.

'If somebody pushed you, would you push them back? It is a yes or no?'

When Sidebottom chose not to give a yes or no answer,

McGeeney said: 'If you are not going to answer my questions, why should I answer yours?' Interview terminated!

Enda McNulty played at club level alongside McGeeney, with Mullaghbawn and Na Fianna, and at county level with Armagh, and knew McGeeney's mindset better than most.

'One of the things that sums Kieran up is that in every one of our big games with Armagh, when he talked to us in the circle beforehand, he'd be nearly crying,' he said.

'That's how emotional he would be. And incredibly focused at the same time. More than anything, Kieran has a desire for excellence and is unwilling to settle for mediocrity in anything he does.

'And you always know that, even when a game looks as if it's gone, he's not going to throw in the towel.'

{ JUDGE, JURY AND EXECUTIONER }

The gritty McGeeney took no prisoners and it was advisable for friend or foe not to incur his considerable wrath. Fellow Armagh great, Stephen McDonnell recounted an encounter on when he fell below the lofty benchmark that McGeeney demanded of his fellow county stars. It was not long after the 'rookie' McDonnell had joined the panel when he unwittingly poked the hornet's nest.

'The Ulster final is always around the time of my birthday. One of the particular years we won Ulster – and we had won a few at this stage – the manager, Geezer and Paul McGrane were happy for us to go out celebrating that night.

'But there was a strict ban, no more drink after tonight as we're preparing ourselves for an All-Ireland quarter-final. But the

Monday after the final happened to be my birthday so myself, Marty O'Rourke and Paddy Watters went on the drink. We weren't back training until the Wednesday night and we had an extra day to recover, but Geezer got wind that we were on the drink.'

'We were coming into Callan Bridge for training, us three boys… we were still young at the time, 24 or 25,' McDonnell continued. 'We were going out to train and Geezer and Paul McGrane pulled us aside and nailed us on it.

'You stepped out of line and it's never happening again, they told us. Made us feel like wee boys. But the big thing that happened in training, that night, was that Geezer circled the senior players – Diarmuid Marsden, Kieran Hughes, McGrane, John Toal – and said, "Nail them boys in training tonight, at every opportunity that you get".

'I'll tell you now, we walked off the training pitch that night knowing that we had stepped out of line. We came off black and blue, blood dripping from us, but that's the way it was. We had to accept that. That's a fair punishment.' McDonnell learned an invaluable lesson that night about upholding the highest standards.

Kieran McGeeney's philosophy of the fabled 300 demanded an unwavering commitment to the Armagh cause. It was a harsh lesson, but it would eventually lead him to a well-deserved Footballer of the Year award.

Kieran McGeeney's love-affair with gaelic football has spanned over three decades. At times it feels like the man they call 'Geezer' has spent a lifetime making sure everything is rosy in 'The Orchard'.

GEEZER'S JOURNEY

HE WAS born in Mullaghbawn, County Armagh and won the 1995 Armagh Senior Championship and Ulster Senior title with them. He later teamed up with Dublin aristocrats, Na Fianna on the northside of Dublin. He enjoyed a successful period in the capital – winning the 1999 Leinster Senior Club Championship and three Dublin Senior Championships.

He was a central figure in the county's most prolific era, captaining the side to their maiden All-Ireland win in 2002. He had all the attributes of a top defender and gained three All Stars (1999, 2000 and 2002).

Armagh were, at the time, Ulster's kingpins and he garnered six Ulster Senior Championship medals (1999, 2000, 2002, 2004, 2005, 2006). McGeeney received the 2002 Texaco Footballer of the Year award after a string of stirring championship displays.

The International Rules Series against Australia was a concept he embraced and relished. He captained his country in the 2006 Series.

He was appointed manager of Kildare in 2007 and lifted 'The Lilywhites' out of the doldrums in his six-year tenure. He led the county to a Leinster final in 2009 and an All-Ireland SFC semi-final in 2010, losing unluckily to Down.

In October 2013, McGeeney joined the management team of his native county Armagh under Paul Grimley, succeeding the incumbent in 2015.

BRIAN McGILLIGAN

(Height 6' 2", Weight 15 St)

Decade... 1980s/1990s

(Position... Midfield)

CHIEF CHARACTERISTIC... UUFFO INTERCEPTOR... UNIDENTIFIED
ULSTER FOOTBALL FLYING OBJECTS

TOP ACCOMPLICES... ANTHONY TOHILL, HENRY DOWNEY,
GARY COLEMAN, TONY SCULLION

BRIAN McGILLIGAN

'ART SAID, "LOOK AT THE BIG DERRY B*****D, THAT'S
THE PLACE FOR HIM, ON HIS KNEES" AND I FELT LIKE
GETTING UP AND STRIKING HIM.''

– BRIAN MCGILLIGAN

BLOOD, thunder… and McGilligan!

The opening, breathless quarter of the 1993 All-Ireland final contained a few snapshots of the tumultuous day ahead.

The Rebels had started like an express train, leading by 1-2 to 0-0. Enter Derry talisman, Brian McGilligan, who flattens Cork's, Barry Coffey. When McGilligan hit you, you stay HIT… just ask anybody in Australia!

Cork had laid down the gauntlet to Derry, and their warhorse McGilligan, but no better man to pick it up. McGilligan appeared to be everywhere early doors. Putting out early bush fires, and lobbing a few grenades behind Rebel lines. He even managed to make a stylish lodgement in the Derry account after assisting Johnny McGuirk in the opening Oak Leaf salvo.

The opening passages of the play were significant, as Cork tested the water. The Rebels furiously eyeballing the upstart Northern raiders.

HARD MAN RATINGS

TOUGHEST: 10/10

MEANEST: 9.1/10

SCARIEST: 9.3/10

HARDEST: 20/20
☠

TOTAL HARD MAN
48.4/50

Cork was a seasoned outfit, who were well versed in the vagaries of All-Ireland day. For Derry, however, this was new territory.

A maiden voyage, that the Rebels were determined to torpedo before it left dry-dock. McGilligan had long been the poster boy for confrontation – if he caved in Derry's hand was significantly weakened, and would soon resemble a busted flush.

It was helter-skelter, head-spinning stuff. Careers are forged on days like these and some careers are lost. The Rebels had raised the stakes, McGilligan never blinked, and the rest was giddy history.

The Derry county final of 1983 spawned the legend.

Dungiven were losing by two points, staring down the barrel of a gun. He was lurking on the edge of the small parallelogram. Magherafelt had both hands on the trophy, as a hopeful punt dropped from the clouds.

The 19 year-old Brian McGilligan soared highest to fist the ball into the Magherafelt onion sack. Game over!

When Derry won an Ulster under-21 title in 1983, as they trounced Donegal, McGilligan's deceptive pace and power – looked tailor-made for football's highest level.

While his totemic presence brought a real edge to the Oak Leafer's, they remained straight-jacketed within the claustrophobic confines of the Ulster Championship.

Brian's provincial vintage led to an unexpected call-up for the International Rules Series against the Aussies, with Dublin supremo Kevin Heffernan placing McGilligan and Dermot McNicholl, behind enemy lines at a Tyrone training session!

The Red Hand were busily preparing for the not-too-inconsiderable challenge of facing Kerry in the 1986 All-Ireland final. Art McRory, the Tyrone manager had received secret strict instructions, to really 'work' the Derry duo in preparation for the three-test Australian tour, as McGilligan ruefully recalled.

'There was no love lost but we were well looked after, we were treated as part of the panel.' McGilligan was pitched against Plunkett Donaghy, Audi Hamilton and Harry McClure in the training 'war' games.

'The only difference was, if we were doing 10 sprints, I was made do five or six more. If there was half a dozen 400s (runs), I would be doing 10 of them. It was the same in the gym sessions.

'I got a lot of abuse. It was bordering on brutality. I remember Art talking to Fr Brian D'Arcy, who was down watching training. Art said, 'Look at the big Derry b*****d, that's the place for him… on his knees' and I felt like getting up and striking him.'

McGilligan's performances at full-back as Ireland recovered from a limp first-test defeat to win the series 2-1 was ample proof that the 'ruse' had paid a rich dividend. He was back in midfield again as Derry powered to an Ulster title in 1987.

He was in imperious form against Meath, in the penultimate stage, but the Royals had too many guns for Derry. By the dawn of the 90s, fresh blood had arrived in the shape of a new midfield partner for Brian. Anthony Tohill lent a considerable presence and those two towering Twin Peaks were the bulwark for defending the walls of Derry, and a sizeable launchpad for initiating lightning counter-attacks.

The foundation for All-Ireland glory was firmly in place. Next up was an equally taxing conundrum… how to Crack the 'Ulster Code'.

When Derry reached the 1993 Ulster Final against Donegal, a

giddy excitement descended on the Oak Leaf County. As Down and Donegal lifted Sam in 1991-1992 respectively, the football universe's balance of power appeared to be shifting significantly, 'North' of the border.

It was a contest balanced precariously on a razors-edge, before Derry, finally shook off a meaty Donegal challenge to triumph by two points, in an instantly forgettable affair.

When Derry edged a photo-finish with Dublin at the penultimate hurdle, there were many golden moments for the highlight reel. Chief among them was McGilligan's earth-shattering shoulder on Dublin's Jack Sheedy, as they progressed to the decider against Cork.

{ THE STRIFE OF BRIAN }

When Ciaran McCabe struck for a late-winning goal as Down stunned the reigning All-Ireland champions in 1994, it felt like the end of the world for Derry. There was no entry through the back door, and in that moment the Oak Leaf's footballing world stopped turning.

The rot that had slowly seeped in – quickly began to manifest itself. Derry had become intoxicated by the sweet scent of success. McGilligan reflected ruefully on the scale of lost opportunity for Derry football, as an exciting future was carelessly traded away.

'Any other county would have got their act together. Too many boys partied, lived the high life and thought it was only matter of turning up. We definitely should have won another one.

The players were good enough, you can't pinpoint any one thing.'

Still, his burning love of GAA sustained him through the highs and lows.

'It kept me on the straight and narrow. Everybody has their vices and the GAA was a vice for me. If it wasn't football, it was hurling.'

Football and hurling up a storm... that was the Life of Brian.

Blood, thunder... and McGilligan!

THE GAME OF
»———→ HIS LIFE ←———«

BRIAN McGILLIGAN was born on December 19, 1963 and is a native of Benedy outside Dungiven. He played a variety of sports during his early schooling at Dernaflaw National School and he also attended St Patrick's College Dungiven.

The dual-playing McGilligan was also a keen and very talented hurler, representing the county at the senior level. He played his club football for St Canic''s GAC Dungiven and also played hurling for Kevin Lynch's club.

McGilligan was part of Derry's triumphant march to the 1987 Ulster Championship where they overcame a spirited challenge from Armagh to prevail by just two points. He produced a string of stellar displays, including a Man of the Match performance against Meath, in the All-Ireland semi-final, earning him a first All Star award.

He added a second All-Star in the 1993 season as the Oak Leaf defeated Cork in the All-Ireland final, to win a first-ever, and only, Sam Maguire Cup.

He won a number of National Football League medals with a very consistent Derry side. The first arrived in 1992, and further successes followed in 1995, and 1996.

RYAN McMENAMIN
(Height 5' 10", Weight 13.5 St)

Decade... 2000s/2010s
(Position... Corner-Back)

CHIEF CHARACTERISTIC... TOUR GUIDE TO
CROKE PARK'S DUNGEONS

TOP ACCOMPLICES... BRIAN DOOHER, KEVIN HUGHES,
PHILIP JORDAN, PETER CANAVAN, CONOR GORMLEY, JOE MCMAHON

RYAN McMENAMIN

'IT'S BEEN SAID TO ME A LOT OF TIMES "YOU'RE NOTHING LIKE THE B***** YOU ARE ON THE FIELD". I'M BIG ENOUGH TO KNOW THAT IF I WENT ON LIKE THAT IN REAL LIFE, I WOULD PROBABLY BE IN JAIL SOMEWHERE, THAT'S THE REALITY OF IT.'

– RYAN MCMENAMIN

HE was small in stature, but the diminutive Ryan 'Ricey' McMenamin was one of the most intimidating, and spine-chillingly scary players of the modern era.

For even the most seasoned of 'marquee' county forwards, the Red Hand's warlord presented a forensic test of their footballing capabilities… and their appetite for the battle.

He was deceptively quick, with a bloodhound's nose for the slightest hint of danger. Despite his small frame, he thrived on physical combat. If a battle of wits, or a 'cupla focal' was your thing, Dromore St Dympna's finest had a flair for in-game conversation and certainly had a way with words!

The Tyrone fireball was famous for the dark art of 'sledging,' and exchanged numerous verbals with opposing forwards during the game. He could read his opponent like a book, and he freely admitted to knowing exactly the personality type

HARD MAN RATINGS

TOUGHEST:
9.2/10

MEANEST:
9.6/10

SCARIEST:
9.9/10

HARDEST:
17.5/20

☠

TOTAL HARD MAN
46.2/50

he could push over the edge. He was constantly probing for chinks in their armour, and ways to get inside his opponent's head.

'Once a forward (Devenney) comes back and tells you that he never missed a free the year before, you kind of say to yourself, "I can make hay with this boy here",' he once explained.

'He spent more time wondering what I was going to say and I was gone up the field more times… and he was coming back answering me with something that I never asked him. I was thinking… *That's a good way to have a man.*'

He was involved in many infamous duels which could have been classified under 'The Good, The Bad,' and The Ugly'. Some days too, his insatiable will to win washed over him in an uncontrollable wave, with disastrous consequences.

An incident Ryan regretted, in particular, occurred during the 2005 Ulster final replay with Armagh's John McEntee, when he landed on the unfortunate McEntee's chest… knees up! Somehow, he escaped with only a yellow card. An apologetic Ryan clearly regretted that rush of blood to the head.

'The game was going away from us and I probably did something I kinda regret, and it caused a bit of fury over the thing. It boils down to frustration. I phoned John and I apologised to him.

'It was my style of play, that I wanted to win everything that was out in front of me and I probably went too intense. I probably did cross the line. I'm big enough to hold my hands up and say "I did wrong…" and rightly so I got punished.'

McMenamin was never predictable and just when a forward was expecting an onslaught from his 'Gift of the Gab', he would pull a rabbit out of the hat, leaving them speechless.

Whenever Tyrone met Armagh, Ryan was often designated to

mark their attacking headline act, Stephen McDonnell.

'I had it in my head that Stevie is probably expecting me to come out with it... full verbals. I thought... *I'll come out, throw him and just say nothing to him* and I think that's what I did. I think Stevie was even trying to get a bit of banter out of me then.'

{ TWO SIDES OF RYAN }

McMenamin was a captivating individual whose personality always appeared to house two completely different characters. One was the 'Pantomime Villian' whom the opposition players and supporters had a wary distrust of, while those who knew him intimately saw a character totally at odds with his stage persona.

He was a stand-up guy for club and county, and saw his Tyrone colleagues as members of his family. If anybody needed help in any shape or form 'Ricey' was the one guy, you could always turn to for assistance.

Former Tyrone minor football manager, Mickey Donnelly saw a different and rather less well-known side of McMenamin.

'But then when anybody gets to know him, they recognise there is a really good human being there. One that genuinely cares about people," says Donnelly. 'When Cathal McCarron reached the very end game of his chronic gambling addiction and the world closed in, it was McMenamin and another Dromore man that lifted him from Dublin airport to bring him to a recovery centre in Newry.'

His on-field alter-ego remained a forward's worst nightmare, however. His game face on match day was genuinely unnerving. He played the role of a snarling psychopath to perfection, with his shaved, tight haircut, and flashing his manic toothless grin.

Kerry's Tomás Ó Sé saw the funny side of it but conceded McMenamin was a real handful.

'I think he was mouthing off at me one day and I just started laughing," said the former decorated Kingdom defender. 'I remember he was foaming at the mouth. I don't even know what he was saying. At the best of times, I'd have a problem with the accent in the north. But Ricey was a fella you obviously went to war with.'

Away from the melting pot of county action, his words revealed a depth of character few of his detractors thought he possessed.

'No one is going to go through their whole life perfect," Ryan admitted in a candid interview after he said goodbye to county football.

'My football career will be remembered more for the off-the-ball stuff. At the end of the day, I don't really care. I played county football to win and that's all I did. I just loved winning. It drove me too far sometimes.'

Ryan McMenamin ruffled more than a few feathers during his colourful Tyrone journey. While his brilliance as a defender may sometimes get lost in translation, his legacy as one of the finest and most feared defenders of Tyrone's 'Golden Generation' is set in stone.

Ricey was a fearless and unapologetic warrior, who was never afraid to walk on the wild side. He was emblematic of a new, never-say-die Tyrone, one who simply refused to accept they were destined to exist on the fringes of football's exalted elite.

THE LIFE
OF RYAN

MCMENAMIN HELPED Dromore win the Tyrone Senior Championship in 2007, beating Coalisland in the final. Dromore returned to the final the following season but were thwarted by Clonoe. McMenamin and Dromore reached their third decider in-a-row in 2009, and wrestled back the crown for the second time in three years.

The flying corner-back gave almost 15 years of unparalleled service to Tyrone in an unforgettable period for the Red Hand. In 2003, he helped Tyrone make history as they followed in Armagh's historic footsteps and won their first-ever All-Ireland senior title. Armagh had started as strong favourites in the first All-Ireland ever between two teams from the same province, but a Peter Canavan skippered Tyrone had not read the script and powered to a coveted first Sam Maguire Cup.

Two years later Ryan struck gold again and won a second All-Ireland medal with Tyrone. In 2006, he was named captain of the side in Brian Dooher's absence, but a much-depleted Tyrone exited the championship in disappointing fashion at the hands of Laois.

He won three All-Ireland Senior Football Championship medals, five Ulster Senior Football Championships and two National League titles with the county. He also won an All Star award in 2005. Post-playing career - he had spells with Fermanagh as manager and Cavan as a coach.

ANTHONY MOLLOY

(Height 6' 1", Weight 14.5 St)

Decade... 1980s/1990s

(Position... Midfield)

CHIEF CHARACTERISTIC... A TRUE LEGEND
WITH ONLY ONE 'GOOD LEG'

TOP ACCOMPLICES... MARTIN GAVIGAN, JOHN JOE DOHERTY

ANTHONY MOLLOY

'MYSELF AND BRIAN (MCENIFF) HAD ALREADY DISCUSSED THIS AND
WE ELECT TO PLAY INTO THE HILL. "DOWN THE F**KING BARREL".
WE'RE READY TO GO... WE'VE NEVER BEEN MORE READY.'
– ANTHONY MOLLOY

ANTHONY Molloy was a war hero for Donegal. The lion-hearted Ard an Rátha soldier was one of the hardest, most totemic players of the 90s. Molloy was a man who would travel to the gates of hell and back for his beloved Donegal.

No one suffered more for his county.

For Molloy, who required six operations on a knee damaged early during his career, walking into the dressing-room was often as painful as anything he ever suffered at the hands of opponents. Training on the knee was simply an unmerciful experience… never mind running out onto the field for a championship game and playing a game for 70 minutes.

It took not just amazing resilience every single day of the week, it took a depth of ambition and hunger which very few gaelic footballers have ever known.

The knee was reduced to 'bone on bone'.

But Anthony Molloy, like his county, knew

**HARD
MAN
RATINGS**

TOUGHEST:
9.4/10

MEANEST:
8.9/10

SCARIEST:
9.1/10

HARDEST:
19.6/20

**TOTAL
HARD MAN
47.0/50**

that he could never turn his back on one more big, painful effort to win the biggest one of all. Donegal's wait for an All-Ireland football title was one of the longest in the history of the football championship. The northern side had taken trophy droughts to a whole new level, living on a spartan diet consisting of the odd Anglo-Celt Cup.

Up to the early 90s, Donegal's provincial haul was in single figures and the road to the county's momentous Sam Maguire heist in 1992 was paved by broken promises.

Donegal was a county built upon easy excuses – a brittle house of cards – easily blown off-course by the rhythms and chimes of distant war drums.

They were a side that lacked fire in the belly, too accommodating to accept their fate. Molloy had soldiered through the indifference, the constant denial and recalls when the penny finally clattered to the floor.

It should have been an occasion to remember for him as he was making his 100th appearance and a weak-looking Fermanagh looked like a sacrificial lamb before an expected duel with Derry in the 1992 Ulster final.

'As I'd been making my way off, I was stopped to be presented with an award to mark my 100th appearance for Donegal. And then it suddenly dawned on me… a century of appearances… not that I was any the wiser. Here I was, presiding over the same kind of crap that had cost us every single time in the past. And believe me, despite the promises of late 1991, here we were in the midst of throwing it all away once again. In the kind of manner only we ever did.

'We might have won by 16 points, but now was the time to

thrash it out. And in the next half hour, Donegal did something really special… we won the All-Ireland.'

Sometimes in sports, it requires the truth, or home truths, to set you free. Donegal's quest for Sam had always been impaired by the 'Law of Inverse Consequences', that curious phenomenon where the all-consuming pursuit of success yields nothing but a vicious cycle of dismal recurring failure.

Having unburdened their souls, they duly held Mayo at arm's length in the penultimate round in 1992 and readied themselves for a crack at Dublin in the decider.

{ TAKING SAM BACK TO THE HILLS }

Anthony Molloy intimated in his searchingly raw and engaging biography, *A Memoir On Life, Glory and Demons*, the earlier introspection had cleansed The Forgotten County's souls!

We go through our warm-up before. I'm finally ushered toward the middle of the field where referee Tommy Sugrue pulls both myself and Tommy Carr together.

I call tails on the coin toss.

As it hits the ground, just like it had every single other time that season, it lands in our favour.

Myself and Brian (McEniff) had already discussed this and we elect to play into the Hill.

'Down the f**king barrel.'

We're ready to go… we've never been more ready.

The cup that cheered Donegal and Molloy so much soon became a different kind of burden for Anthony, as the endless requests led to late nights and drinking binges galore, with no end in sight.

Donegal was a county not used to such dizzying heights and wherever Anthony went, inevitably, Sam would surely follow. For a time, the unthinkable occurred, as he began to despise his illustrious travelling companion.

It's dark, but the little bit of early morning light that is beginning to creep in the window suddenly hits the Sam Maguire and... there it is once again. It's mid-February of 1993 and I've long since had enough. Physically, I'm exhausted and mentally... I'm completely spent.

We're a duo now... and the truth is, it's become like a ball and chain around my ankle. I'm sick looking at that damn cup at the bottom of the bed.

At the end of his unparalleled stint in the green and yellow geansaí, he could look back with a real fondness on those extraordinary days – when Sam made it home to the hills.

The greatest thing I've ever done in my lifetime is lift Sam Maguire, after Donegal's first-ever All-Ireland title, high into the Croke Park air. That moment back in 1992, the one immortalised on so many walls throughout the world, that is me. Or, it was me.

New York, London, Sydney... even a bar in Kerry of all places... every now and then, it crops up in the most unlikely of locations. But I can look at it now and smile. I can let my mind wander back and remember that exact moment. It still has the power to warm me.

And the whole of Donegal...

PEAKS HILLS AND VALLEYS

ANTHONY MOLLOY was born on May 28, 1962. He played his club football with Ard an Rátha. The club has won numerous Ulster titles and Anthony was on-board for his sole success in 1981.

Anthony really came to prominence for Donegal when he was a member of their All-Ireland under-21 winning side in 1982. It was the first time Donegal had won the competition, courtesy of a three-point win over Roscommon.

Molloy went on to play for his county at senior level for over a decade. In a 12-year career span, he amassed an astounding 123 appearances, beginning in 1982.

He has won three Ulster titles, the first of which arrived against Cavan in the 1983 Ulster final, and he captained Donegal to the 1992 Ulster crown against Derry and led the county to a first-ever Sam Maguire triumph.

He lifted the trophy with the famous words after a stirring speech 'Sam's for the hills'.

After a terrific campaign in 1992, he was duly honoured with an All Star award.

He also played in America for a spell and won two New York Senior Championships, in 1986, and 1992, while playing for the Donegal club.

BRIAN MULLINS

(Height 6' 2", Weight 15 St)

Decade... 1970s/1980s

(Position... Midfield)

CHIEF CHARACTERISTIC... BOSS OF BOSSES DUBLIN ENGINE ROOM

TOP ACCOMPLICES... JIMMY KEAVENEY, TONY HANAHOE, SEÁN
DOHERTY, DAVID HICKEY, GAY O'DRISCOLL, PAT O NEILL

BRIAN MULLINS

'IN THE RECENT PAST, IT HAS BEEN OFTEN SAID THAT
DUBLIN TEAMS STOOD ON THE SHOULDERS OF GIANTS.
TODAY WE LOST ONE OF THOSE GIANTS. BRIAN MULLINS
WAS A COLOSSUS AND A DUBLIN GAA LEGEND.'

– DUBLIN GAA

THE year is 1974. Platform shoes and Rubik's Cubes were all the rage. Love and peace were the mantra for a new generation, and Dublin football was back in vogue.

A new breed of gaelic footballers had risen from the ashes in the capital city and a precocious young man from Clontarf... was brewing up a storm.

It was the era when Heffo's Army were on the march and nobody walked taller than the totemic Sky Blues' midfield giant, Brian Mullins.

Mullins, first and foremost, was a Vincent's man, as he proved in a lifetime dedicated to the bluebloods of Dublin football. His son Bernard witnessed this love first-hand at the Marino-based football hotbed.

'At St Vincent's matches or with St Vincent's people, he was a true clubman in every sense of the word. He would do anything for the club, I mean anything.

'Whether as a player, coach, selector, fundraiser,

**HARD
MAN
RATINGS**

TOUGHEST:
10/10

MEANEST:
9.0/10

SCARIEST:
9.5/10

HARDEST:
20/20

**TOTAL
HARD MAN**

48.5/50

organiser, committee member, adult games director, chairman…
or even watering the pitch with his own car and a hose, he did
everything and loved every minute of it too.'

He was, of course, the fulcrum that a classy Malahide Road-
based Vincent' revolved around, and featured in three All-Ireland
Club finals for 'Vinnies'.

It would be a tale of contrasting emotions on All-Ireland day
for Brian and Vincent's, as they succumbed to Nemo Rangers
in their first appearance in 1972, after a replay. They returned to
the decider in 1975 against Roscommon Gaels and produced a
breath-taking display, to emerge victorious by 17 points. They
again emerged from Leinster in 1984, and squared off against
Castleisland Desmonds of Kerry in the national final. It was a
nail-biting, see-saw affair with a dramatic, but ultimately heart-
breaking conclusion for the Dublin side.

With two minutes left, Mullins' side had a 0-7 to 1-2 lead.
A line ball by Castleisland's Willie O'Connor found Donie
Buckley, who sent the ball into the net.

St Vincent's were stunned and had no time to respond, as
the Kerrymen completed a remarkable 'smash 'n' grab raid to
wrestle the trophy from the blue and whites on a 2–2 to 0–7 final
scoreline.

Mullins had exploded onto the county scene in 1974 when his
swashbuckling all-action style would power Dublin to one of the
unlikeliest All-Ireland triumphs in recent memory.

Dublin had been on the floor in 1973 – after a shock
defeat in the Leinster Championship saw them exit in rather
underwhelming circumstances again Louth.

If you had said to any of the Dublin faithful leaving Páirc

Tailteann in Navan in 1973 that the Dubs would be crowned All-Ireland champions a year later, and a 19-year-old programme-seller would be the 'Messiah,' who would lead them to the promised land, they may well have questioned your sanity.

The catalyst for a footballing dynasty, who had worked in the shadows around Croke Park for over a decade... paused for a second. Brian Mullins, the programme-seller, considered the question posed by John Harrington on *GAA.ie*.

'Ah sure, if I thought about it... and I don't remember thinking too much about it, but if I did I would have said they'd be miles away from it. I would have attended every All-Ireland as a programme-seller for 10 or more years beforehand.'

It certainly was stranger than fiction. The totemic Dublin midfielder outside Croke Park selling programmes, the year before he won an All-Ireland title, but for Brian Mullins it was the natural thing to do.

'That's just what you did when you were around here and you were so close to Croke Park.'

He considered the intriguing question again... the football pundit stirring within his soul.

'The '73 All-Ireland was Cork and Jimmy Barry Murphy and Ray Cummins... and looked like they were world-beaters. The previous year's Offaly... Offaly had to some extent... dominated would be the wrong word... but they had a big presence from 1969 through to '75/'76.

'How far Dublin would have been away from it? God, I don't know.

'So, in looking at other teams around at the time, I wouldn't have believed that it was possible to sell programmes in 1973 and be out on the pitch in '74. Like that would have been a total crackpot proposal.'

{ THE 1974 RISING }

Luckily for Dublin, iconic supremo Kevin Heffernan was a man that never baulked at crackpot proposals. He refocused and reimagined an ageing side – with 19-year-old Mullins infusing the team with the brash confidence and boundless energy of fearless youth.

He also added a layer of steel to the city side, which had often been perceived of having a soft underbelly. When the going got tough, the granite-like Mullins ruled the engine-room with an iron fist, and Dublin were once again top-of-the-pile as they defeated Galway on September 22, 1974.

After crushing Kildare in the Leinster final in 1975 (3–13 to 0–8), Dublin were red-hot favourites going into the All-Ireland final against a talented, but callow Kerry team.

On a rain-soaked pitch, John Egan and substitute Ger O'Driscoll scored two goals for Kerry and the Dubs were ambushed, 2–12 to 0–11. It was a bitter pill for Mullins and a Dublin team from whom so much had been expected.

In 1976, Dublin returned to the decider and once again it was Kerry who provided the opposition, as one of the great rivalries of football entered an epic new phase. Both sides were confident of success, however, a 3–8 to 0–10 scoreline gave Dublin the title and Mullins a second All-Ireland winners medal. He rounded off the year by collecting his first All Star award.

His fighting spirit and toughness were sorely needed when

a serious car accident very nearly derailed his career. Typical of the man, Brian Mullins fought his way back to full fitness. And fought to an unlikely All-Ireland title for 12-man Dublin in the 1983 All-Ireland final.

The emblematic Mullins was the face of a new Dublin football empire. A legendary warrior and an exemplary sportsman. He passed away on Friday, September 30, 2022.

Brian Mullins was an officer and a gentleman.

'Ar dheis Dé go raibh a anam dílis.'

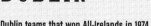

KING OF DUBLIN

BRIAN MULLINS was born in 1954. He received his primary and secondary education in Dublin, before later attending Thomond College in Limerick. Mullins completed a Bachelor of Arts in physical education and Irish there.

He played his club football with the powerful St Vincent's club, a career that spanned three decades. Mullins lined out in his first county championship decider against college side UCD - which Vincent's won by 2-8 to 0-9. Mullins would garner five county titles, three Leinster Club Championships and an All-Ireland Club title with Vincent's during a glorious career.

Brian was *the* vital cog on the pioneering Dublin teams that won All-Irelands in 1974, 1976, 1977 and 1983.

He made a total of 97 league and championship appearances for Dublin between 1974 and 1986, winning nine Leinster titles. He was also honoured at the All Star awards ceremony when selected in 1976 and 1977.

Mullins retired from county football in 1985 and became the caretaker manager for Dublin in 1986, along with former teammates Sean Doherty and Robbie Kelleher. Early in 1996, he was appointed senior manager of the Derry County team where he was in charge for three seasons. He won a league title in 1996 and an Ulster crown in 1998.

BARNES MURPHY

(Height 6' 0", Weight 14 St)

Decade... 1970s/1980s

(Position... Centre-Back/Midfield)

CHIEF CHARACTERISTIC... DELIVERING DEFENSIVE
MASTERCLASSES IN BLACK AND WHITE

TOP ACCOMPLICES... JOHN BRENNAN, BOBBY LIPSETT,
MATTIE BRENNAN, TOMMY CUMMINS, FRANK HENRY,
TOM COLLEARY, PADDY HENRY

BARNES
MURPHY

'IT WAS OUR FIRST CONNACHT WIN IN 47 YEARS, THE
CELEBRATIONS PERHAPS WENT ON FOR TOO LONG. I TRIED IN
VAIN TO PUT A STOP TO THEM, BUT WINNING ONE CONNACHT
TITLE WAS LIKE WINNING FIVE ALL-IRELANDS TO US.'
– BARNES MURPHY

HE was as imposing as the county's mighty Knocknarea
(Cnoc na Riabh), and might as well have been forged
from its steep limestone cliffs. The towering Cnoc na Riabh
means Hill of the Kings, and peers imperiously over the Cúil
Irra peninsula, overlooking the Atlantic coast.

If there were a referendum held for King of Sligo football
there would be no need for snap elections or
hasty coronations. The goliath that was Barnes
Murphy was one of the Yeats County's most
ravenous warriors and would likely be one of the
poll-toppers in most constituencies.

When the 'Yeats' won their second Connacht
title, Murphy brought multi-tasking to a whole
new level, as he coached, captained, and likely
ironed the jerseys – as Sligo finally got their paws
on the elusive Nestor Cup.

The Enniscrone native was a force of nature as
the men from Markievicz Park finally escaped
from the clutches of those formidable ruling

HARD
MAN
RATINGS

TOUGHEST:
9.6/10

MEANEST:
9.5/10

SCARIEST:
9.3/10

HARDEST:
19.5/20

TOTAL
HARD MAN
47.9/50

Connacht families, Galway and Mayo, to finally reach the West's version of Shangri-la. The seeds of that long overdue success had been sewn on Barnes' All-Star trip the year previously. The All Star centre-back in 1974 had travelled on tour to San Francisco and Los Angeles in April of 1975, as he later recalled.

'I was on the All Star trip in April of '75 and all the Galway lads were talking about how they were going to hammer us in the first round of the championship that year.

'When I came home, I told the Sligo team what I had been listening to and we ended up having the last laugh. Kerry beat us in the All-Ireland semi-final but, seeing as it was our first Connacht win in 47 years, the celebrations perhaps went on for too long. I tried in vain to put a stop to them, but winning one Connacht title was like winning five All Irelands to us.

'I was the team's coach, but I got James Tierney, who was masseur with the Sligo Rovers soccer team at the time, to do the training. He'd be better known for his involvement with Sligo Rovers but he's very well thought of in Sligo GAA circles.'

The cross-code collaboration worked a treat for a fired-up Sligo outfit. Barnes was incensed at his charges being taken so lightly. It was just the material he had been seeking to ignite his hungry flock, whom he was convinced had all the raw materials to usurp the fattened kings of Connacht football.

Galway were a hotly fancied visitor to Markievicz Park for the provincial semi-final. Sligo had exited at the same juncture the previous year after a replay, and looked set to perish at the penultimate stage once again.

Few would have predicted, not only the victory but the manner of it, as Sligo sauntered into the Connacht final, 1-13 to 0-6.

When Sligo and Mayo played out a highly entertaining draw in the decider on Sligo's home patch, it appeared the ship had sailed on the Yeats' men – with the Nestor Cup on board!

A third encounter with one of those leviathan Connacht beasts beckoned and avoiding defeat seemed a very remote prospect indeed.

{ THE WONDER YEARS }

Barnes was stationed at centre-back and if ever Sligo needed their talisman's legendary powers of resistance, this was the occasion. Sligo scribes could have written many painful volumes on the county's visits to those twin 'heartbreak hotels,' in Castlebar and Tuam.

Two weeks later, 20,000 spectators at MacHale Park, witnessed another nail-biting encounter, where fortunes fluctuated wildly in the final 15 minutes. Those final fraught moments were a snapshot of Murphy's distinguished career.

There was tough, there was tougher, and then there was Barnes Murphy! As the onslaught intensified, Barnes faced Sligo's *High Noon* with all guns blazing. The man blessed with the strength of an ox repelled wave after wave of Mayo attacks. In the air and in the trenches, it mattered little what artillery reigned down on Murphy.

The human shield from Enniscrone stood as tall as Cnoc na Riabh and drove the green and red invaders back from when hence they came.

Aided by two crucial second-half goals, the Yeats plundered the trophy to end a 47-year-old drought, and finally be crowned kings of the West. The fairytale for Barnes and his doughty Sligo men ended there. A ruthless Kerry dismantled them in the All-Ireland semi-final, putting them to the sword, 3-13 to 0-5. The final tally is hard to comprehend as by the mid-point of the second period, Kerry was only six points to the good, but then the floodgates well and truly opened.

Sligo's 1975 triumph was the pinnacle for Barnes and company, as further provincial crowns proved a bridge too far. He lamented some lost opportunities that could have yielded an ever even greater bounty for the Yeats men.

'During my time as a player with the county between 1968 and '75, we had a very good team. We were very consistent and were always there or thereabouts, getting to the league semi-final in 1968, '72, and '74. We were also beaten in the provincial final, after a replay, by Galway in 1971. We ran a very good Mayo team to several replays and were very unfortunate not to have won something in the early part of the 70s.

'I think we had a far better team before 1975, as others on the team at the time would surely acknowledge. Some of our footballers would have got on any team at that time. Several were on the Connacht team which won the Railway Cup in 1969. With others like Danny McHugh and Brendan McCauley also on the scene then it was a purple patch for Sligo that time.'

As Sligo football finally emerged from the shadows in 1975, Barnes Murphy put in some shift at the coalface. His unbridled passion relit the fire in the Yeats County's belly.

A warrior's tale… recounted in Black and White.

LIFE IN MONOCHROME

BARNES MURPHY excelled at underage before progressing to the county senior side in 1967.

He went on to become an integral part of one of the finest teams that ever represented the Yeats County, retiring from the game in 1981.

One of the county's most successful-ever footballers, he won five county championships(with Craomh Rua and St Mary's), and five League medals (also with Craomh Rua and St Mary's). Murphy also tasted success at provincial level, winning three Connacht Club Championships and an All-Ireland 'Sevens' title in 1980. He also won junior titles with St John's, the new club that had emerged after the old Sligo borough boundaries were divided.

Barnes began his incredible Sligo odyssey in 1967, and after a number of lean years guided Sligo to a rare Connacht Senior Championship win in 1975. The inspirational Murphy both captained and coached Sligo to that stunning success that season. It was Sligo's first Connacht Championship in nearly half a century - the last time they lifted the Nestor Cup came back in 1928.

A regular on the Connacht Railway Cup side, he was the first Sligo player to captain his province in the competition. Murphy's brilliance extended well beyond the county's wild and beautiful walls and his enduring excellence was rewarded with a well-merited GAA All Star award in 1974.

MICHAEL MURPHY

(Height 6' 1", Weight 15 St)

Decade... 2000s/2010s/2020s

(Position... Full-Forward)

CHIEF CHARACTERISTIC... TEACHING OPPOSITION DEFENCES
THE REAL MEANING OF MURPHY'S LAW

TOP ACCOMPLICES... PATRICK MCBREARTY, RYAN MCHUGH, NEILL
MCGEE, LEO MCLOONE, COLM MCFADDEN, NEIL GALLAGHER

MICHAEL MURPHY

'THE STRONGEST PERSON I HAVE EVER COME UP
AGAINST ON A FOOTBALL PITCH, HE JUST GRABBED
ME AND YOU COULDN'T MOVE.'

– MATTIE DONNELLY

THE young man studied the outline of the stadium and his heart almost skipped a beat. His father grasped his hand tightly as they approached a stern-looking security guard, enquiring would there be any possibility of admission to the 'magic castle'?

The duo were ushered to a reception area and informed that admission to Croke Park was not on an ad-hoc sort of basis! It appeared the adventure would end there, but this outpatient was no ordinary day tripper and was not about to give up on his dream.

Endless Trips to the Mater Hospital for corrective therapy on his hips had unearthed a deep-seated yearning inside the youngster – he had to set foot inside the hallowed stadium walls.

The boy recognised a famous-looking figure loitering inside with a face that wore a thousand welcomes. The man broke into a gentle smile when his eyes fell upon those distinctive county's colours, there would be no need to enquire what

**HARD
MAN
RATINGS**

TOUGHEST:
9.6/10

MEANEST:
9.1/10

SCARIEST:
9.0/10

HARDEST:
19.8/20

☠

TOTAL
HARD MAN

47.5/50

part of the country they hailed from.

'Do you know Anthony Molloy?' the man enquired, smiling broadly? The young boy's eyes widened at the mention of his hero.

'I do!' replied the young man his eyes shining brightly. 'He is the captain of Donegal.'

As the celebrated broadcaster led them down the tunnel and onto the playing surface at GAA headquarters, he had no idea they would meet again at Croke Park with unerring regularity.

The Jones; Road venue was a place Mícheál Ó Muircheartaigh had the occasion to frequent quite a lot… but then again so did the future captain of Donegal.

The kid grew up impatiently. That's the thing about being young; yearning for the clock to tick a little faster… and then as you grow older, imploring it to slow down!

Michael Murphy was the boy who would be king. He travelled the country with his parents to attend Donegal games when he was a child. He had vivid memories of many of those heady days, some a little darker than others.

He painfully recalled the 1998 Ulster final and the moment the tide rolled out for his beloved Donegal.

'I remember exactly where I was sitting in the Gerry Arthurs Stand, watching out and seeing Geoffrey McGonagle's infamous dunt on Noel McGinley, and all the dreams went.'

School interceded for a while, but for young Murphy, education in secondary school was destined to be of the sporting variety.

'Secondary school to me was just football, football… football.

'Most people try and make football fit around school or work, but I tried to make the Leaving Cert fit around football and it doesn't really work that way. I repeated the Leaving Cert because I really just let my studies take a back seat the first time around. All I wanted to do was play for Donegal. I wasn't bothered about the books.'

Learning came easy for the Glenswilly giant and the football came even easier. He made his senior county debut at the tender age of 17 and would be voted 'Young Footballer of the Year' just two seasons later.

He was the 'Big Flaming Green and Yellow Clad Football Giant.' Trying to stop him was a bit like trying to flag down a herd of stampeding Buffalo.

Tyrone's Mattie Donnelly ruefully recalls an encounter from early in his minor career.

'The strongest person I have ever come up against on a football pitch,' he remarked, years after encountering a 17-year-old Murphy at underage level. 'He just grabbed me and you couldn't move, like... I have to admit I think he was on one leg that night. They were peppering every ball in on top of him. I think he got five frees that night... I might have fouled him for all five of them.'

Michael Murphy was always destined to lead from the front and while his appointment as captain in 2011 was a major surprise given his age profile, it also made perfect sense.

Jim McGuiness' gamble as manager would bear glorious fruit, as Donegal won only their second-ever All-Ireland in 2012 against a hapless Mayo. Michael Murphy struck a telling blow early on after collecting a high ball delivered by Karl Lacey.

The audacious smash 'n' grab was widely hailed as 2012's Goal of the Season. Upon making the pilgrimage up the revered stairway of the Hogan Stand, Murphy proclaimed to Donegal's ecstatic fanbase… 'We have him' in reference to the Sam Maguire Cup.

Such was his sustained level of brilliance, he retained the captaincy throughout his county career.

{ A GIANT AMONG MEN }

Murphy's capacity to absorb physical punishment had by now assumed mythical proportions, so it came as no surprise when he was selected to star in the reality sports documentary *The Toughest Trade* in 2017. He exchanged places with rugby star Shane Williams and spent a week at the French rugby team, Clermont while Williams joined up with Glenswilly.

While he struggled with the intricacies and technique of the oval ball game, not even the most combative rugby players on the Clermont books, most of whom were seasoned internationals, could extract any change out of Murphy. It was a huge testament to both his conditioning as an amateur sportsman, and ferocious robustness.

Donegal and Murphy came agonisingly close to another All-Ireland title in 2014, but a freak concession of a goal to Kerry's Kieran Donaghy scuppered their hopes in a largely underwhelming performance by the Northern Kingpins.

Murphy represented Ireland in five International Rules Series, starring in a number of unforgettable victories against the invaders. His silky skillset and explosive power were ideally matched to the rigours of the high-octane hybrid game.

THE BOY
▶━━━▶ WHO WOULD ◀━━━◀
BE KING

MICHAEL MURPHY was born on August 4, 1989 in Letterkenny. He was part of Donegal's 2006 Ulster Minor Championship-winning side. He then captained Donegal's 2010 Ulster under-21 Championship winning squad.

At club level with Glenswilly, in 2011, Murphy was part of the team that won its first-ever Donegal Senior Football Championship title and contributed 1-7 of his team's 1-8 total in the decider.

Further county titles would duly follow in 2013 as Glenswilly defeated Killybegs by 3-19 to 2-6, and again in 2016. He made his senior debut for Donegal in January 2007 in the Dr McKenna Cup and he made his All-Ireland Senior Championship debut later that year.

In December 2010, manager Jim McGuinness selected Murphy as captain ahead of the 2011 season. Donegal ended a four-year drought without silverware winning the National Football League Division 2 title. Murphy also led Donegal to their first Ulster Senior Championship title in 19 years with a win over Derry in Clones.

In 2012, he became the first player to captain Donegal to back-to-back Ulster titles, and later that year an All-Ireland title – only the second Donegal captain to lift the Sam Maguire Cup after Anthony Molloy in 1992.

He won a total of five Ulster titles, one All-Ireland medal, and three All-Star Awards. He was Donegal's all-time scorer amassing over 500 points.

JOHNNY NEVIN

(Height 5' 9", Weight 13.5 St)

Decade... 1980s/1990s/2020s

(Position... Corner-Forward/
Centre-Forward)

CHIEF CHARACTERISTIC... LIKED TO SETTLE OLD
SCORES - AND NEW ONES!

TOP ACCOMPLICES... WILLIE QUINLAN, NOEL DOYLE,
ANTHONY KEATING, HUGH BRENNAN

JOHNNY NEVIN

'Q: WERE YOU EVER SENT OFF?
A: ONCE, IN A CHALLENGE GAME WITH MY CLUB ABOUT EIGHT OR
NINE YEARS AGO FOR DEFENDING MYSELF. A GUY MADE A BOX AT
ME AND RATHER THAN STAND THERE LIKE A
DUMMY AND GET TWO BOXES...!'

– JOHNNY NEVIN

THROUGH ADVERSITY TO THE STARS.'

The motto of the Royal Australian Air Force could well have been tattooed on his arm. The Latin 'per ardua ad astra' embraces a stirring call to arms to the members of the regiment.

The message is stark and powerful. Fight courageously through any adversity and eventually you will gain your reward.

No man raged harder against adversity than Carlow 'giant', Johnny Nevin. Fighting under the long and ominous shadows of provincial hurling and football superpowers was a journey through adversity of the highest magnitude.

The warrior who wore the tricolours of his beloved 'Barrow' in both codes never buckled under the weight of an unrelenting onslaught. On and on, he fought manfully until he finally reached the stars.

HARD MAN RATINGS

TOUGHEST:
9.2/10

MEANEST:
8.5/10

SCARIEST:
9.2/10

HARDEST:
19.6/20

TOTAL HARD MAN

46.5/50

By the end of his career which had been fought in the foxholes that existed far away from the main stage he carved out an impressive reputation as not just one of Carlow's greatest ever GAA players – but one of the finest dual performers in the history of the Leinster Championship.

He forged his name with heroic deeds; the letters boldly engraved from blood, sweat, and tears.

He spent a career wrapped in the Carlow tricolours. At times it was a blessing, at times it was a curse for the Old Leighlin legend. 'The Scallion Eaters' were always held hostage to others' fortune. Bound and chained in a provincial prison, held under the tyrannical rule of the Meath 'Royals' and the Dublin 'Jacks', and even the lesser lights of the 'Lilywhites' and the 'Faithful.' Carlow seemed eternally cursed to spend a life exiled from the Delaney Cup.

The intrepid Nevin had proudly worn the tricolours against almost every county in Ireland. He was still performing at the highest level into his 40s – more of a vintage car than one of the classic varieties at that stage!

Nobody has done more to spread the county's hurling and football gospels than their inspirational dual-performing legend. He started his incredible odyssey at the age of 17 – when stepping out for the senior football panel, and ditto the senior hurlers the following season.

His football debut arrived against Limerick in February 1988 at Askeaton, with his first full appearance for the hurlers arriving against Offaly in Division 2 league tie in October 1989.

He had earlier made a substitute appearance against Wicklow in the All-Ireland B Championship replay at Dr Cullen Park in

May 1989. Such longevity is a rare and beautiful thing, especially when it isn't based on lining your pockets with Celtic Crosses.

Keeping count of Johnny's appearances in those three colours could well have been beyond the finest statisticians on the planet! While it would be folly to predict the exact total for perspective purposes, these figures are truly off the charts.

Since his first outing with the footballers in the late 80s, he had racked up over 150 appearances by August 2003. While he could always be relied upon to put in a shift in the backline, Johnny brought his football shooting boots in his preferred mode as a free-scoring forward, and would finish his career with an estimated total of over 300 points.

Seldom has a county had a player that has given so much to its cause. If Carlow went into battle, Johnny invariably answered the call. His career was almost split evenly between the codes, his commitment never wavering despite his advancing years.

When he wasn't performing in his day job with the footballers, he was moonlighting as a hard-nosed defender on the hurling side. it goes without saying his football incarnation went along the famous lines of Marvel's Incredible Hulk character.

'You wouldn't like me when I'm angry.'

Johnny was not the tallest or even the strongest - but he hit the hardest. He was a man transformed when he slipped on the Carlow sash, a man possessed with an insatiable lust for physical combat.

He panned for gold on barren hills and slippery inclines for decades. Aside from the odd nugget of an All-Ireland B title and a Kehoe Cup medal, nuggets were invariably of the Dutch gold variety – all that glittered – but rarely gold.

{ FLYING THE PROVINCIAL FLAG }

Johnny was a rare shining light in Carlow's valiant struggle to painfully inch up the provincial pecking order. While he has missed a handful of games in both codes, not a single season pass had expired without Johnny's name stamped somewhere upon it.

His appearances for the province show proved that however far you perform from the main stage, talent and tenacity which he had in abundance will always find a way.

Johnny became one of only three Carlow footballers who have ever been voted into the Leinster football Hall of Fame, along with fellow legends, Cyril Hughes and Paddy Quirke. It is his fervent belief that success, however small, will someday inspire future Carlow generations.

'If they see the generation ahead of them winning, they'll want to have a piece of that. They'll want to emulate those before them.'

When once queried about ever being sent off, he was slow to claim any liability!

'Once, in a challenge game with my club about eight or nine years ago, for defending myself. A guy made a box at me and rather than stand there like a dummy and get two boxes…'

Against all odds, Nevin waged a magnificent war on two fronts for his beloved Carlow. After 14 years, 177 appearances for the county footballers and 155 for the hurlers,he finally called it a day.

It had been an extraordinary journey. The man from one of the forgotten teams in GAA who rose to be one of its finest.

'THROUGH ADVERSITY TO THE STARS.'

»——→ A LIFE IN ←——«
THREE COLOURS

JOHNNY NEVIN excelled at both hurling and football for his native Carlow. He was born in Old Leighlin, whom he represented in senior football and Naomh Bríd in the small ball game.

Nevin is a dual Carlow medallist, winning two senior titles in football and adding another three in hurling. Naomh Bríd was only founded in February 1996, when Parnells of Leighlinbridge and St Fintan's of Ballinabranna decided to join forces.

Former Wexford star, Christy Keogh was the team's first manager, who sensationally guided the new entity to a Carlow SHC title in his very first season in charge, defeating St Mullin's.

The club claimed further Carlow SHC titles in 2004 and 2008, with Johnny Nevin playing a starring role in all three successes, and the club has the unique distinction of having never lost a county final.

Johnny is one of a very select cohort of players who represented their province in the Railway Cup in both codes. Despite comparative lack of success at national level, he still managed to win an All-Ireland B football medal in 1994.

He has played against almost every county in Ireland between both codes, bar Cork.

STEPHEN O'BRIEN

(Height 6' 1", Weight 15 St)

Decade... 1980s/1990s

(Position... Corner-Back/Full-Back)

CHIEF CHARACTERISTIC... SHORT STOP AND LANDING
SITE OPERATOR FOR FLYING FORWARDS

TOP ACCOMPLICES... NIALL CAHALANE, JIMMY KERRIGAN, TONY
DAVIS, CONOR COUNIHAN, JOHN KERINS, TEDDY MCCARTHY

STEPHEN O'BRIEN

'I'M DELIGHTED IT'S BACK TO ITS RIGHTFUL OWNER, ONE OF THE GREATEST UNSUNG HEROES OF CORK FOOTBALL.'

– BERNARD FLYNN

AT the end of the 1990 All-Ireland football final, they both shook hands and exchanged jerseys. The age-old tradition of swapping shirts has always been a gesture of universal respect, after the battle has ended.

The first sharing of jerseys in soccer is thought to have begun when France played England in a friendly encounter in 1931, but this most personal of moments shared between gladiators can certainly be traced back much further than that…

All-Black No 97 as he would come to be known, took off his mud-spattered jersey and exchanged it with his Welsh counterpart Gwyn Nicholls. It was a moment that would echo across time.

The New Zealand 'original' touring party had lost the only game of their historic first ever tour of these islands. Dave Gallagher, the Irish emigrant who captained New Zealand, embraced his opposite warmly and departed into the mists of time. They would never meet again, yet the

HARD MAN RATINGS

TOUGHEST:
9.6/10

MEANEST:
9.0/10

SCARIEST:
9.0/10

HARDEST:
19.8/20

TOTAL HARD MAN

47.4/50

story didn't end there...

As Cork's full-back took off his shirt and extended it to Meath's fallen hero Bernard Flynn, it was a symbol of a timeless tale. One warrior handing his blood-stained shield to another.

The instant bond forged from the blood, sweat, and tears of the battlefield.

The Nemo Rangers titan basked in the glory of a hard-earned victory over Meath – 'hard-earned' and 'Meath' always seemed to run concurrently in the same sentence!

While Meath would return the following season, the Rebels would experience plenty of provincial strife before returning to the big stage.

As Flynn and O'Brien left the battleground, the rivalry that had been at its zenith during the mid-1980s had by 1990 run its course. The sides that had faced off in four finals in the space of five years, spanning 1987-91, were finally running out of gas.

As Flynn and O'Brien departed the stage. they would never cross swords again in an All-Ireland final, yet, their personal story didn't end there.

Stephen O'Brien's Cork football journey started as a toddler aged five when he began playing football with his local club, Nemo Rangers. It was the start of a head-spinning 28-year playing association with the Cork southside powerhouse.

O'Brien took the game like the proverbial duck to water and by the age of 16, his exploits with Coláiste Chríost Rí had alerted the attention of the Cork minor football management.

O'Brien was a steely cog in the Turner's Cross school's wheel as they defeated Spioraid Naoimh, in the Corn Uí Mhuirí Munster Senior Colleges final. Coláiste Chríost Rí, and O'Brien didn't stop there, as after an enthralling All-Ireland decider, they beat Summerhill College Sligo.

O'Brien was naturally parachuted into the Nemo Rangers senior side after another impressive set of cameos in Cork's losing minor All-Irelands in 1986 and 1987.

He could do no wrong as his immense contributions over the years powered Nemo Rangers to six Cork Senior Championships, as well as three All-Ireland club titles.

He had by now migrated to the Rebels under-21 side and was seen as the natural fit for captaincy. The talismanic figure was about to experience one of his greatest-ever seasons in the red and white.

His outstanding efforts yielded medals from an All-Ireland under-21, an All-Ireland senior, National Football League... and All-Ireland club championship in 1989.

'To win that many championships in one year was absolutely brilliant and I certainly look back on that year with a lot of pride, as it's a record that won't be achieved by too many players,' he recalled.

O'Brien's and Cork's hot streak showed no sign of slowing down, as the following season produced an incredible double as both 'Sam' and 'Liam,' were paraded by the banks of the River Lee.

The victory over old adversaries Meath was particularly sweet, as the Rebels had suffered more than most at the hands of the Royals. O'Brien, however, did not buy into the narrative about Meath being a cynical team, and was always of the mind that in order to match them teams needed to bring the very best version of themselves.

'There was a lot of talk in the press about our clash with Meath, because of previous games against them and with the Cork hurlers' great win. The build-up and the tension gripped Cork for weeks.

'A lot of silly things were said in the press that only added fuel to the fire before the game, but, at the end of the day, we knew that we needed a top-class display to win that final.'

{ THE ARMOUR OF WAR }

Dave Gallagher's jersey remarkably surfaced 110 years after he had taken it off in Cardiff.

Welsh skipper, Gwyn Nicholls had taken the shirt back to his family laundry business in the city, before making a gift of it to rugby-mad van boy, Thomas Mahoney. It stayed in his family for over a century, before fetching an astounding £180,000 at auction in October 2015.

The men who had clashed in five All-Ireland SFC finals (one replay) were reunited on television almost 30 years later. Bernard Flynn arrived bearing gifts, and O'Brien's eyes widened in disbelief as Flynn handed him a framed jersey – the one O'Brien had famously handed to him almost three decades before.

'I'm delighted it's back to its rightful owner, one of the greatest unsung heroes of Cork football.'

Having witnessed O'Brien's herculean efforts for the Rebels at close hand, Flynn had perfectly summed up an often-forgotten Cork hero. The Nemo Colossus was immense as the Cork footballing empire struck back. His was the adhesive that bound a formidable back six into one of the most stingy and robust defences the county had ever produced.

The symbolic exchanging of jerseys has been an unwritten

contract between sporting warriors for well over a century. When Bernard Flynn presented Stephen O'Brien with his famous shirt from 1990, it was a gesture that All-Black number 97 would surely have approved.

»——→ CAPTAIN NEMO ←——«

STEVEN O'BRIEN was born on December 28, 1969. He played his club football with Cork kingpins Nemo Rangers, joining the club's juvenile ranks aged five. He was a standout schoolboy performer with Coláiste Chríost Rí and was a member of the side that won the Hogan Cup in 1987. Late that season he made his senior debut for the Nemo Senior side - kickstarting a 15-year tenure at the level.

On March 17, 1989, Nemo won a fifth All-Ireland Club title with O'Brien on board. It was the first title for the Cork giants since 1984, as they defeated Roscommon's Clan na Gael by a comfortable 10-point margin.

O'Brien would collect a total of three All-Ireland club titles with Nemo and also won six Munster club, and six Cork senior finals.

He made his Cork debut for the minor footballers and was part of a side that lost two All-Ireland finals in-a-row. He then captained the under-21 side to the All-Ireland title in 1989, and was by then a member of the senior panel.

He won six Munster medals and one National League title. He was part of the famous Rebel outfit that garnered two Sam Maguire Cups in quick succession, in 1989, and in 1990, and he also won a very impressive three All Star awards.

MARTIN O'CONNELL

(Height 6' 0", Weight 14.5 St)

Decade... 1980s/1990s

(Position... Wing-Back/Full-Back)

CHIEF CHARACTERISTIC... HEAD PERCUSSIONIST
WITH THE MEATH BAND 'THE KILLERS'

TOP ACCOMPLICES... LIAM HARNAN, MICK LYONS, GRAHAM
GERAGHTY, COLM COYLE, KEVIN FOLEY

MARTIN O'CONNELL

'THOSE TWO INCIDENTS PROBABLY LOOKED BAD, BUT THEY WEREN'T
REALLY. I STAMPED ON NOBODY, THAT WASN'T MY FORM. JOHN
MCDERMOTT ALSO GOT A BIT OF CRITICISM OVER THE TACKLE ON
CANAVAN WHICH INJURED HIM, BUT TYRONE WEREN'T ANGELS, WE
WEREN'T ANGELS... THAT'S JUST THE WAY IT WAS.'

– MARTIN O'CONNELL

SOME may have smiled at the gentle irony of his employment status – Martin O'Connell was a butcher by trade!

He hailed from St Michael's, a small rural club from outside Kells. The tiny club had such a small membership, the younger members had to line out with the adult teams.

'Training with older fellas and that, you earned your ball and you got tougher really... it was *tough* football. You had to get tough because if not, you were going to be wiped out.'

O'Connell's apprenticeship in the bearpit of the Meath club scene stood him in good stead for the fire and fury of county football. He was called into the Meath minor set-up, quickly migrating to the senior ranks. His meteoric progress didn't last and, in 1986, he became disillusioned by his lack of

**HARD
MAN
RATINGS**

TOUGHEST:
9.3/10

MEANEST:
8.8/10

SCARIEST:
9.2/10

HARDEST:
19.5/20

☠

TOTAL
HARD MAN

46.8/50

progression and sensationally departed the squad.

Sean Boylan undeterred by his departure, reinstated O'Connell.

'I thought I was doing the right thing, but I soon realised it was the wrong thing and I was praying Sean would ring me back. Thank God he did. Ever since that, if he asked me to play in the goals, I would have played in the goals, if you know…'

Martin was true to his word as he just about played in every position on the club and county teams – right-back, left-back, full-back, midfield, half-back and, even on occasions, full-forward.

His performances all contained the same recurring theme, nothing could quell the Carlanstown native's lust for the battle, not even broken bones.

'I broke the collarbone, broke my hand, broke my ribs naturally enough of course, sure everyone breaks ribs. I had a disc removed in 1997 but I did well really with injuries, I didn't really get them until the end of my career.

'I had an awful lot of tough fellas around me and that made the game a little easier for me too. When you play with the likes of Liam Harnan and Mick Lyons… now people say they were dirty, they weren't dirty, it was just that toughness and that rawness that whatever was in their way, it wouldn't matter because they'd go through it to win that ball anyway.'

Meath's mighty warrior piled into the challenges with a nerveless abandon. The scene often resembled the aftermath of a car crash, such was the carnage Martin's involvement ensured.

{ MEETING JOE DUFFY }

One such incident occurred in the 1996 All-Ireland semi-final against Tyrone. It all appeared to be innocuous enough, but then things quickly unravelled for Carlanstown's finest, as he revealed in his incredible memoir *Royal Blood*.

He was a yard or so in front. I knocked the ball out of his hand and, as I did, he fell over in front of me. The ball was hopping and, as I was going over him to try to win it back, I caught him on the head with my boot. I certainly didn't stamp on him. A stamp is looking down on a fella and putting real force into it. I clipped him with my stud, but my eyes were on the ball.

There certainly was no stamping motion involved, and I would defy anyone to say otherwise.

I was in two minds that day whether to wear moulded or studs, and in the end, I wore studs. If I'd have worn moulded, I probably wouldn't have cut him at all. It was definitely accidental.

Like McBride, Dooher went off with blood everywhere. Like McBride, Dooher came back out with a big bandage. Only for the bandages, people wouldn't have noticed anything at all. It certainly wasn't my form to intentionally injure someone, it was just one of those things, unfortunately.

When the game was over, I was enjoying the victory and didn't give a moment's thought to the incidents with McBride and Dooher. Little did I know how bad it was going to get. That evening, The Sunday Game was inundated with calls, and letters started flooding into the newspapers. There was a big discussion about it on Liveline on the Monday.

Those two incidents probably looked bad, but they weren't really. I stamped on nobody, that wasn't my form. John McDermott also got a bit of criticism over the tackle on Canavan which injured him, but Tyrone weren't angels, we weren't angels, that's just the way it was.

For Martin and Meath, the controversy was only starting....

After a tepid enough draw against Mayo on the first day in the 1996 final, the replayed game duly exploded into life with a ferocious melee involving 30 players. Both sides remarkably only had one player dismissed, and it was the Royals who coped better with 14 players – as Martin collected a third Celtic Cross. The bad blood didn't end there, with Martin picking up the story.

The next day, when the dust settled – or so we thought – both teams were brought back to Croke Park for a function. You could cut the tension with a knife.

There was a bit of friction between players from both teams, and words were said. The president of the GAA, Jack Boothman got up to say a few words and Seán said a few words.

Next, it was John Maughan's turn. He never congratulated us properly, I felt. He spoke about how great the Mayo team was – which you would expect – then at the very end he just said, 'Well done Meath'.

That didn't go down too well. There was a bad atmosphere across that whole function, and it raised its head at different times. I saw a few of the Mayo lads at the All Stars do a few months later, but there was no talk with them or Tyrone. I don't know if they didn't want to talk to us or we didn't want to talk to them, or both!

Broken bones, melees, medals, and even an appearance on Liveline! Life in the fast lane with the Millennium Man... the only modern-day player to take his place on the GAA's Team of the Millennium.

THE
»———→ MILLENNIUM ←———«
MAN

MARTIN O'CONNELL was born on August 29, 1963 in Carlanstown, County Meath. He played football with his local club St Michael's. The side competed in the intermediate tier of the county's club scene.

He was part of the Meath senior squad for a 13-year period from 1984 until 1997.

O'Connell was one of Meath's most decorated defenders and was selected for the Football Team of the Millennium.

In a senior county career that touched two different decades the imperious O'Connell won every major honour in the game at senior level with the Royal County, including three All-Ireland titles.

O'Connell was an integral part of the Meath side that claimed a record of six Leinster football titles. He also won the National Football League on three different occasions.

He was also the recipient of a number of individual awards including four All Star awards. He was also named Texaco Footballer of the Year in his final playing season in inter-county involvement in 1996.

The GAA community was shocked to learn that the All-Ireland medal he won in 1987 was stolen during a burglary in November 2020. Happily, the missing medal was recovered a short time later and reunited with its rightful owner.

GAY O'DRISCOLL

(Height 6' 0", Weight 15 St)

Decade... 1960s/1970s

(Position... Corner-Back)

CHIEF CHARACTERISTIC... DUBLIN DEFENSIVE
SOLUTIONS RAPID RESPONSE UNIT

TOP ACCOMPLICES... PAT O'NEILL, BRIAN MULLINS, ROBBIE
KELLEHER, SEAN DOHERTY, FRAN RYDER

GAY
O'DRISCOLL

'I WAS DRAINED BOTH PHYSICALLY AND MENTALLY. IT WASN'T AN
EXHAUSTING GAME TO PLAY IN. JUST REALLY ENJOYABLE AND AT THE
TIME I REALISED I WAS PART OF SOMETHING SPECIAL AND IN LIGHT OF
WHAT HAPPED BETWEEN OURSELVES AND KERRY, I SUPPOSE IT'S EASY
TO UNDERSTAND WHY PEOPLE WOULD COME TO REGARD IT AS A CLASSIC.'
– GAY O'DRISCOLL

HE was a man who solved problems. Problems arrive in many shapes and forms on a football field. Sometimes they can be tactical, sometimes they can be self-inflicted. A lot of problems can be solved by a cerebral approach.

A quick consultation with fellow selectors can often be just the panacea for a wide range of ills. The subtle movement of the playing pieces around on the chess board can also often have the required effect.

For everything else... there was Gay O'Driscoll!

Kevin Heffernan had a fetish for players who were consumed by a touch of darkness.

Gay O'Driscoll was one of Heffo's most trusted generals, and as sure as night followed day the St Vincent's destroyer could always be called upon to generate a little darkness.

In 1976, the situation had festered to the

HARD
MAN
RATINGS

TOUGHEST:
9.5/10

MEANEST:
9.8/10

SCARIEST:
9.6/10

HARDEST:
19.7/20

TOTAL
HARD MAN

48.6/50

point where Cormac Row of Meath was now becoming a serious problem. He was causing mayhem within the Dublin rearguard, and the Leinster final had started to tilt more than a little sideways, with the Dubs staring down the barrel of a gut-wrenching reversal at the hands of those Royals.

Cormac Rowe carried on his killing spree, oblivious to the fact that the clock was ticking on his involvement in this particular Leinster final. The time had arrived for Denis Gabriel O'Driscoll to do his thing…

The following extract is from *Heffo*, Liam Hayes' exhilarating account of one of the most iconic managers in GAA history…

Rowe had the ball.

The noise level in the ground soared every time he took the ball into his giant hands, and made one of his big, defiant turns, shoulders first, in the direction of Paddy Cullen. Kelleher had pawed at him.

Rowe was moving towards the Dublin goal with some speed, when…

BANNNGGGGG!

Gay O'Driscoll had charged straight at Rowe. He came in from an angle and struck Rowe just underneath his left shoulder. Except O'Driscoll didn't bounce off Rowe. O'Driscoll's right shoulder connected just under Cormac Rowe's chin. Rowe had gone down. That was hard to believe.

Harder still was the sight of Rowe crumpled up on the ground.

He wasn't getting up.

There wasn't a stir out of him.

Referee Seamus Aldridge from Kildare had not stopped play. Seán Doherty had gathered up the ball that had fallen out of Rowe's hands, and lashed it up the field. Gay O'Driscoll reported back to his own corner to check on Mattie Kerrigan.

Half of the population of Meath was stunned.

Those who sat in the Cusack Stand stopped watching the game. Two Meath selectors were bringing Cormac Rowe off the field.

He was being dragged off.

There was no stretcher in Croke Park in the summer of 1976.

With his feet dragging along the ground, and with his head slumped over his own right shoulder, Cormac Rowe was brought over to the Meath dug-out. His jersey was covered in sweat, mixed with a good amount of blood. Cormac Rowe was laid out on the Meath sideline, directly in front of all of the Meath substitutes sitting in the dug-out.

Rowe was gone.

Problem solved! Heffo was a man that always chose his trusted generals wisely, Gay O'Driscoll was a soldier that always carried out his instructions with a surgical level of efficiency, and the minimum of fuss.

O'Driscoll had left a serious calling card that would put the brakes on the head of steam Meath had stock-piled in the preceding minutes.

With the man mountain-Rowe out of the way, the skies overhead rapidly tinged to a sky blue pastiche. Gay was a man that never over thought the process. He who hesitates is truly lost in the high-voltage world of county football. Heffo appreciated his specialist man-marking skills, and his capacity for smelling clear and present danger. Most that were present to witness his confrontation with the unfortunate Rowe likely never saw the culprit, just a light blue blur.

No need to send out an APB however, just round up the usual suspect!

Gay O'Driscoll kept doing his thing for nearly 14 punishing seasons. In a stellar career littered with so many titanic struggles, the tenacious corner-back plumped for the 1977 All-Ireland semi-final against Kerry as one of his most treasured days at the office.

'I was drained both physically and mentally. It wasn't an exhausting game to play in. Just really enjoyable and at the time I realised I was part of something special and in light of what happened between ourselves and Kerry I suppose it's easy to understand why people seeing in on the telly for periods afterwards would come to regard it as a classic.'

The Heffo years provided a rich harvest for the capital crew. The wily old fox had struck the perfect balance in the blue machine. A side stacked with silky skills and heavy hitters like Tommy Drumm, Dr Pat O'Neill, Brian Mullins, and one that needed little introduction!

He reflected on those halcyon times and the incredible effect it had on life in the 'big smoke'.

'When we came to the forefront there was almost a cultural type revolution. All of a sudden gaelic football started to get a hearing amongst the youngsters in the city. It was a watershed moment in the promotion of football in Dublin.'

Gay had slugged it out one round too many with Father Time and cashed in his chips in 1979. The speedometer had only hit 33, but every fighting dog has had its day.

'I wasn't too disappointed after our defeat in 1979 and to be honest I wasn't particularly looking forward to another year of having to settle for a place on the bench on occasions. I got a calf injury before the 1979 All-Ireland semi-final and had to make do with coming on as a substitute in the final, so the writing was on the wall.'

Every inter-county forward in Ireland worth his salt slept a little easier… upon hearing that welcome news!!

»———→ URBAN YEARS ←———«

GAY O'DRISCOLL was born in 1946. His championship career at senior level with the capital's inter-county team spanned 13 seasons from 1966 until 1979.

He was born in West Cork, and O'Driscoll was the son of a Royal Navy serviceman. He moved with the rest of his family to Marino in Dublin at an early age, attending St Joseph's Secondary School in Fairview.

O'Driscoll was a member of the famous St Vincent's club who were serial winners of the Dublin Football Championship. His club career spanned three decades, with the undoubted highlight arriving in 1976 when he won an All-Ireland medal with the club.

O'Driscoll also won two provincial Leinster medals and an astonishing 10 county senior championships.

He was an excellent dual performer, and first arrived on the county scene as a hurler at minor and under-21 levels. An All-Ireland runner-up in the under-21 grade in 1967, he spent over a decade in sky blue despite not featuring on the minor or under-21 football teams.

O'Driscoll first pulled on the senior shirt during the 1966-67 league. Over the course of the next 13 seasons he won three All-Ireland medals between 1974 and 1977.

Dublin were the dominant force in Leinster, and he also won six successive Leinster medals and two National League medals, and collected two All Star awards.

NOEL O'LEARY

(Height 6' 0", Weight 14.5 St)

Decade... 2000s/2010s

(Position... Corner-Back/Half-Back)

CHIEF CHARACTERISTIC... PROVING DISPOSSESSION
WAS NINE-TENTHS OF THE LAW

TOP ACCOMPLICES... ANTHONY LYNCH, NICHOLAS MURPHY, GRAHAM
CANTY, JOHN MISKELLA, PAUDIE KISSANE, MICHEAL SHIELDS

NOEL O'LEARY

'YOU'D MEET HIM OFF THE FIELD AND HE'S SO
QUIET. HE WAS TOUGH... THE PHYSICALITY, AND HE
COULD PLAY BALL AS WELL. HE JUST GETS IN THE
ZONE. HE DOESN'T EVEN SAY HELLO TO YOU.'

– GRAHAM GERAGHTY

KILNAMARTRA is located halfway between Killarney
and Macroom. The picturesque village is part of the
townland associated with the barony of Muskerry West.

Like every village, Kilnamartra descants a captivating tale. It
is home to Ireland's only toy-soldier factory that
manufactures a range of military and fantasy
figurines.

St Lachtin is believed to have found a monastery
in the area in the 8th century, which was almost
destroyed by raiding Vikings in 832AD, but it
was subsequently restored and continued as a
place of pilgrimage.

This majestic Cork heartland has been
immersed in gaelic football since the dawn of the
GAA. The first recorded victory of the club in
1887, was in a 21-a-side match versus Ballinagree.

The village has produced some fine footballers

**HARD
MAN
RATINGS**

TOUGHEST:
9.5/10

MEANEST:
9.9/10

SCARIEST:
8.8/10

HARDEST:
19.5/20

**TOTAL
HARD MAN
47.7/50**

and Mick Goold won a National League title in 1952 with Cork before winning a Munster SFC title as a substitute later that season. He enjoyed further inter-county success throughout the 1956-57 season, winning a second league title and consecutive Munster SFC medals. Goold and Cork suffered back-to-back All-Ireland final defeats by Galway in 1956 and Louth in 1957.

Kilnamartra however, would not be denied its day in the sporting sun. A remarkable young warrior named Noel O'Leary would wage war on the football behemoths – to eventually take Kilnamartra all the way to the promised land.

Former Meath legend, Graham Geraghty was asked to choose the three toughest defenders he faced during a decorated county football career that lasted nearly 20 years.

After a lifetime of facing the bullets and the barbs, the full forward took us to his inner-sanctum, and revealed his number two selection on the BBC Northern Ireland sports podcast – Cork's beating heart, and Rebel fan favourite, Noel O'Leary.

The rugged defender spent 14 years at the Cork coalface, winning an All-Ireland minor title in 2000 and a senior All-Ireland medal a decade later.

'Let's put it this way, if you didn't come off without a few bruises on you, you weren't in a game,' said Geraghty.

'You'd meet him off the field and he's so quiet. He was tough… the physicality, and he could play ball as well. He just gets in the zone. He doesn't even say hello to you.'

It was a perfect summation of the Cork 'cult figure'. A quiet unassuming hero, who once he crossed the whitewash was transformed into a mighty mythical warrior.

Former Armagh star, Óisin McConville gleefully retold a

story about Noel's almost fanatical dedication to the 'Blood and Bandages'.

'Noel O'Leary, he was working in Dublin,' said the retired Crossmaglen great. 'He was picking two boys up for training. They were on the Naas dual-carriageway and a stone came up from a lorry in front, hit the windscreen and the windscreen shattered. He stopped the car on the side of the road, pushed the windscreen out (while) pulled over on the side of the road.

'The two boys were in the car, and he drove to Cork with no windscreen. The two boys were lying down in the back of the car. That's the sort of boy he was.'

Noel's debut in the Munster Senior Championship was one to forget, however, as Cork were hammered by a rampant Limerick. The following season was nothing to write home about either, as Fermanagh slammed the 'back door' firmly shut to end Cork's sorry season.

Cork reached the Munster final in 2005, losing inevitably to Kerry. Bit by bit the Rebels reeled Kerry in over the course of the following seasons, and emerged as All-Ireland contenders in 2009, and 2010.

In 2010, Noel and Cork would finally make it to the summit of Everest. Cork wrestled manfully with formidable northern raiders Down, with Noel O'Leary's titanic battle with Down talisman Marty Clarke one of the defining duels of a fiercely fought contest.

Subduing Clarke was never going to be an easy task, but Kilnamartra's finest gave as good as he got, as Cork edged a nervy, attritional war.

His late father, Donal, who was also an accomplished

footballer, revealed what the win would signify in the village and surrounding areas.

'It means everything really because from the day we came out of the cradle, we live for football… that gives you an idea of what it means to us.'

{ FASHION AND FISTYCUFFS }

Noel O'Leary painfully rolls his eyes, a mischievous twinkle slowly forming at the notion.

'If I had a penny for every time Paul Galvin's name was mentioned…'

They were chalk and cheese. One quiet, modest, and unassuming – the other brash, cocky and full of mischief. It seemed they had been rubbing each other up the wrong way since the dawn of time.

Galvin, the 'fashionista', really got under Noel's skin and O'Leary, the Rebel enforcer, was a red-rag to that particular Lixnaw bull. The only attempts to bury the hatchet by the combustible duo… were in each other!

From 2005-2010, the pair clashed 14 times, with O'Leary quite literally landing the knockout blow. The pair regularly clashed over that series of games, culminating in both of them being dispatched to the line in the 2009 Munster semi-final replay, won comprehensively by Cork.

Noel on that occasion connected with a right hook, which had the effect of helping thaw relations between the two warring factions. In truth, the only way was up from there, and O'Leary revealed a text he got from Galvin after his Sam Maguire success.

Congrats – now would you please retire and leave me alone!

O'Leary always had a grudging respect for his old nemesis, as he admitted to Galvin's teammate, Tomás Ó Sé.

'To be fair to the man, I'd have great respect for him. Obviously, a brilliant footballer... a brilliant footballer and certainly a driving force on your team at the time.'

A LIFE ON LEESIDE

NOEL O'LEARY began his Rebel career with the Cork under-16 team, winning a Munster title in the grade. In 1999 O'Leary joined the Cork minor football team, lining out as a corner-back as Cork beat Kerry by 2-16 to 1-9.

In 2000 he was a member of the Cork minor football team that qualified for a second consecutive Munster decider, and defeated Kerry. Cork later qualified for the All-Ireland final, beating Mayo by 2-12 to 0-13. The win gave Noel an All-Ireland minor winners' medal in his final appearance for Cork in that grade.

He also won Munster and All-Ireland Championship medals with the Cork junior team in 2001.

Noel established himself as a regular on the senior side, reaching his first Munster final in the grade in 2005. He won his first Munster medal in 2006, but missed the final, before returning as Cork bowed out to Kerry in the All-Ireland semi-final.

He won his only All-Ireland senior medal in 2010 after Cork defeated Down, and retired on October 17, 2013. He was nominated for an All Star on three occasions.

With Kilnamartra, he won a 1999 Cork Minor C Football Championship and in 2002, O'Leary enjoyed his first major success with Cill na Martra, winning a divisional junior football championship, and doubling up in 2023.

COLM O'ROURKE

(Height 6' 2", Weight 15 St)

Decade... 1970s/1980s/1990s

(Position... Corner-Forward)

CHIEF CHARACTERISTIC... GENERAL ROYAL
ARTILLERY ARMOURED DIVISION

TOP ACCOMPLICES... DAVID BEGGY, PJ GILLIC,
JOE CASSELLS, GERRY MCENTEE

COLM O'ROURKE

'WITH THAT, O'ROURKE HIT ME A SHOULDER AND TO THIS DAY I'VE
NEVER BEEN HIT AS HARD. MY SOUL LEFT MY BODY FOR A MOMENT
AND CAME BACK TO ME WHEN I HIT THE GROUND.'
– VINNIE MURPHY

KILLING them softly…

James 'Jim' Brown Miller was a study in never judging a book by its cover. Miller was often impeccably dressed with good manners, he didn't smoke or drink and often attended church – earning him the nickname 'Deacon Miller'.

The Texas Ranger and outlaw was also one of the most prolific killers in the history of the Wild West, who was said to have killed 12 people during gunfights, and more in other outlaw activities and assignments.

Most never saw James 'Jim' Brown Miller coming and even if they did, he hardly had them quaking in their boots. That's the thing about hit-men… they can appear in all shapes and guises…

He always looked a cut above the muddy trenches and hand-to-hand combat of county football. This Royal could kill you in a variety of different ways. A lethal assassin from play and placed balls, every indiscretion was ruthlessly punished in a game of death by numbers.

HARD MAN RATINGS

TOUGHEST:
9.5/10

MEANEST:
9.0/10

SCARIEST:
9.2/10

HARDEST:
19.5/20

TOTAL HARD MAN

47.2/50

If none of the above worked, Colm O'Rourke was never afraid to get his hands dirty. Dublin's Vinnie Murphy was no choir boy. Vinnie was always big and bold when he stepped into the Colosseum of Croker for a taste of being fed to the lions… namely Meath!

He detailed in the *Game of my Life* series what it was like to get down and dirty with the Royal's, and one man in particular.

'What I found about stepping up to playing Meath wasn't necessarily how hard you were getting hit, but how clever they were with what they did and how they did it. The pulling and dragging, the little pull or nudge at just the time… I wasn't used to that. Meath were a fantastic football team, and they don't get enough credit for that, but they were definitely masters at the dark arts.

'There was a big row in the league final replay in 1988. Kevin Foley hit Kieran Duff and I came in briefly and got involved, but I thought I'd be sent off, so I tried to meander away. Then, I got sandwiched between Mick Lyons, Harnan, and Colm O'Rourke. You couldn't have picked three harder lads if you tried. I ended up on the deck.

'The blood was boiling at that stage, and I won the next ball that came out and got around O'Connell and let it into the full-forward line. With that, O'Rourke hit me a shoulder and to this day I've never been hit as hard. My soul left my body for a moment and came back to me when I hit the ground.

'The thought did cross my mind… is this where you really want to be?'

{ LIFE IN THE FAST LANE }

O'Rourke found the initiation into the fast and furious world of elite football a struggle for the first few seasons and admitted some games passed him by. Gradually he absorbed the lessons of soft skills and dark arts, and offered a compelling insight into life in the fast lane of county football in his autobiography *The Final Whistle.*

'Early on with Meath I was not strong enough to hit hard, and I can quite well remember getting tough wallops in contesting possession which would leave me unable to play for about 10 minutes. As time went by, I got stronger and by the mid-80s I was weighing in at a fit fourteen and a half stone and was so unlikely to be pushed around by a back unless I let him. There is a very thin line between not taking any messing and being dirty. Every corner-back in the country will grab the forward for a second to prevent him getting a clear run out. 'That's if they know that the forward is not going to lash back with a fist or an elbow in the mouth! To get the sort of respect from backs that allows you to play means that you have to "bust" a few of them in high-profile games, and the word quickly spreads around that any back grabbing your jersey runs the risk of having a few teeth dislodged.

'Naturally, it is something you have to do when the referee is not looking. If a back was giving me a lot of hassle and there was nothing being done, I often let him go out in front for the ball and just at the right moment, I'd give him an unmerciful box behind the ear.'

By the late 80s, Colm was a totemic presence in one of the

greatest football teams of all time. He was a pure footballer with a stylish, purring Rolls Royce engine. Meath won a couple of All-Irelands and left a couple behind them. Three would probably have been about right for Sean Boylan's fighters, but accountancy has never been a particular strength of the sporting gods.

The general perception was Meath bamboozled their path to Jones' Road, one that Colm strongly disagreed with in the Meath edition of the *Game of my Life* series.

'We always felt that it was a case of "Give a dog a bad name" about our team. No matter how good our football was, we were still going to retain the image of being a fairly hard outfit.

'There was a hard edge to us. The two Lyons, Foley, Harnan… they were really tough hard men, so maybe some of the reputations were deserved, but it came at the price where our good football was often forgotten. To some extent, that perception worked in our favour because some teams approached us and didn't seem to understand that we could also play football too and ended up taking their eye off the ball.'

Most defenders never saw Colm O'Rourke coming until it was too late. His languid style could lull you into a false sense of security. Nothing appeared hurried, rushed, or forced.

He was the ultimate marksman, who lived by the Assassins Creed.

Killing Them Softly…

DIARY OF
⟫———⟶ A FOOTBALL ⟵———⟪
KILLER

COLM O'ROURKE played league and championship at senior level for Meath for two decades, starting in 1975. He was born in Aughavas, County Leitrim, but his family relocated to Skryne in County Meath. In the football-mad county, he played schools competitive gaelic football with Patrick's Classical School in Navan.

O'Rourke was a product of the Skryne underage system before he graduated to the senior side. The club are second on the Royal County's list of all-time winners to Navan O'Mahony's. O'Rourke won back-to-back senior titles in 1992 and 1993.

He represented University College Dublin and won a Sigerson Cup medal in 1979.

He enjoyed little success at underage level with the Royal County. Colm made his senior debut arrived during the 1975-76 league. He won back-to-back All-Ireland medals in 1987 and 1988. During his career, he accumulated five Leinster Championship titles, three National Football League medals, and the 'Footballer of the Year' award in 1991.

He embarked on a career in sports broadcasting with RTÉ, as an analyst on *The Sunday Game* for over 25 years. He also pens a column for *The Sunday Independent*.

He took up the position of manager of the Meath senior team in July 2022.

PÁIDÍ Ó SÉ
(Height 5' 10", Weight 14.5 St)

Decade... 1970s/1980s
(Position... Wing-back/Corner-back)

CHIEF CHARACTERISTIC... DEFUSING EXPLOSIVE FORWARD LINES.

TOP ACCOMPLICES... JIMMY DEENIHAN, JACK O'SHEA,
TIM KENNELLY, BOMBER LISTON

PÁIDÍ
Ó SÉ

'WE WERE WALKING DOWN THE CORRIDOR WITH MR. HAUGHEY,
WHO WAS ON CRUTCHES AT THE TIME. HE ASKED HIM "PÁIDÍ
DID YOU BREAK ANY BONES DURING YOUR CAREER?" AND HE
SAID, "YES TAOISEACH, BUT NONE OF MY OWN"'

– ANONYMOUS

PÁIDÍ Ó Sé was the 'Kingdom of Kerry' personified. The combative all-action defender housed a relentless fire, that burned brightly for Kerry football for nearly two trophy-laden decades. He was one of the unshakable pillars that a star-studded Kerry four in-a-row team was built upon.

He was the kingdom's 'Mr Consistency.' When Kerry's need was most acute, he was as steady as the white sands of Ceann Trá, his beloved Ventry.

Páidí was a man that took no prisoners. Hard, but scrupulously fair, he had no fears of sailing close to the wind if an errant opponent stepped over the line.

Cork and Kerry battles over the decades, fell into one very distinct category – shrinking violets need not apply! When these fiercest of Munster rivals clashed there were numerous flashpoints, otherwise known in the GAA world as 'shenanigans'.

Páidí always held firm in the eye of the storm

HARD MAN RATINGS

TOUGHEST:
9.9/10

MEANEST:
9.5/10

SCARIEST:
9.7/10

HARDEST:
19.8/20

TOTAL HARD MAN
48.9/50

and if justice needed to be served, the publican was more than willing to dispense it! He became a YouTube sensation when his flooring of Cork's Dinny Allen in the 1975 Munster final was uploaded several decades later. Allen and Páidí had been getting to know each other intimately during a fractious encounter.

Tempers had reached boiling point by this stage and the normally reserved Allen's patience finally evaporated!

The Cork man flung an elbow backwards, striking Páidí in the jaw. Páidí was shaken for a few brief moments, then he let fly with a haymaker of a punch,sending a bemused Allen into orbit and almost pole-axing the match official.

When queried about the incident in a post-match interview as gaeilge, Páidí responded succinctly, as béarla, with one of the understatements of the century.

'I was very lucky not to be sent off by the referee!'

Páidí was in the words of the Edmund Burke famous saying, 'Not merely a chip off the old block, but the old block itself'. His playing career and numerous adventures off the pitch, were the stuff of GAA folklore. His larger-than-life persona was enhanced by some hilarious events that were, quite simply, stranger than fiction.

Ripley's Believe It or Not, was an American TV Series created by Robert Ripley that first screened in the early 1930s. The programme was hosted in later years by Hollywood acting legend, Jack Palance. It dealt in bizarre events and items so strange and unusual, that viewers might question their claims. Páidí could well have supplied enough material for an entire season of the hit show with some of his side-splitting stories.

The great man recounted a famous story in the *Irish Examiner* about his obsession with lucky charms and superstitions (piseógs). Páidí had struck up an unlikely friendship with controversial former Taoiseach, Charles Haughey. The colourful politician was a regular visitor to his pub in Ventry.

'In 1985, I was captain of Kerry. I was not that long married and my wife packed my bag for me the day before the All-Ireland final when we headed to Dublin. That night, I discovered to my horror that she hadn't packed my lucky underpants. I had worn them in each of my previous six winning All-Ireland finals and I was absolutely convinced that if I didn't wear them, we wouldn't win the final again.

'So, in a panic, I rang my mother. She told me to leave it with her. I rang her back an hour later. She said: "I have arranged for them to travel up on the train in the morning. I rang Charlie Haughey. He will send his car to Heuston Station to collect them and he will have them in Croke Park for you in plenty of time for the game".'

Kerry went on to defeat Dublin in the 1985 All-Ireland final. Páidí's 'lucky underpants' duly worked the oracle as he won the seventh of his eight All-Ireland medals.

{ HOLLYWOOD MEETS THE WEST KERRY GAELTACHT }

Páidí's pub in Ventry was the epicentre of the local community. It was a place where you always received a warm 'Céad Míle Fáilte'. A visit to Páidí's pub was never dull. He was a natural story-teller who had a wonderful sense of charm and always had a roguish twinkle in his eye.

Kerry great, Marc Ó Sé remembers his uncle was a man who had your back. 'He'd back you to the hilt,' says Marc. 'We were close, fierce close. He'd pop round the house almost daily and have you in stitches with his stories. He was larger-than-life, a rogue... an absolute rogue.'

He fondly remembers the great man in an interview with *the42 ie*, which recalls the famous day when a Hollywood A-lister enters Páidí's bar one November.

Marc, seeing an incredible advertising opportunity, rushes upstairs to inform his uncle.

'Martin Sheen is in the pub!!'

'Who the f**k is Martin Sheen?'

'Hollywood... Jesus. *The West Wing*, Páidí!!'

'Oh Jesus Christ... I'll be down in five minutes.'

Páidí marched over to Sheen and introduced himself, pointing to the wall of his pub where there were photos of him with Dolly Parton and Tom Cruise.

'Martin, how are you doing? Nice to meet you, you're welcome.'

'You know Tom?' Sheen asked.

'Oh yeah, Tom and myself are personal friends,' said Páidí, who'd met Cruise only the once.

He asked Sheen if he'd like a drink?

'No thank you,' replied the Hollywood legend.

'Ah sure look, it is not every day we have a Hollywood celebrity into the bar. Look... you'll have a drink?'

'No, thank you, I'm an alcoholic,' explained Sheen.

At this point, the story appeared to have run its course with Hollywood's finest threatening to spoil the party. 'No' was a word, however, that never existed in Páidí's vocabulary. He was not about to give up on his prize catch… of that all-important 'celebrity has a drink in Páidí's Ó Sé's Ventry pub photo'.

Marc Ó Sé continues the story…

'So, Páidí says, "No problem, no problem…Yerra Christ, you'll have ONE!'

On or off the pitch. Páidí always had the last word!

PÁIDÍ'S PILGRIMAGE

HE MADE his first senior appearance at just fourteen years of age for An Gaeltacht senior football team in 1970. He won numerous divisional championship titles and was also selected for the West Kerry divisional team.

Páidí Ó Sé won Kerry Senior Championship medals in consecutive campaigns in 1984 and 1985, to complete back-to-back championship-winning seasons.

He won every honour at senior level with The Kingdom, including eight All-Ireland football titles, 11 Munster Championships, four National League titles, four Railway Cups, and five All Stars.

As a manager, he won two All-Ireland football titles with Kerry and added six Munster titles, and a National League. He was also a surprise appointment for the Westmeath senior football team, and sensationally guided the Lake County to the Leinster Championship title in 2004. It was their first-ever title, in only his first season in charge.

In 2007, he was also linked with a potential return to Kerry as manager, however, there would be no reunion with his native county, as he took over the reins with the Clare senior footballers instead. On and on…

TOMÁS Ó SÉ
(Height 5' 11", Weight 14 St)

Decade... 1990s/2000s/2010s
(Position... Wing-back)

CHIEF CHARACTERISTIC... KEEPING THE Ó SÉ FLAG FLYING HIGHEST

TOP ACCOMPLICES... AIDAN O'MAHONY, TOM O'SULLIVAN,
MARC Ó SÉ, SEAMUS MOYNIHAN, MIKE MCCARTHY

TOMÁS
Ó SÉ

'I DON'T THINK I WAS HARD TO MANAGE. I THINK I WORKED HARD.
I'D GET PISSED OFF WITH CERTAIN STUFF. I DIDN'T LIKE LONG TEAM
MEETINGS. IT JUST SEEMED EVERYTHING WAS GETTING DRAWN OUT
AND LONGER. SESSIONS WENT FROM AN HOUR AND 20 MINUTES, UP
TO AN HOUR AND 45 MINUTES. EVERYTHING WAS LONGER. MEETINGS
AFTERWARDS WERE LONGER. THE TIME YOU HAD TO PUT IN TO BE AN
INTER-COUNTY PLAYER, ALL THAT STUFF MADE ME CRANKY.'

– TOMÁS Ó SÉ

HE titled his memoir *The White Heat*. And why not? Throughout his career, on every field he graced with his heroic athleticism, Tomás Ó Sé always appeared to have his fingers on the thermostat. He was also the picture of his beloved uncle – the man who strode like a colossus across the gaelic football landscape.

While the great man had sadly departed... he could still feel *him*. Marching purposefully along the Ventry Strand. They say you cannot know a man unless you have walked a mile in his shoes, but ask any Kerry warrior, and they would freely have soldiered for a million miles with Páidí Ó Sé.

The roguish smile, that twinkle in his eye, and then the steely, defiant gaze. If any man could fill the imprints which his uncle's famous shoes left, you just knew it would be him.

His nephew could still glimpse his uncle in the

HARD
MAN
RATINGS

TOUGHEST:
9.7/10

MEANEST:
9.2/10

SCARIEST:
9.5/10

HARDEST:
19.4/20

TOTAL
HARD MAN

47.8/50

half-light – peering across the water – all introspection and deep concentration, meticulously planning the next campaign. Hands in pockets, kicking every ball in his head, living every game-day moment. Then he'd be off. Marching boldly along the sand.

Every time you saw the Ó Sé brothers performing in the Kingdom colours, it was like looking in the family mirror. Marc, Darragh and Tomás, all performing in the likeness of their exalted uncle. The family's gift to Kerry football was a gift that kept on giving.

For the Ó Sé clan, football was the family business. Their youngest brother Marc picked up a fifth All-Ireland medal against Donegal in 2014. That impressive tally left the immediate family on 16 Celtic Crosses between them. The brothers also topped the charts on the all-time list of championship appearances for Kerry, no family has togged more for the Kingdom's cause.

Of all the siblings, Tomás possibly encapsulated his uncle's freewheeling defensive style more than most. Once Páidí let the handbrake off, all hell followed with him! Tomás would give a very good impression of his famous uncle during his stellar shift in the Kingdom colours, as the blood that coursed through his veins would also be of the volcanic variety, and in the later stages of his momentous career, he became involved in a number of controversial flashpoints.

Before then, however, he had already left his mark on the game as a man who sometimes considered the ball of secondary importance. In the 2000 All-Ireland final against Armagh, he was one of a half dozen Kerry players who were booked for late hits on Kieran McGeeney. 'I wouldn't say we decided five or six fellas to hit him. If I got a second chance to hit him I probably would have taken that as well, and probably got another yellow card,' he told one interviewer upon publication of his memoir.

'I do think we recognised that he was their spiritual leader. We needed to stop him if we wanted to stop Armagh. And that was probably our thinking. We got hurt badly by Armagh in 2002. There was a feeling… "We're not going to lie down this time". Now, sometimes that doesn't work. Against Tyrone in 2005 and 2008 it didn't work.

{ THE OLD GUNSLINGER }

The 2010 season was the start of a tailspin for the celebrated half-back, and one clouded in controversy. Kerry beat Cork in the Munster Championship semi-final and on the face of it looked to have a straightforward assignment against Limerick.

The 'Treaty' led early on, but ran out of bluff and bluster, as their challenge petered tamely out. In the aftermath of the game, the footage suggested Tomás had made a number of illicit challenges on Limerick star forward Stephen Kelly. The CCCC (Central Competitions Control Committee), handed him a ban a week later, as Kerry limped tamely out of the championship at the hands of Down, 1-10 to 1-16 staring the defeated from the scoreboard.

The suspensions flowed like confetti as though the incident with Kelly opened 'Pandora's Box'. In 2011, Ó Sé lined out against Tipperary in the Munster Championship quarter-final, in a contest littered with off-the-ball incidents.

Tomás became entangled with Hugh Coghlan in front of the stands just before half-time. He appeared to strike the Premier player, and the altercation left the match official, Maurice Condon with no option but to red-card him.

When you do the crime, you have to do the time. The jail time was adding up by now, as this was the second such offence for Ó Sé in the space of a year – the mandatory ban was applied on the double, and this led to him taking up a watching brief for the remainder of the Munster Championship.

The year 2012, was groundhog season for Tomás as the Kingdom's first outing in the National League was against Tipperary. The bad blood awash between him and Tipp continued to fester, and another flashpoint was swiftly followed by another straight red card.

Tomás Ó Sé returned to the 'ring' in Kerry's league tie with Laois. Less than 10 minutes had expired when Ó Sé became involved in some extracurricular, with the referee brandishing a red card for a 'striking' offence.

Tomás's three convictions in the space of 10 months were growing signs of an itchy trigger-finger, and the GAA hierarchy produced a lengthy sentence that saw him sit out the remainder of the league campaign.

The following year, Kerry started the league with an unwanted four in-a-row of losses against Mayo, Dublin, Kildare and champions Donegal, and staring down the barrel of an unprecedented relegation battle. During the 'joust' against Donegal, Ó Sé was red-carded for an off-the-ball incident with Ryan McHugh!

The incident duly yielded Tomás's fifth red card between 2010 and 2013. All the infractions were of a variety the normally imperious Ó Sé would have avoided with a bargepole in his pomp.

In October 2013, the old gunfighter realised he was starting to lose too many shoot-outs in one-horse towns, and announced his retirement from county football.

Kerry manager Éamonn Fitzmaurice struck the right pitch and tone as he weighed up the gravity of Tomás's tumultuous impact on the Kerry cause… 'The best wing-back that I have seen play the game'… and no doubt in sight.

FAMILY
FORTUNES

TOMÁS Ó SÉ was born on June 21, 1978 in Ard an Bhóthair, Ceann Trá, County Kerry.

Ó Sé played his club football with An Ghaeltacht, making his debut with the club's senior team in the mid-1990s. He also represented Cork giants, Nemo Rangers, after a hugely successful career at senior level for the Kerry County team from 1998, until he retired in 2013.

In 2000, an Ghaeltacht reached the county senior championship for the very first time in its history. They were installed as the red-hot favourites, but their opponents, Dr Crokes triumphed by the bare minimum.

In 2001, an Ghaeltacht returned to the decider against Austin Stacks. Ó Sé and Co. made no mistake on this occasion winning by six points, 1-13 to 0-10. An Ghaeltacht surrendered their crown the following season but reached the final again in 2003, defeating Laune Rangers. They advanced to the Munster club final, where they defeated Clare representatives, St Senan's.

An Ghaeltacht's journey would take them all the way to the All-Ireland Club Championship final against Caltra from Galway, where they were edged out by a single point, 0-13 to 0-12.

At senior level for Kerry, Ó Sé won 5 All-Ireland titles, and 8 Munster titles, and was Footballer of the Year in 2004. He also won five All Star Awards.

JACK O'SHEA

(Height 6' 1", Weight 14.5 St)

Decade... 1970s/1980s/1990s

(Position... Midfield)

CHIEF CHARACTERISTIC... CHIEF CO-ORDINATOR
KINGDOM ARMOURED TANK DIVISION

TOP ACCOMPLICES... PAT SPILLANE, OGIE MORAN, GER POWER,
EOIN LISTON, MIKEY SHEEHY, SEAN WALSH

JACK
O'SHEA

"HE HAD A ROLLS-ROYCE ENGINE AND SO MUCH SKILL AND
DETERMINATION THAT HE NEEDED NO INSTRUCTIONS...
"OFF YOU GO JACK, DO YOUR THING" '

– MICK O'DWYER

TRACK and Trails…

The hunter mopped his brow and gazed down at the misty blanket that enveloped Cahersiveen. The terrain was rugged, with the mountainside dotted with sharp ragged rocks and stones. He inhaled, his breath sharpening as the air began to thin… close to the summit.

The sun slipped low as he eased his aching muscles onto a narrow track. There was something about the chase that consumed him.

Soon the proud son of the Kingdom would have bigger fish to fry, and bigger prey to ensnare. A shiny silver pot… that was one of the most sought-after prizes in Irish sport.

As a boy, Jack O'Shea loved to hunt in the mountains close to his home. He relished the physical and mental challenge of tracking down his quarry. The excitement of the hunt intrigued him. In later years, he conveyed to a teammate how it had shaped him to withstand the physical

HARD MAN RATINGS

TOUGHEST:
9.9/10

MEANEST:
8.9/10

SCARIEST:
9.5/10

HARDEST:
19.9/20

**TOTAL
HARD MAN
48.2/50**

and mental duress of county football at the highest level.

The suffering came easily for Jacko, pre-schooling for the long road ahead involved pounding the roads and the fields as a middle-distance runner. He showcased that athleticism when he once finished on the podium behind Olympic silver medallist and two-time World champion John Treacy in a Munster schools' event.

Born to run... Born to hunt.

Jack O'Shea was ready for the ultimate pursuit. It was time to become 'King of the Gaelic Football Jungle'. The hunt for Sam Maguire was on!

It proved to be a very successful expedition for O'Shea, as he won seven 'Sams' as part of one of the greatest footballing sides of all time. Jack was a central brick in the Kingdom wall.

He had all the tools required to rewrite how modern-day midfielders should operate. His time tracking John Treacy was well spent as he hurtled from box-to-box, building attacks and extinguishing the incoming enemy fire. The 'hunter' that was forged from the rocks around Cahersiveen might as well have been insulated with boron, for he was built like an armoured combat vehicle.

Jacko rarely crossed the line in terms of his physicality; he was as tough as elephant hide but never needed to invoke the darker side of his game.

His sheer will to win and all-round strength was more than enough for whatever 'kitchen sinks' were aimed in his direction.

Jack lived outside the Kingdom which was a real test of his commitment to the cause, but his passion for the green and gold shirt was such that he hardly missed a beat in 16 years.

'He had a Rolls-Royce engine and so much skill and

determination that he needed no instructions. Off you go Jack, do your thing,' his legendary manager for all seven of his All-Ireland medals, Mick O'Dwyer wrote in his outstanding autobiography *Blessed and Obsessed*.

Jack lived in Kildare and it was a really taxing commute between the two counties, but he rarely missed a match. He stitched almost 53 championship games together for Kerry between 1977 and 1992, the outlier being the 1982 Munster final semi-final against Clare.

His approach to All-Irelands was of the Zen Buddha-like variety as the big Cahersiveen legend took it all in his stride.

'My approach to an All-Ireland final might have been a bit different to other lads. I lived in Dublin, so I'd drive up to the hotel in Malahide on the Saturday night before the game and meet up with the team.

'At around half past nine we'd go down to the beach in Malahide and sit on the wall in the dark. You couldn't see who was next to you. All you could hear was Micko's voice.

'That was our pre-match team talk... on the beach, in the dark.'

It must have been an incredible scene, the mighty Kingdom huddled on the dark beach preparing for battle as their legendary leader rallied the troops. The following day the Kerry machine was well-oiled and ready for war.

'Then I'd get into my car with John Egan, Charlie Nelligan, Tommy Doyle and a buddy of John Egan's from Cork. We'd follow the team bus into Croke Park. John's buddy would sing songs the whole way in. I'd park under the old Hogan Stand and take my spot in the dressing-room next to Mikey Sheehy. I never thought about the match until that point.

'I loved the build-up. I couldn't wait to get behind the band, and I wanted to be in that position every year. I was enjoying it so much, if I saw someone I knew in the crowd I'd give them a wave. By the time I competed for the first ball, I was relaxed and ready. It's why I can remember every moment of those games... none of it passed me by.'

{ MÍCHEÁL Ó MUIRCHEARTAIGH TO THE RESCUE }

In any man's darkest hours before the battle dawns, what solace a simple relic can convey to the soul. Like many elite athletes, Jacko had a fetish for superstitions and lucky charms.

'I had my few superstitions too. I always polished my boots the night before. I never moved until the national anthem was finished. I always wore a Celtic Cross and chain that my mother gave to me.

'During the 1979 All-Ireland final, I went into a tackle on the 21-yard-line over near the Cusack Stand and I felt the chain go from my neck. After the match, the fans ran onto the pitch to celebrate... people everywhere. I met Mícheál Ó Muircheartaigh and I told him what happened to my cross and chain. He went over to the '21' at the Cusack and about a yard in from the sideline didn't he find it. I still have the cross and chain to this day.'

Jacko's journey was an inter-county trek for the ages. From the mountains around Cahersiveen, to the lofty peaks of the Hogan Stand. The ultimate big game hunter was always on the prowl.

Tracks and Trails...

A HUNTER'S
LIFE

HE PLAYED with his local clubs St Mary's in Kerry and Leixlip in Kildare. Upon joining the Kingdom senior squad in 1976, he embarked on a journey that would last 16 sensational seasons.

O'Shea first came to prominence on the Kerry minor football team, making his minor debut against Waterford in 1974. He won an All-Ireland minor medal the following season, and three under 21 All-Irelands as part of a hugely talented Kerry underage squad. O'Shea made his senior county debut in 1976 versus Meath in Navan.

He won a National Football League medal in 1977 and a Munster title following a win over Cork. From 53 championship games, he scored an impressive 11-55. Jacko also maintained an amazing league scoring ratio of 16-110 from 102 games.

For a total of 15 consecutive championship games, from the All-Ireland final defeat to Offaly in 1982, to the All-Ireland semi-final replay win over Monaghan four seasons later, he raised a white or green flag.

At the conclusion of Jacko's glittering career, he had amassed seven senior All-Ireland medals. He also won six All Star awards in-a -row, and captained Ireland to victory against Australia on enemy soil in the International Rules Series in 1986.

GLENN RYAN

(Height 6' 1", Weight 15 St)

Decade... 1900s/2000s

(Position... Centre-Back)

CHIEF CHARACTERISTIC... ENSURING EVERYTHING
WOULD BE ALL WHITE ON THE NIGHT

TOP ACCOMPLICES... CHRISTY BYRNE, BRIAN LACEY,
SEAMUS DOWLING, ANTHONY RAINBOW, NIALL BUCKLE

GLENN
RYAN

'GLENN HAD BEEN SUCH A HUGE PART OF KILDARE FOOTBALL
FOR SO MANY YEARS THAT IT'S VERY DIFFICULT TO
CONTEMPLATE THE INTER-COUNTY TEAM WITHOUT HIM.'

– ANTHONY RAINBOW

'**T**Á an brón agus an briseadh croí thart.'

An immensely proud and passionate Round Towers' club man nailed the seismic moment as gaeilge.

('The sadness and heartbreak is over')

It was a walk that was 42 years in the making. Judging by Glen Ryan's initial progress up the steps of the Hogan Stand, it was likely going to be another eternity before he got his hands on the Delaney Cup.

Kildare's supporters and players could have waited another lifetime for their lion-hearted captain to put his fingerprints all over history, and finally take possession of the provincial trophy. After several false dawns during the 90s this was the moment Lilywhite supporters could unleash the frustrations of over four decades of Eastern strife. Louth, Dublin, Offaly, Meath, and even Longford, had pilfered the provincial silver since their last victory in 1956 when they prevailed over Wexford. There followed a never-ending book of

HARD
MAN
RATINGS

TOUGHEST:
9.9/10

MEANEST:
8.5/10

SCARIEST:
9.1/10

HARDEST:
19.4/20

TOTAL
HARD MAN
46.9/50

sorrows, with the opening chapter seeing them fall to Meath in the 1966 final.

Next up were Offaly in 1969, 1971, and 1972. Dublin lowered in 1975, 1978, and again in 1992. The following season Dublin dished up losing final number eight in the sorrowful sequence.

In 1997, they fought a furious battle with Meath over three pulsating semi-final games only to miss out by a whisker. There seemed to be nothing left for it only a bottle of holy water and a copy of the Golden Pages to locate the services of a decent exorcist.

Kildare football could by now have written a thesis on the fine art of extracting defeat from the jaws of victory – such were the many and nuanced ways they were finding to lose!

When Glenn Ryan lifted the trophy and imparted a profound cúpla focal nobody could doubt the sincerity of the Round Towers' man's poignant rhetoric. Ryan had often resembled a practitioner of one-man wars in the Lilywhite jersey, a raging face of steely defiance.

His Kildare journey had begun at under-14 level and continued impressively up to his county debut vs Derry in December 1990 in Newbridge. From there, he became the defensive rock the county could build a solid foundation upon.

He came from blue-chip GAA stock, as Kildare All-Ireland winner from 1928 Billy Mangan was a branch of his family tree. That was the last time the Lilywhites lifted the trophy, and Kildare football had not witnessed an All-Ireland final appearance since 1935.

Incredibly Kildare had won six Leinster titles in-a-row during the 20s, from 1926-31 and were the dominant force in the province.

Ryan's unwavering consistency and sheer bloody-mindedness provided echoes of another Kildare legendary centre-back, Jack Higgins of Naas, who battened down the hatches for the county during the halcyon days of Kildare football in the late 20s and early 30s.

If any dynamic duo could lead Kildare back to the promised land, the shrewd old fox, O'Dwyer and the emblematic Round Towers centre-back ticked all the right boxes.

O'Dwyer had experienced the fragile psychology of Kildare football in his previous incarnation as coach in 1991. The proud footballing coach was lost in a provincial halfway house, and O'Dwyer's magic wand had malfunctioned on that occasion, failing to extract any silverware when the Waterville sorcerer's three-year tenure expired in 1994.

O'Dwyer, however, was convinced that Kildare could scale the provincial peaks again and returned in 1997 for one more attempt at leading the Lilywhites across the Rubicon.

While his second coming stalled in a shattering loss to Meath at the penultimate provincial stage, the county were emboldened by the impressive showing against the Royals, and approached the 1998 season in high spirits.

{ PROVINCIAL GAINS AND NATIONAL LOSSES }

Their optimism proved to be well-founded as they advanced to the decider, which was inevitably against Meath. There would be no requirement for three takes on this occasion as Kildare held the whip-hand in an absorbing contest to triumph by five points.

O'Dwyer was a man who choose his generals well and in Glenn Ryan he had the kind of leader that would inspire a new generation of Kildare warriors. As Ryan made his way back down the steps of the Hogan Stand, Kildare set off on a fantastic voyage.

It had to be Kerry tanks that barred the road to All-Ireland Sunday when Kildare rolled into town on August 30,1998. Both sides arrived bristling with intent and the game went down to the wire, with O'Dwyer's charges emerging by the bare minimum to journey back-to-the-future, as Kildare football finally inscribed a perfect circle.

Galway duly spoiled Glenn and Kildare's coronation to deny the fairytale finish it seemed destined to deliver. Kildare scaled Leinster again in 2000, only for the Tribesmen to rain on their parade in the All-Ireland semi-final.

With that reversal, the stars went seriously out of alignment and not even the celebrated All-Ireland winning coach and his inspirational captain could chart a course back to All-Ireland Sunday.

Glen Ryan raged against the inevitability of decline until October 2006, when like all great 'Spartans' he was carried out on his shield.

On the occasion of his retirement, another Lilies' great Anthony Rainbow recalled his footballing life and times with a true footballing warhorse.

'I first came across Glenn when I was playing in under-16 schools' football for Patrician, Newbridge and he for the Academy, Kildare Town, and even at that stage he stood out as an exceptionally talented footballer, who always gave 110 percent.

'Glenn has had a fantastic career, and it was a real pleasure playing beside him in the half-back line.'

Not even the vice-like grip of history could derail 'Micko,' Glen Ryan, and Kildare's charge towards the Delaney Cup in 1998.

'The long wait is over,' Ryan had announced on the steps of the Hogan Stand. 'It has been 42 years since a Kildare man has had the honour to stand up here... so I'm going to take my time to go through everybody.'

Go through everybody? That sounds like a mantra for the great man's career!

A KILDARE
»——→ CALLING ←——«

GLENN RYAN was born on October 20, 1972. He played his club football with Round Towers club and was part of a Round Towers' squad that won three Kildare senior titles during his stellar club career. The club has won 10 Kildare senior titles, the last of which arrived in 2003.

He was called into the Kildare senior set-up while he was still a minor and he captained the Lilywhites during one of their best spells in recent memory, with the side managed by former Kerry legend Mick O'Dwyer reaching an All-Ireland final.

He also won two Leinster Championship medals, with the first arriving in 1998, and the second in 2000. Ryan was one of the finest centre-backs in the country and it was no surprise when he was honoured with two All Star awards, in 1997 and 1998.

Glenn Ryan's outstanding contribution to Kildare GAA was recognised when he was selected on the Kildare Football Team of the Millennium.

He was appointed manager of the Kildare team in 2021, having previously managed the Longford senior side. He also managed the Kildare under-21 team, leading them to the All-Ireland final where they were defeated by Kerry.

TONY SCULLION

(Height 6' 0", Weight 15 St)

Decade... 1980s/1990s

(Position... Corner-Back/Full-Back)

CHIEF CHARACTERISTIC... THE WARRIOR WHO WAS THE 'OAK'

TOP ACCOMPLICES... KIERAN MCKEEVER,
FERGAL MCCUSKER, JOHNNY MCGURK, HENRY DOWNEY,
GARY COLEMAN, ANTHONY TOHILL

TONY SCULLION

'THEM WAS TERRIBLE TIMES. TAKING A GAA BAG IN A CAR...
IT WASN'T RIGHT HOW WE WERE TREATED. IT WASN'T RIGHT
HOW OUR COMMUNITY WAS TREATED. THROWN OUT OF CARS,
BAGS SEARCHED, HELD UP FOR TRAINING SESSIONS... IT WAS
ABSOLUTELY TERRIBLE WHAT THEY GOT AWAY WITH.'

– TONY SCULLION

RADIO days…

They always gathered around the wireless on matchdays. John Scullion Snr was head of the posse as they clamoured for a ticket to the only show in Ballinascreen.

Before he got chronic arthritis, he used to hop up on the old bike and set sail to Dean McGlinchey Park, the old county grounds, to watch Derry playing in the flesh.

Those days were a distant memory now as his arthritic condition worsened, and the old bike was gathering rust in the yard. His tour of duty among the faithful on the terraces was over, but for one of his sons, the Oak Leaf journey was just beginning.

Tony Scullion grew up on a family farm with no running water. All the family had to their name was an old Dexta tractor – 'It was supposed to be blue, but there was more rust on it than blue!' –

HARD MAN RATINGS

TOUGHEST:
9.8/10

MEANEST:
8.5/10

SCARIEST:
9.0/10

HARDEST:
19.7/20

TOTAL HARD MAN

47.0/50

and that lone bicycle! If it was a test of character, Tony would pass with flying colours. He faced the hardships with little complaint, playing soccer with his barefoot mates on the undulating banks of the 'Moocher' Groogan's field.

Tony would reveal the trials and tribulations of growing up in the often marginalised world of rural Ireland. 'Where I grew up at, I could have very easily hid in the rushes and not come out of it. I'd say for many a year I did, hide in the rushes. Felt inferior to people because of where I came from. No doubt about it.'

Tony never played for Derry in the minor ranks. He would have to bide his time before he announced himself within the football-mad county, and eventually progressed to the county under-21 side. It was clear from an early stage that Scullion was made with different gravy. The inter-county football 'meta-verse' is no country for old men... or young guns trying to make a dollar.

If Tony Scullion had a hint of inferiority, it was about to be exposed in the bear-pit of one of the most unforgiving environments in intercounty football... the Ulster Championship.

The Anglo Celt Cup is a daunting assignment in any era. The ultra-competitive competition is the ideal stress test for the rocky road to Croker. Tony Scullion had worked his way onto the senior side by 1987 and 12 years had crawled by since the last time the Oak Leaf County had snaffled the trophy.

Tony had announced himself to the GAA fraternity with a bang. The hardest men in the province were food and drink to the 'Tiger' Scullion. As hard as he was hit, Scullion bounced back for more. He could run rings around you – or just plough straight through you. His enduring excellence powered Derry to its first Ulster title in 11 years in 1987. Meath the eventual winner of

Sam Maguire Cup would prove too strong for Tony Scullion's bravehearts in the All-Ireland semis, but hopes were high that Derry would make a swift return to Jones' Road.

Those expectations were firmly put to bed the following season as the Oak Leaf limped out, with a last eight-stage elimination in Ulster at the hand of Down. Tony's star was far from waning, however, and he was bestowed with all the tools required to mix it at inter-county and international level. Scullion's skillset was perfectly aligned for the rough and tumble of the annual 'bloodbath' with the Aussies.

If ever an applicant fitted a job description, Derry's demolition man was always going to represent his country against the Australians in the hybrid contest. Tony was duly selected for the 1990 International Rules Series, the first of his two appearances in the controversial cross-code game.

Things took a serious turn one evening as Tony, who also hurled with Ballanascreen, was returning from a hurling game down south. Along with three teammates, he was stopped at the checkpoint in Aughnacloy. They were forcibly removed from the car and led into a big shed, where they were interrogated by soldiers.

'Them were terrible times. Taking a GAA bag in a car... it wasn't right how we were treated. It wasn't right how our community was treated. Thrown out of cars, bags searched, held up for training sessions... it was absolutely terrible what they got away with.' It was a sobering reminder to Tony and his Ulster teammates about the great divide that still existed within Erin's sacred shores and the inherent dangers of border-crossings within the island at the time of the troubles. Derry were struggling to regain former glories, and at various stages it was beginning to look like Sam had bolted from Tony Scullion. Finally, in 1993 opportunity knocked for Derry as they advanced to face Donegal in St Tiernach's Park, Clones. Derry and Tony Scullion had all their ducks in a row this time as they seized the day winning by two points. The Oak Leaf was now inching ever closer to a first-ever Sam Maguire.

In the All-Ireland semi-final, Tony was moved from the corner to deal with some business – namely the metropolitan talisman, Vinnie Murphy. Tony did a job on Vinnie and was in his element at full-back, as Derry safely negotiated the shark-infested waters to reach landfall on the Jones' Road…

{ 22 CARNAMONEY LANE }

He smiled as he saw his family home. There was something about the man that strode down the grassy laneway. He had a quiet power, that hinted at a man you would not want to cross.

There was a glint of silver in his hands as the sun eased lazily towards the mountains. The birds sang and the fields swayed and danced as he swung into the old farmyard. He could have punted a football from where he stood to the Moocher's field.

Tony could picture his father there in the bedroom, on All-Ireland final day, and his mother rushing in with the updates. His dad would be clutching the rosary beads in hand, desperately seeking divine intervention for Derry.

Tony Scullion had not arrived home empty-handed. He was carrying one of the most sought after items in Irish sports. There were warm embraces, and a few tears also, before he handed the precious silverware over to his father.

He peered around the old kitchen and could almost hear the strains of Michael O'Hehir warming up the listeners who had tuned in to the 1993 All-Ireland football final in which Derry proved too brave and bold for Cork.

In a dusty corner of his mind, he had never left at all, the logs sparking and cracking in the hearth, his eyes widening with wonder as the stirring images from the radio conveyed all chaos and camaraderie from the battlefield.

A rosy haze swirled around the cottage walls. At that moment, Tony Scullion hitched a ride back in time.

The old wireless was belting out the strains of Amhrán na bhFiann.

Radio Days…

»——→ THE DERRY HEIR ←——«

TONY SCULLION was a late arrival to football and was not a member of the minor football squad for Derry. He did feature at the under-21 level, however, and they went on to be crowned 1983 Ulster football champions. National honours evaded his grasp as Derry were edged out by Mayo after a replay.

Tony joined the senior panel in 1983, and he anchored the Derry rearguard from full-back. He was voted Man of the Match in both the 1987 and 1993 Ulster Championship finals.

He made a crucial intervention in the 1993 Ulster final with a famous diving block as Derry prevailed and went on a run to the All-Ireland final. Tony won his only Celtic Cross that year as Derry defeated Cork to lift Sam Maguire for the first time. Tony joined fellow Derry compatriot Anthony Tohill, winning four All Stars in 1987, 1992, 1993 and 1995.

Derry were on the crest of a wave during his career with Tony winning four Ulster titles and, three National Football League medals in 1992, 1995, and 1996.

Scullion won a record six consecutive Interprovincial Championship Railway Cup medals with Ulster between 1989 and 1995.

LARRY TOMPKINS

(Height 6' 1", Weight 15 St)

Decade... 1980s/1990s

(Position... Centre-Forward)

CHIEF CHARACTERISTIC... PLAYING THROUGH
THE PAIN FOR REBEL GAIN

TOP ACCOMPLICES... CONOR COUNIHAN, NIALL CAHALANE,
STEPHEN O'BRIEN, BARRY COFFEY, TONY DAVIS

LARRY TOMPKINS

'I SAID TO MYSELF... IF THIS IS THE LAST GAME I PLAY,
I'LL WIPE THE PAIN OUT OF MY HEAD'

– LARRY TOMPKINS

IN his stirring account of his playing career, in *Believe*, Larry Tompkins details how far he was willing to go to get his hands upon the 'Holy Grail,' known as the Sam Maguire Cup.

As Cork's talisman Tompkins lay on the treatment table in Old Trafford, and he was about to demonstrate that whatever the price of victory, he was more than willing to pay it.

'Jim McGregor took a look at me and he was shocked. He said it was the worst hamstring tear he'd ever seen in his life, that I had a lump the size of his fist.'

'How the hell did you play on?' McGregor wanted to know.

Suffering was the name of the game for Tompkins after sustaining a serious tear of his hamstring in the 1988 All-Ireland final against Meath.

'I was doing okay physically, but then a ball broke around the middle and I felt the hamstring go. I headed for the sideline, to tell Billy I was

HARD
MAN
RATINGS

TOUGHEST:
10/10

MEANEST:
8.5/10

SCARIEST:
9.0/10

HARDEST:
19.3/20

TOTAL
HARD MAN

46.8/50

gone, but before I got my words out, Billy was roaring at me to swap with Teddy.

'I said to myself... "If this is the last game I play, I'll wipe the pain out of my head".

'On the 70th minute mark, Dave Barry was fouled and a free awarded. Dave gave me the ball. "Whatever you do... put it over!" he said.

'Tommy Sugrue from Kerry was refereeing, and I thought I heard him say, "Time is up!" I put down the ball and I turned to Hill 16 and I blessed myself.

'I knew as soon as I had kicked the ball that it was going over.'

Larry had hauled Cork back from the brink and into the Promised Land. The unbearable pain he had endured had not been in vain.

For Larry Tompkins and Cork, the moment that would live long in the memory, but someone forgot to tell Kerry official Tommy Sugrue to blow his whistle!

Larry continues the story with more than a hint of regret tinged within his words.

'Then, McQuillan kicked the ball out and the ref let play go on. Shea Fahy caught it cleanly and went to fist it to Tony Nation, but the ball went out over the sideline at the Cusack side.

'Still, he still let play go on.

'Martin O'Connell sent a massive kick in and everyone went for it, before David Beggy threw himself on the ball. And Sugrue gave a free. It was easy for Stafford and that was it... a draw... 1-9 to 0-12. Sugrue came in for some stick. I remember Conor (Counihan) trying to keep the peace.'

There was hardly a word spoken in the dressing-room afterwards.

'I was banjaxed. I could hardly walk and Dr Con was saying that there was no way I'd be able to play in the replay.'

Things were looking bleak for Larry and Cork. The general prognosis was Meath had been off-colour and the gift horse had firmly bolted. Then the story took an extraordinary twist as Larry was about to get help from an expected source – Manchester United's legendary manager Alex Ferguson.

Larry was flown to Manchester and met at the airport by another United great, Paddy Crerand, and taken to their famous training complex known as The Cliff.

'Paddy brought me to meet the physio, a Scotsman named Jim McGregor, up in the treatment area on the first floor. Norman Whiteside and Clayton Blackmore were being treated and Alex Ferguson popped in.

'I heard you were coming,' Fergie said. 'You're one of us now… anything you want, just ask, but you're to be here at quarter to nine in the morning like any other player.'

The treatment was intense and agonizing, but highly effective. Larry's description is applied minus sugar coating. With little time to spare, McGregor informed him cheerfully, 'If you're willing to suffer, we have a chance.'

'I'll have to sign a form declaring that you're able to play and I'll have to be truthful,' and he immediately set about 'Operation Larry Tompkins'… like a man possessed!

'I lay down and he handed me a strap, and said, "Bite on that!" I noticed a bucket on the ground under my head. I learned later that it was there to mop up the sweat and the sick because of the severity of the treatment. He went at it hard, and my screams were loud.

'Norman Whiteside was lying beside me, getting treatment, and he was laughing at me.

'You GAA lads must be made of paper,' he told me. 'I didn't try to hide the pain from him, or anybody else. The pain was brutal. I was taken back to the hotel in a taxi, but even after two treatments, it was beginning to feel better.

'Jim put me through 50 minutes of a fitness test at Old Trafford in the morning and I came through that fine; I was sprinting and the hamstring felt great. He signed the letter clearing me to play and told me I'd worked really hard.'

After an epic voyage, Larry was ready for the replay and another shot at an elusive All-Ireland medal, but his extraordinary efforts would all be in vain.

'They were definitely more geed up and it felt like there was a fight every 10 minutes... they wanted to make it a physical battle. Gerry McEntee was sent off early on for a kick on Niall, but we couldn't make use of the extra man.'

For Larry and Cork, the bitter pill would have to be swallowed twice as Meath laid down the rules of engagement, yet again. Larry Tompkins absorbed the crushing defeats like all great champions to win two All-Irelands back-to-back – which went a long way to redressing the balance of the previous two years.

Mick O'Dwyer was best placed to pass judgement at the end of the great man's career... 'Heart of a Lion...one of the true greats!'

It was hard to argue with the assessment.

LARRY'S
DOUBLE LIFE

LARRY TOMPKINS was born on June 13, 1963 in Naas, County Kildare. He began his storied career with his local club Eadestown. He played the majority of his club football which spanned two decades with his adopted club Castlehaven.

He won three Munster Club Championship titles with Castlehaven, and contested three All-Ireland Club semi-finals, losing to Wicklow champions Baltinglass in 1989 and Dublin's Kilmacud Crokes in 1994, just failing to clear the penultimate hurdle, and make a historic appearance in an All-Ireland Club football final.

He started his county career with Kildare before transferring to Cork with fellow county colleague Shay Fahy. Cork would lose two consecutive All-Ireland finals to Meath (1987/88), both were ill-tempered affairs with the 1988 final going to a replay.

Larry would not have long, however, to finally get his hands on a Celtic Cross with Cork winning the next two finals - against Mayo in 1989, and then defeating Meath in 1990. It was a crowning moment for Larry as he proudly lifted 'Sam' as Cork captain.

In all, he won two All-Irelands, six Munster titles, a National League, and was crowned an All-Star on three occasions. Tompkins, who also entered the rarified surroundings of the GAA Hall Of Fame, managed Cork the 1999 All-Ireland where they lost to Meath.

BIBLIOGRAPHY

Keith Barr: Interview in the *Irish Mirror*

Francie Bellew Interview in the *Irish Independent*, *Balls.ie*

Colm Boyle: Interview on *GAA.ie*

Niall Cahalane: Interview in the *Irish Examiner*

Jonny Cooper: From column in *The Irish Times*

Colm Coyle: Interview in *The Irish Mirror*

Conor Counihan: Interview in *Irish Examiner*

Paul Curran: Interview in the *Irish Independent*

Graham Geraghty: Interviews in *Irish Examiner/GAA.ie/Irish News*

Conor Gormley: Interview with the *Irish News*

Keith Higgins: Interview in the *Irish Independent*

DJ Kane: Interview on *BBC Northern Ireland Sport*

Lee Keegan: Interview on *Boylesports*

Tim Kennelly: Interview from *Joe.ie*

Sean Lowry: Interview with *Clubforce.com*

Mick Lyons: Interview in the *Irish Independent*

James McCarthy: *Interview in Irish Daily Mail with Philip Lanigan*

Gerry McCarville: Colm O'Rourke column in the *Sunday Independent*

Paddy McCormack: Interview on *Hogan Stand*

Kieran McGeeney: Interviews from *Buzz.ie.*, *Sportsjoe.ie*

Brian McGilligan: Interview in *Derry Now*

Ryan McMenamin: Interviews with *The GAA Hour*, *the42.ie*

Barnes Murphy: Interview from *Hogan Stand* website.

Johnny Nevin: Interview in the *Irish Independent*

Stephen O'Brien: Interview with *EchoLive.ie*

Gay O'Driscoll: Extracts from *Heffo: A Brilliant Mind* published by Transworld

Noel O'Leary: Interview with *BBC Northern Ireland Sports Podcast*

Tomás Ó Sé: Interview with the *Irish News*

Páidí Ó Sé: Interview with the *Irish Examiner, the42.ie*

Glenn Ryan: Interview in the *Irish Independent*

Tony Scullion: Interview with the *Irish News*

Larry Tompkins: Extracts from *Believe: Larry Tompkins, The Autobiography* published by Hero Books

Printed in Great Britain
by Amazon